I0006203

Android App Mastery: Developing for the Modern User

Biagio Palazzo

In the dynamic world of mobile app development, Android stands tall as a dominant platform, powering billions of devices worldwide. From smartphones and tablets to wearables and smart TVs, Android offers developers unparalleled opportunities to craft innovative and impactful applications for a global audience. Yet, with this potential comes the challenge of staying ahead in a rapidly evolving ecosystem.

Android App Mastery: Developing for the Modern User is your comprehensive guide to navigating the complexities of Android app development. Whether you're a beginner taking your first steps or an experienced developer looking to sharpen your skills, this book equips you with the knowledge, tools, and strategies needed to build cutting-edge apps that captivate users.

This journey begins with the fundamentals, introducing the Android platform and development environment, and gradually progresses to advanced topics like performance optimization, integrating modern technologies, and designing for diverse audiences. Along the way, you'll learn how to implement intuitive user interfaces, handle complex data storage, and create apps that stand out in a competitive marketplace.

What sets this book apart is its focus on the modern user—an audience that demands seamless, visually appealing, and accessible experiences. By blending technical expertise with user-centric design principles, you'll learn to create apps that not only function flawlessly but also resonate with the needs and preferences of today's users.

Each chapter builds on the last, culminating in a complete understanding of the Android ecosystem. By the end, you'll be equipped to develop professional-grade apps, deploy them on Google Play, and even explore monetization opportunities to turn your passion into profit.

The world of Android development is constantly changing, but with the right foundation, tools, and mindset, you can master it. Let's embark on this journey together and transform your ideas into reality.

Welcome to Android App Mastery: Developing for the Modern User.

Biagio Palazzo is a seasoned software developer, educator, and technology enthusiast with over a decade of experience in mobile application development. Specializing in Android, Biagio has designed, developed, and deployed a wide range of apps across various industries, from innovative startups to Fortune 500 companies. His passion for crafting seamless and user-friendly applications has earned him recognition as a thought leader in the Android development community.

Biagio's journey into the world of technology began with a curiosity about how software shapes our lives. This curiosity led him to a career where he not only builds solutions but also shares his knowledge with others. As a mentor and speaker at numerous tech conferences and workshops, Biagio has guided aspiring developers in mastering Android development, emphasizing both technical expertise and user-centric design.

Beyond coding, Biagio is deeply interested in the intersection of technology and human behavior. He believes that great apps are not just functional—they are intuitive, accessible, and transformative. This belief drives his commitment to empowering developers to create apps that truly make a difference.

When not immersed in code or mentoring developers, Biagio enjoys exploring the latest technological trends, contributing to open-source projects, and sharing his insights through articles, tutorials, and now, this book.

With **Android App Mastery: Developing for the Modern User**, Biagio brings together his years of experience, practical knowledge, and passion for teaching to provide a comprehensive guide for developers eager to excel in the Android ecosystem.

Part 1: Foundations of Android Development

Every great app begins with a solid foundation. Part 1 of this book lays the groundwork for your Android development journey, introducing you to the tools, concepts, and languages that form the core of the Android ecosystem. From setting up your development environment and exploring the architecture to mastering Kotlin basics, this section ensures you're equipped with the essential knowledge and skills to build robust and user-friendly applications. Whether you're a beginner or refreshing your fundamentals, this is where your path to Android app mastery begins.

1. Introduction to Android Development

Android has revolutionized the way we interact with technology, becoming the backbone of billions of devices worldwide. This chapter introduces you to the vibrant world of Android development, exploring its history, significance, and role in shaping the digital age. Whether you're drawn by its global reach, diverse applications, or promising career opportunities, this chapter provides the context and motivation to embark on your journey as an Android developer.

1.1 History and Evolution of Android

Android, as we know it today, is a global powerhouse in the world of mobile operating systems, powering billions of devices across a variety of platforms—from smartphones and tablets to wearables, smart TVs, and even cars. However, Android's history and evolution are deeply tied to a series of technological advancements, visionary ideas, and business decisions that have shaped the mobile industry. This section will take you through the fascinating journey of Android's history, from its humble beginnings to its dominant position in the global tech ecosystem today.

The Birth of Android: 2003-2005

The story of Android begins in 2003 when Android Inc. was founded by Andy Rubin, Rich Miner, Nick Sears, and Chris White. The company was initially focused on developing an advanced operating system for digital cameras, but they soon recognized the much larger potential of creating a mobile OS for smartphones. The vision behind Android was simple: to create a robust, open-source platform that would make smartphones more affordable and accessible to consumers. At the time, the mobile market was dominated by closed systems like Nokia's Symbian, Microsoft's Windows Mobile, and Apple's proprietary iOS.

In 2005, Google, seeking to expand its reach into mobile, acquired Android Inc. for an undisclosed sum, believed to be between $50 million and $100 million. With this acquisition, Google brought Rubin and his team aboard to develop the Android platform under the company's auspices. Rubin's vision for an open, customizable, and extensible platform would lay the groundwork for Android's success.

Android's Public Debut: 2007-2008

Android's true public debut came in 2007, when Google, along with other industry giants such as Intel, HTC, Sony, Dell, and Samsung, formed the Open Handset Alliance (OHA). This alliance was established to promote Android as a viable mobile operating system, built on open-source principles, with a goal to compete against the closed ecosystems of Apple's iOS and other mobile platforms. The OHA would help Android gain significant momentum by attracting major hardware manufacturers who would produce devices powered by Android.

In 2008, Android made its first official appearance with the launch of the Android 1.0 operating system, and the first Android-powered smartphone, the T-Mobile G1 (also known as the HTC Dream), was released. The G1 featured a touchscreen interface, a full QWERTY keyboard, and access to the Android Market (now the Google Play Store), which allowed users to download and install third-party apps. Android 1.0, while basic by today's standards, introduced many core elements of the operating system that are still in use today, including the notification system, web browser, and Google Maps integration.

The Rise of Android: 2009-2011

As Android gained traction, Google released several important updates, each adding new features and improving performance. Android 1.5 Cupcake (2009) introduced features such as an on-screen keyboard, support for widgets, and the ability to upload videos to YouTube. Android 1.6 Donut (2009) expanded the operating system to support a wider range of screen sizes and added features like a quicker search interface and the ability to view Google Maps in a full-screen mode.

The most pivotal update came in 2010 with Android 2.0 Eclair, which brought significant improvements such as support for multiple accounts, better camera functionality, and Google Maps Navigation. This update set Android apart from other mobile operating systems, as it demonstrated Google's ability to continuously improve and innovate its platform.

2010 was also the year that Android's market share began to grow exponentially. Several manufacturers, such as Samsung, Motorola, and HTC, embraced Android and released a wide range of devices, each targeting different segments of the market. This proliferation of Android devices resulted in Android surpassing other mobile operating systems in terms of sales and market share. By 2011, Android had become the dominant smartphone platform worldwide, a position it continues to hold to this day.

Android Becomes the Leading Mobile Platform: 2012-2014

The period between 2012 and 2014 marked Android's rise to dominance in the mobile market. The launch of Android 4.0 Ice Cream Sandwich (2011) was a significant milestone, introducing a complete redesign of the user interface with a focus on a cleaner, more modern aesthetic. The update introduced features such as facial recognition for unlocking the device and a refined notification system.

In 2012, Android's market share surged, with the platform powering over 50% of smartphones worldwide. Google had also established a strong presence in the tablet market with the release of the Google Nexus 7 in 2012, which ran a pure version of Android without any manufacturer-specific modifications. The Nexus series became known for its close-to-stock Android experience, giving users the latest software updates directly from Google.

With the launch of Android 5.0 Lollipop in 2014, Android underwent another significant transformation. Lollipop introduced Material Design, a unified design language that focused on clean, flat, and vibrant interfaces, as well as a more intuitive user experience. This update also brought improved performance and better battery life through Project Volta, a set of features that optimized power consumption.

Android's Continued Growth and Android 6.0 Marshmallow to Android 10: 2015-2019

By 2015, Android had firmly established itself as the leading mobile operating system, with more than 80% of smartphones worldwide running on Android. Android 6.0 Marshmallow (2015) brought important new features, such as Doze mode (which helped conserve battery life) and granular app permissions, giving users more control over what data apps could access.

With the release of Android 7.0 Nougat (2016), Android became even more powerful, introducing features like split-screen multitasking, improved notifications, and Vulkan API support for better gaming performance. Android 8.0 Oreo (2017) focused on speed and efficiency, including faster boot times and improved battery life, as well as introducing features like picture-in-picture mode and notification channels.

Android 9.0 Pie (2018) continued the focus on usability and performance, introducing features like gesture navigation, adaptive battery, and digital wellbeing tools. Android also embraced AI more heavily, with features such as adaptive brightness and app actions that used machine learning to improve the user experience.

In 2019, Android 10 was released, marking the first time that Android adopted a more straightforward naming scheme, moving away from the dessert-based names to a numeric system. Android 10 introduced Dark Mode, a system-wide UI update designed to reduce eye strain and save battery life, and added enhanced privacy features, such as location access controls.

The Era of Foldables, 5G, and Android 12 and Beyond: 2020-Present

In recent years, Android has continued to evolve in response to new technological trends. The rise of foldable devices, powered by Android 10 and later Android 11, showcased Android's ability to adapt to new form factors, providing developers with the tools to create seamless experiences across foldable and flexible screens.

The release of Android 12 in 2021 marked a dramatic redesign of the user interface, with Material You, a new design system that offered dynamic theming based on the user's wallpaper. Android 12 also focused heavily on privacy features, such as the Privacy Dashboard and microphone and camera indicators.

As 5G networks began to roll out, Android adapted by supporting 5G connectivity, allowing developers to create apps that take advantage of the higher speeds and low latency that 5G promises.

Looking ahead, Android is poised to continue its evolution with the advent of Android 13 and beyond, focusing on better performance, enhanced privacy features, and deeper integration with emerging technologies like augmented reality, AI, and more.

From its humble beginnings as an open-source project to its current status as the world's most widely used mobile operating system, Android's journey has been nothing short of remarkable. With its open-source nature, continuous innovation, and global reach, Android remains at the forefront of mobile technology, offering developers and users a platform that is dynamic, flexible, and constantly evolving.

1.2 Market Share and Popularity of Android Apps

Android's success is deeply tied to its market share and the popularity of its apps. Over the years, Android has grown from a niche operating system into the dominant force in the global mobile ecosystem. This chapter explores Android's market share, its rise to dominance, and the factors that have made Android apps popular among developers and users alike.

Android's Global Market Share

Since its launch in 2008, Android has steadily gained ground in the smartphone market. By 2010, Android had captured around 3% of the global market share, but its rapid growth began in earnest after 2011. According to various research firms like IDC, Statista, and Canalys, Android overtook Symbian in 2011 to become the most widely used mobile operating system.

By 2014, Android had surpassed 80% of global smartphone market share, a position it has maintained to this day. As of 2023, Android holds around 70-75% of the global smartphone market share, far ahead of its closest competitor, Apple's iOS, which accounts for roughly 20-25%. This market share dominance is not limited to smartphones but extends to tablets, wearables, and other connected devices. Android has also emerged as the dominant operating system in emerging markets, where low-cost devices running Android provide affordable access to the internet and smartphones.

One key factor in Android's dominance is its accessibility to a wide range of manufacturers. Unlike Apple's iOS, which is confined to Apple devices, Android is an open-source platform that can be licensed by any hardware manufacturer. This has resulted in a vast array of devices running Android, ranging from high-end flagship smartphones to budget-friendly entry-level models. Manufacturers such as Samsung, Xiaomi, Huawei, Oppo, and many others have built Android-powered devices, contributing to the platform's widespread adoption and helping it penetrate virtually every region globally.

Additionally, Android's open-source nature allows for a level of customization that appeals to manufacturers and users alike. This flexibility has helped Android gain a significant share in countries with emerging economies, where price sensitivity plays a major role in purchasing decisions.

The Growth of Android Apps

The growing popularity of Android is also reflected in the vast number of apps available on the Google Play Store. Android's open ecosystem has fostered an environment where developers can create a wide variety of apps, ranging from simple utilities to complex, feature-rich applications. By 2023, the Google Play Store had surpassed 3 million apps, making it the largest app marketplace in the world, ahead of Apple's App Store.

There are several factors that have contributed to the explosion of Android apps:

Open Ecosystem: Android's open-source model allows developers to build and distribute apps with fewer restrictions compared to iOS. This has led to a wider variety of apps, including niche and experimental apps, which may not be allowed in the more regulated App Store.

Developer-Friendly Tools: Google has provided developers with a suite of powerful tools to build, test, and deploy their apps, including Android Studio, the official integrated development environment (IDE), and a wide range of libraries and frameworks such as Jetpack Compose for UI design. These tools have made Android development more accessible, fostering an ever-growing community of developers.

Cross-Platform Development: Tools like Flutter, React Native, and Xamarin allow developers to create apps for both Android and iOS with a single codebase, further increasing the appeal of Android app development. This cross-platform approach allows developers to reach a larger audience while minimizing development costs.

Monetization Opportunities: Android offers a range of monetization options for developers, such as in-app purchases, advertisements, paid apps, and subscriptions. The lower barrier to entry on the Google Play Store allows even smaller developers to enter the marketplace and generate revenue.

Global Reach: Android's open-source nature and affordability have made it the preferred platform in developing countries, where cost-effective smartphones are crucial. This has opened up new markets for Android apps, expanding the user base and driving further growth in app downloads and engagement.

Android App Usage and Popularity Among Users

Android apps are widely used across the globe, with millions of users interacting with apps daily. In fact, according to various reports, Android users spend an average of 4 to 5 hours per day on their devices, with a significant portion of that time dedicated to using apps. The sheer variety and availability of apps have made Android the platform of choice for millions of users, offering everything from entertainment and social media to productivity and health management.

Some of the most popular categories of Android apps include:

Social Media and Communication: Apps like WhatsApp, Facebook, Instagram, and Snapchat have massive user bases, providing platforms for communication, social networking, and content sharing.

Entertainment and Streaming: Android users also flock to apps like YouTube, Netflix, Spotify, and TikTok for entertainment. These apps have become integral parts of modern life, offering on-demand access to music, movies, and videos.

Productivity and Utilities: Android is home to a range of productivity apps, from Google's suite of tools (Gmail, Google Drive, Google Docs) to third-party solutions like Microsoft Office and Evernote. Additionally, utilities such as file managers, antivirus apps, and battery optimization apps remain popular.

Gaming: Mobile gaming is one of the largest categories in the Google Play Store, with millions of games available for download, from casual titles like Candy Crush to more complex games like PUBG Mobile. Android's versatility allows games to run on a variety of devices, from high-end smartphones to budget models, which has contributed to the popularity of gaming on the platform.

E-Commerce and Finance: Apps such as Amazon, eBay, and Google Pay have transformed the way people shop, manage money, and invest. The rise of mobile commerce and the ability to shop on-the-go has led to increased usage of e-commerce and finance apps.

Why Android Apps Are So Popular

There are several reasons why Android apps continue to be popular among both developers and users:

Customization: Android offers a high degree of customization, allowing users to personalize their app experiences by changing themes, settings, and even the user interface.

Affordable Devices: With Android being the operating system of choice for many budget-friendly smartphones, users in emerging markets have greater access to Android apps. This has contributed to Android's enormous user base across all regions.

Open Source Nature: Android's open-source platform allows developers to experiment with new ideas and features, leading to the creation of a wide range of apps that serve the needs of diverse user groups.

Google Integration: Android is tightly integrated with Google's services and apps, such as Google Search, Google Maps, YouTube, Gmail, and Google Assistant. This seamless integration creates a user-friendly ecosystem that makes it easier for users to access content and services across devices.

Wide Device Compatibility: Android apps run on a wide variety of devices, including smartphones, tablets, wearables, TVs, and even automotive systems. This broad compatibility ensures that developers can reach a massive, diverse user base.

Android's market share and the popularity of its apps are a testament to the success of its open-source model, developer-friendly tools, and the extensive hardware ecosystem built around it. With its vast global reach, Android continues to dominate the smartphone market and maintain a strong presence in many other categories of connected devices. The Android app ecosystem, with its ever-growing number of developers and users, shows no signs of slowing down. As technology continues to evolve, Android is positioned to remain at the forefront of mobile innovation, driving the future of app development and usage.

1.3 Key Players in the Android Ecosystem

The Android ecosystem is a vast and dynamic network of companies, developers, and technologies that collectively shape the development, distribution, and use of Android devices and apps. As the most widely used mobile operating system in the world, Android's ecosystem is influenced by several key players, each contributing to its growth and success. This section delves into the main participants in the Android ecosystem, from operating system developers to hardware manufacturers, app developers, and service providers, all of whom play a critical role in Android's global dominance.

1. Google: The Creator and Custodian of Android

At the core of the Android ecosystem is Google, the company that developed the Android operating system and continues to maintain and update it. Google's influence on Android is profound, as it controls the direction of the platform, from core system features to app distribution and services. Here are a few ways Google shapes the Android ecosystem:

Android Development and Updates: Google is responsible for developing the Android operating system itself. The company releases regular updates, each bringing new features, security patches, and performance improvements. These updates ensure that the platform remains competitive with other mobile operating systems and continues to meet the evolving needs of users and developers.

Google Play Store: As the official app store for Android, the Google Play Store is a central hub where users can discover, download, and update apps. Google manages the Play Store's policies, ensuring that apps meet certain standards for quality, security, and functionality. With millions of apps available, the Play Store has become the largest mobile app marketplace in the world.

Google Services and APIs: Google provides a suite of services and APIs that developers integrate into their Android apps, such as Google Maps, Google Drive, Firebase, Google Cloud, and Google Analytics. These services enhance app functionality and improve user experience, and they are central to the Android ecosystem's interconnectedness.

Android Hardware Integration: Google has also ventured into hardware with its Pixel line of smartphones and other devices like the Google Nest smart home products. These devices run a "pure" or "stock" version of Android, providing an experience closely aligned with Google's vision for the platform.

2. Device Manufacturers: Hardware Makers Driving Android's Reach

A defining characteristic of Android is its open-source nature, which allows numerous manufacturers to use the operating system on their devices. These device manufacturers play a crucial role in bringing Android to the masses and shaping how Android is experienced by users. Some of the biggest names in the Android hardware ecosystem include:

Samsung: As the largest manufacturer of Android smartphones worldwide, Samsung has a significant influence on the Android ecosystem. Samsung produces a wide range of devices, from budget smartphones to flagship models like the Galaxy S series and Galaxy Note. The company also offers a custom version of Android called One UI, which adds additional features and design elements over stock Android. Samsung's influence extends beyond smartphones to wearables, tablets, and smart TVs, all of which run Android or Google's Wear OS.

Huawei: Despite facing challenges due to political tensions and restrictions from the U.S. government, Huawei remains a key player in the Android ecosystem. The Chinese tech giant produces a variety of smartphones that run Android, though it uses its own version of Android (with a custom user interface called EMUI) due to its exclusion from Google's services. Huawei has also made strides in other areas like 5G and artificial intelligence, shaping the Android experience with its hardware innovations.

Xiaomi: Known for offering high-quality devices at affordable prices, Xiaomi has become one of the most prominent Android smartphone manufacturers. With its custom MIUI interface on top of Android, Xiaomi provides a highly personalized user experience. The company has gained massive popularity in emerging markets and continues to expand into Europe and other regions.

Oppo, Vivo, and Realme: These brands, all owned by BBK Electronics, are major players in the Android space, particularly in Asia. Oppo and Vivo offer a wide range of smartphones with custom Android skins, while Realme targets budget-conscious consumers with high-performance devices. All three brands contribute to Android's diversity by offering different user experiences and features, such as advanced camera technologies and fast-charging capabilities.

LG and Sony: While no longer as dominant as they once were, LG and Sony still contribute to the Android ecosystem with their smartphones, particularly in the premium and mid-range segments. LG has since exited the smartphone business, but its innovations in mobile technology, such as wide-angle cameras and modular designs, have had a lasting impact. Sony's Xperia line, known for high-quality displays and cameras, continues to cater to niche markets.

3. App Developers: Creators of the Android Experience

App developers are essential to Android's success, as they build the applications that drive user engagement and enhance the platform's utility. The Play Store is home to millions of apps, created by independent developers, startups, and large corporations. Android's open ecosystem has attracted a diverse community of developers, fostering innovation and competition. Key aspects of the developer ecosystem include:

Independent Developers and Startups: A significant portion of Android apps are created by individual developers or small teams. Android's open nature and user-friendly development tools, such as Android Studio and the Kotlin programming language, have lowered the barriers to entry for developers. Independent developers can create apps ranging from simple utilities to complex, high-performing applications, often reaching a global audience through the Play Store.

Large Corporations and Enterprises: Many large tech companies, such as Facebook, Microsoft, Amazon, and Netflix, have embraced Android to reach their customers. These companies develop apps that integrate with their services, leveraging Android's flexibility to offer a consistent experience across smartphones, tablets, and other devices. For example, Facebook, Instagram, and WhatsApp (all owned by Meta) are some of the most popular apps on Android.

Cross-Platform Development Tools: Frameworks like React Native, Flutter, and Xamarin have made it easier for developers to create apps that run on both Android and iOS, expanding the potential market for apps and making development more efficient. These tools enable developers to write code once and deploy it across multiple platforms, streamlining the development process.

4. Google's Partners: Telecom Operators and Cloud Providers

Android's success is also supported by a wide array of partners in the telecommunications, cloud computing, and internet services industries. These partners help distribute Android devices and services to a global audience, as well as provide necessary infrastructure for Android apps to function smoothly.

Telecom Operators: Mobile carriers and telecom companies play a critical role in the Android ecosystem by selling Android-powered devices to customers, offering data plans, and supporting app distribution. Telecom operators also partner with manufacturers to bring exclusive features, promotional content, and custom-branded versions of Android to users. Companies like Verizon, AT&T, T-Mobile, Vodafone, and China Mobile are key players in Android's global reach.

Cloud Providers and Services: Android apps increasingly rely on cloud computing services to provide data storage, synchronization, and processing capabilities. Google Cloud, Amazon Web Services (AWS), and Microsoft Azure are the primary cloud platforms used by Android app developers to host back-end infrastructure and manage app data.

5. Android Users: The Ultimate Drivers of the Ecosystem

Finally, at the heart of the Android ecosystem are the users themselves. With billions of active Android users worldwide, these individuals not only drive demand for Android devices but also influence app development trends through their feedback, preferences, and usage patterns. Android's widespread appeal among consumers—due to its affordability, customizability, and wide selection of devices—ensures that the ecosystem remains robust and dynamic. Users' preferences and behavior help shape what features, apps, and devices become successful in the Android space.

The Android ecosystem is a vibrant and interconnected network of players, each contributing to the platform's success. Google, as the platform's creator and custodian, sets the direction for Android, while device manufacturers bring the operating system to life on a wide range of devices. App developers create the content and functionality that users rely on daily, and telecom operators and cloud service providers ensure that the ecosystem runs smoothly. Together, these key players continue to propel Android forward, ensuring its dominance in the mobile world and beyond.

1.4 Why Choose Android for App Development?

Android has firmly established itself as the dominant operating system for mobile devices, holding a significant share of the global smartphone market. With over 2.5 billion active Android users worldwide and an ecosystem that extends beyond smartphones to tablets, wearables, and smart TVs, choosing Android for app development is a decision that offers immense potential. This section explores the compelling reasons why developers should consider Android as their platform of choice when building mobile applications.

1. Massive User Base and Market Reach

One of the primary reasons for choosing Android for app development is the platform's enormous global user base. As of 2023, Android holds a market share of approximately 70-75% in the smartphone industry, a dominant position that offers developers access to a vast audience. Android is not only popular in developed markets but also has a strong presence in emerging economies, where affordable Android devices offer millions of users access to the internet and mobile services.

The sheer volume of active Android devices means that developers have the potential to reach a broad and diverse audience. This large user base opens up numerous opportunities for app monetization, whether through ads, in-app purchases, subscriptions, or paid apps. The ability to develop apps for both entry-level and high-end devices further extends the market reach, allowing developers to target various segments of the population.

2. Open-Source and Customizable

Android's open-source nature is a key factor in its popularity. The operating system is developed and maintained by Google, but the Android Open Source Project (AOSP) allows anyone to contribute to its development, modify its source code, and build their own custom versions of the OS. This open-source model has led to a highly flexible and adaptable platform that can be customized according to specific needs, whether it's for individual users, specific devices, or unique use cases.

For developers, this open-source nature means they can freely access the Android source code and tailor the operating system to suit their app development requirements. Custom ROMs, custom user interfaces, and specialized features can all be implemented with Android, providing flexibility that is not available with more closed systems like iOS. Additionally, the open-source model encourages innovation and allows developers to experiment with new ideas and functionalities without being bound by restrictive guidelines.

3. Developer-Friendly Tools and Resources

Android offers a rich set of development tools that make building mobile apps easier, faster, and more efficient. Android Studio, the official integrated development environment (IDE) for Android, provides everything developers need to create, test, and debug Android apps. With features like code completion, debugging tools, and performance analysis, Android Studio simplifies the app development process and boosts productivity.

Android also supports several programming languages, most notably Java and Kotlin. While Java has been the traditional language for Android development, Kotlin, introduced by Google as a first-class language for Android, has quickly gained popularity. Kotlin offers modern language features, better readability, and improved safety compared to Java, making it a preferred choice for many developers. The language's seamless integration with existing Java-based Android apps allows developers to adopt Kotlin incrementally, making it easier for teams to transition and enhance their apps over time.

Beyond Kotlin and Java, Android development also benefits from Jetpack, a suite of libraries and components designed to make Android app development more efficient. Jetpack libraries provide developers with pre-built solutions for common challenges, such as handling background tasks, managing UI components, and implementing navigation. These tools not only accelerate the development process but also ensure that apps follow best practices for stability and performance.

4. Wide Range of Devices and Customization

Unlike iOS, which is limited to Apple devices, Android runs on a vast array of devices from different manufacturers. This includes flagship phones, budget devices, tablets, wearables, TVs, and even automotive systems. This diversity offers developers the ability to create apps that work across a broad spectrum of devices, from high-end smartphones with cutting-edge technology to budget-friendly phones in emerging markets.

Android's customization options also enable developers to optimize their apps for various screen sizes, resolutions, and hardware specifications. Whether an app is designed for a large tablet display or a small, entry-level phone, Android's flexibility allows developers to create tailored experiences. Moreover, Android's support for multiple device types, such as smartwatches (Wear OS), Android TV, and Android Auto, extends the reach of Android apps beyond smartphones to other forms of connected technology, opening new avenues for app innovation.

The ability to customize the Android experience further extends to the user interface (UI). Developers have the freedom to design unique and personalized user interfaces, using XML for layout design and tools like Jetpack Compose for building modern, declarative UIs. This level of customization is a significant advantage for developers who wish to offer users a distinctive and engaging experience.

5. Strong Support for App Monetization

Android provides multiple avenues for monetizing apps, giving developers flexibility in how they generate revenue. The Google Play Store is the largest mobile app marketplace globally, offering developers access to millions of users. Developers can monetize their apps in various ways:

In-App Advertising: Android supports integration with Google's AdMob platform, which allows developers to display ads within their apps. This is an effective revenue model for free apps that aim to generate income through impressions or clicks.

In-App Purchases (IAP): Android provides robust support for in-app purchases, allowing developers to offer digital goods, premium content, or subscription services. This model is widely used in mobile gaming and other app categories.

Paid Apps and Subscriptions: Developers can also choose to charge users for downloading their app or offer a subscription-based model. The Play Store's billing system simplifies the process of handling payments, subscriptions, and renewals.

Freemium Model: Many apps combine free access with premium features, offering users basic functionality for free and charging for advanced features or exclusive content. Android's infrastructure makes it easy to implement this model and handle user transactions securely.

6. Integration with Google Services and APIs

Android offers seamless integration with Google's services, making it easy to incorporate a variety of features into apps. Key Google services and APIs that enhance Android app functionality include:

Google Maps API: The ability to integrate location-based services is a core feature for many apps. With the Google Maps API, developers can provide mapping, navigation, and location tracking features.

Firebase: Firebase is a suite of cloud-based tools provided by Google for app development. It offers services like real-time databases, authentication, analytics, cloud storage, push notifications, and app quality monitoring. Firebase simplifies backend development and helps developers build robust, scalable apps quickly.

Google Analytics: With Google Analytics, developers can track user behavior within their app, gaining valuable insights into how users interact with features. This helps in making data-driven decisions to improve app performance and user engagement.

Google Assistant: Integration with Google Assistant allows developers to create voice-controlled apps that respond to user commands, enhancing user interaction and accessibility.

These services allow developers to add powerful features to their apps without having to build them from scratch, making Android a more efficient platform for app development.

7. Active Community and Resources

The Android developer community is large, diverse, and highly active. From official Google forums and Stack Overflow to various subreddits and developer meetups, the Android community provides ample resources for support and collaboration. Developers can find solutions to common problems, share best practices, and contribute to open-source projects that help improve the Android ecosystem.

Google's official documentation and resources, such as Google Developer Training and Codelabs, provide in-depth tutorials and guides for developers of all skill levels. The extensive resources and active community make it easier for developers to stay up-to-date with the latest trends, tools, and best practices in Android development.

Android provides a wealth of advantages for app developers, from its massive user base and open-source nature to its flexibility, developer-friendly tools, and robust monetization options. Whether you're a beginner or an experienced developer, Android offers the resources, community, and ecosystem needed to build innovative, high-performing apps. Its open and customizable platform, combined with powerful tools like Android Studio, Kotlin, and Jetpack, gives developers the freedom to create tailored experiences for a wide range of devices and users. Choosing Android for app development is a decision that opens up opportunities to reach billions of users worldwide, ensuring the growth and success of your app in a competitive marketplace.

1.5 Overview of Career Opportunities and Trends

The rapid growth of mobile technology and the dominance of Android as the leading operating system for mobile devices have created an expansive array of career opportunities for Android developers. The demand for skilled Android developers has surged as businesses and startups continue to focus on mobile-first strategies. As Android continues to evolve and innovate, developers also face a wide range of exciting new trends and advancements that shape the career landscape in the field. This section provides an overview of the career opportunities within Android development, the trends shaping the industry, and how developers can position themselves for success in this dynamic field.

1. The Growing Demand for Android Developers

The mobile app development industry is booming, and Android remains the leading platform for mobile applications worldwide. This growth has resulted in a significant demand for skilled Android developers across various industries, including technology, healthcare, finance, entertainment, e-commerce, and more. Organizations are constantly seeking talented Android developers who can create high-quality, user-centric applications to engage customers, boost productivity, and drive business growth.

Android developers can find opportunities in a variety of settings:

Tech Companies and Startups: Leading tech companies like Google, Samsung, and Facebook, as well as smaller startups, are always on the lookout for skilled Android developers to build innovative mobile apps. Startups, in particular, offer a dynamic and creative work environment, where developers have the opportunity to work on cutting-edge technologies and bring new ideas to life.

Freelance and Contract Work: Freelancing offers Android developers the flexibility to work on a variety of projects across different industries. Freelance developers can take on contracts with clients ranging from small businesses to large enterprises, creating custom Android apps tailored to specific needs. Freelancing can be a lucrative career path, especially for developers who have a strong portfolio and a network of clients.

Large Enterprises: Many large corporations have in-house teams of Android developers who create and maintain mobile applications for internal operations or customer-facing solutions. Enterprises in industries like finance, retail, and healthcare seek experienced Android developers to build secure, reliable, and scalable apps to serve their customers and employees.

App Development Agencies: App development agencies, which cater to clients looking for custom-built mobile applications, offer another career path for Android developers. Working at an agency allows developers to work on a wide range of projects and interact with clients from various industries.

2. Key Roles and Career Paths in Android Development

Android development offers multiple career paths, ranging from technical roles to managerial positions. As the industry matures and expands, developers can specialize in different aspects of Android development or progress into leadership positions. Some key roles and career paths in Android development include:

Junior/Entry-Level Android Developer: Junior Android developers are often new to the field and work under the guidance of senior developers. They focus on building foundational skills, learning Android frameworks, coding languages (Java/Kotlin), and contributing to the development of apps. It is a great starting point for individuals looking to establish a career in mobile app development.

Senior Android Developer: Senior developers have advanced knowledge of Android development and can design, implement, and optimize complex Android applications. They work on larger projects, mentor junior developers, and are often responsible for leading the technical direction of the team. Senior Android developers are expected to have expertise in multiple Android frameworks, libraries, and best practices.

Android Architect: Android architects focus on the design and architecture of mobile applications. They are responsible for ensuring that apps are scalable, maintainable, and optimized for performance. Android architects work closely with both developers and stakeholders to define the structure of the app and ensure that it meets technical, functional, and user experience requirements.

Mobile Development Manager/Lead: A Mobile Development Manager or Lead is a leadership position responsible for overseeing the Android development team. They handle project management, coordination, resource allocation, and strategic planning. In this role, developers must have strong leadership, communication, and organizational skills, as well as a deep understanding of Android technologies.

Android UI/UX Designer: While developers primarily focus on writing the code for Android apps, UI/UX designers are responsible for creating visually appealing and intuitive interfaces. For developers with a keen interest in design, this role can be a good fit, allowing them to combine their technical skills with creativity to enhance user experiences.

Mobile App Tester/QA Engineer: Quality Assurance (QA) engineers and testers play a crucial role in ensuring that Android apps are bug-free, secure, and high-performing. These professionals are responsible for testing apps under various conditions, identifying potential issues, and working with developers to resolve them before apps are released to the market.

Android Consultant: With deep expertise in Android development, consultants offer specialized advice and guidance to companies looking to build or improve their mobile apps. They often work with businesses to identify pain points, offer solutions, and implement best practices for app development.

3. Career Trends in Android Development

As the Android ecosystem continues to evolve, there are several emerging trends that will shape the future of Android development and offer new opportunities for developers. Staying ahead of these trends will help developers remain competitive and future-proof their careers:

Kotlin Adoption: Kotlin has become the preferred programming language for Android development, and its adoption is expected to continue to grow. Kotlin offers a modern, concise syntax with built-in safety features, making it easier for developers to write clean and error-free code. As more companies adopt Kotlin, developers with Kotlin expertise will be in high demand.

Jetpack and Modern Android Tools: Jetpack, a suite of libraries and components from Google, is revolutionizing Android development by providing tools that streamline app creation and maintenance. Jetpack Compose, a modern UI toolkit, is quickly gaining popularity for creating responsive and declarative user interfaces. Android developers who master these new tools will be better equipped to build scalable and maintainable apps.

Cross-Platform Development: While Android-specific development remains highly popular, cross-platform frameworks like Flutter, React Native, and Xamarin are gaining traction. These frameworks allow developers to write code once and deploy it on both Android and iOS platforms, reducing development time and cost. As businesses increasingly look for cost-effective solutions, cross-platform development skills are becoming a valuable asset for Android developers.

Android for IoT and Embedded Systems: The Internet of Things (IoT) is expanding, and Android is increasingly being used to power IoT devices and embedded systems. With Android Things, developers can create apps for smart devices like wearables, home automation systems, and connected vehicles. This growing field presents new career opportunities for developers interested in embedded development and IoT.

Artificial Intelligence and Machine Learning: AI and machine learning are becoming integral to mobile app development, and Android is no exception. With tools like ML Kit and TensorFlow Lite, developers can integrate machine learning models into their Android apps, enabling features like image recognition, natural language processing, and predictive analytics. As AI and machine learning continue to shape mobile experiences, Android developers with expertise in these areas will be highly sought after.

App Security and Privacy: With increasing concerns about data privacy and security, developers are placing more emphasis on building secure Android apps. Understanding Android's security features, best practices for securing data, and compliance with privacy regulations like the GDPR will be crucial for Android developers as the industry becomes more focused on privacy-conscious development.

4. Continuous Learning and Professional Development

Android development is a field that constantly evolves, and developers must commit to lifelong learning in order to stay current. The introduction of new tools, languages, libraries, and frameworks ensures that Android development is always advancing. Therefore, developers who continue to update their skills, explore new technologies, and contribute to the Android community will have the best opportunities for career growth.

Online Courses and Certifications: Many online platforms offer courses in Android development, and obtaining certifications can help developers stand out in a competitive job market. Google offers the Associate Android Developer certification, which is a recognized credential that demonstrates proficiency in Android development.

Community Involvement and Open-Source Contribution: Contributing to open-source projects, participating in developer communities, and attending conferences or meetups can significantly enhance a developer's career. Networking with peers, sharing knowledge, and staying informed about the latest industry trends are key to success in Android development.

Android development offers a wide range of career opportunities across various industries, roles, and career paths. The platform's massive market reach, combined with emerging trends like Kotlin adoption, cross-platform development, and machine learning, presents Android developers with abundant prospects for career advancement. By staying up-to-date with the latest tools and technologies, developers can position themselves to take advantage of new opportunities and carve out a rewarding career in the ever-evolving field of Android app development.

2. Setting Up Your Development Environment

Getting your development environment ready is the first crucial step toward building Android apps. In this chapter, you'll learn how to download and install Android Studio, the primary tool for Android development, and configure the necessary SDKs and emulators for testing. With a fully set-up environment, you'll be able to create, test, and refine your apps efficiently. This chapter ensures you're well-equipped to begin your Android development journey with a solid foundation in place.

2.1 Downloading and Installing Android Studio

Android Studio is the official Integrated Development Environment (IDE) for Android development, offering a comprehensive suite of tools for building, testing, and debugging Android apps. It's an essential tool for Android developers, providing features like code completion, UI design tools, device emulation, and real-time performance monitoring. This section walks you through the process of downloading and installing Android Studio, ensuring you're ready to start developing Android apps on your machine.

1. System Requirements

Before you begin downloading and installing Android Studio, it's important to ensure your system meets the minimum requirements. Android Studio can be installed on Windows, macOS, and Linux operating systems, but the hardware and software specifications vary for each platform.

For Windows:

- **OS**: Windows 8/10 (64-bit)
- **Processor**: x86_64 or ARM processor with 2 GB RAM or more (4 GB recommended)
- **RAM**: 4 GB minimum (8 GB recommended)
- **Hard Disk**: 2 GB of available disk space (minimum)
- **Java Development Kit (JDK):** Android Studio comes bundled with an embedded JDK, so you don't need to install it separately.

For macOS:

- **OS**: macOS 10.14 (Mojave) or later

- **Processor**: Intel-based or Apple Silicon (M1/M2 chip)
- **RAM**: 4 GB minimum (8 GB recommended)
- **Hard Disk**: 2 GB of available disk space (minimum)
- **Java Development Kit (JDK):** Bundled with Android Studio

For Linux:

- **OS**: 64-bit version of Linux (Ubuntu, Debian, or similar)
- **Processor**: 2 GB of RAM or more (4 GB recommended)
- **RAM**: 4 GB minimum (8 GB recommended)
- **Hard Disk**: 2 GB of available disk space (minimum)
- **Java Development Kit (JDK):** Bundled with Android Studio

Make sure that your machine meets or exceeds these specifications for the best performance.

2. Downloading Android Studio

Now that you have verified your system meets the necessary requirements, you can begin downloading Android Studio from the official website.

Steps for Downloading:

Visit the Android Developer Website: Go to the official Android developer website to download Android Studio: https://developer.android.com/studio.

Choose Your Platform: On the website, you'll be presented with options to download Android Studio for Windows, macOS, or Linux. Select the appropriate option for your operating system.

Download the Installer: Click the Download Android Studio button, and the installer file will start downloading. Be sure to agree to the terms and conditions when prompted.

- **Windows**: The file will usually be named something like android-studio-ide-xxxx.xxxxx-windows.exe.
- **macOS**: The file will be a .dmg disk image file, such as android-studio-ide-xxxx.xxxxx-mac.dmg.
- **Linux**: The file will typically be a .tar.gz archive, like android-studio-ide-xxxx.xxxxx-linux.tar.gz.

Wait for the Download to Complete: The file size can vary depending on the version and platform, but generally, it should take a few minutes to download, depending on your internet connection.

3. Installing Android Studio

Once the download is complete, you can proceed with the installation process. The steps vary depending on your operating system.

For Windows:

Run the Installer: Double-click the .exe installer file that was downloaded. The Android Studio Setup Wizard will launch.

Choose Installation Options: The installer will ask you to choose the installation options. You can typically go with the default options:

- **Install Android Studio**: This is the main installation of the IDE.
- **Android Virtual Device (AVD):** This is optional but recommended as it will allow you to test your apps on an Android emulator.

Begin Installation: Click on Next and follow the prompts to complete the installation. The process should take a few minutes, depending on your system's performance.

Launch Android Studio: Once the installation is complete, you can launch Android Studio. You'll be asked if you want to import previous settings (if you've used Android Studio before), but if this is your first time, you can simply choose Do not import settings.

For macOS:

Open the .dmg File: Double-click the downloaded .dmg file. This will mount the Android Studio disk image.

Drag and Drop to Applications Folder: In the window that opens, drag the Android Studio icon into the Applications folder. This installs Android Studio on your Mac.

Launch Android Studio: Go to your Applications folder and double-click Android Studio to launch the application. You may be prompted to confirm opening the app since it was downloaded from the internet. Click Open to proceed.

For Linux:

Extract the .tar.gz File: Open a terminal and navigate to the directory where the .tar.gz file was downloaded. Use the following command to extract the contents:

tar -xvzf android-studio-ide-xxxx.xxxxx-linux.tar.gz

Move the Folder: Once extracted, move the Android Studio folder to a location where you want to store it (e.g., /opt/):

sudo mv android-studio /opt/

Run Android Studio: Navigate to the Android Studio directory and run the following command:

./studio.sh

This will launch Android Studio. You may want to create a symbolic link or a desktop shortcut for easier access.

4. Initial Setup and Configuration

After installing Android Studio, you'll need to complete some initial setup and configuration steps to prepare the IDE for your Android development needs.

Welcome Screen: Upon first launching Android Studio, you'll be greeted by a welcome screen that allows you to configure the IDE. If this is your first time setting up Android Studio, select Standard installation for the recommended settings.

Install Required SDK Packages: Android Studio will prompt you to install the Android SDK (Software Development Kit) and other essential components, such as the Android Emulator. These tools are necessary for building and testing Android apps. Click Next to start the SDK installation process.

Download and Install Updates: Android Studio may check for any updates, and it's a good idea to install them before continuing. It's important to keep Android Studio and SDK components up to date to ensure compatibility with the latest Android features.

Create a Virtual Device (Optional): If you plan to test your apps using an Android emulator, you can configure a Virtual Device (AVD) during setup. This allows you to simulate Android devices on your computer, which is useful if you don't have a physical Android device for testing. Alternatively, you can create an emulator at any time later from the AVD Manager in Android Studio.

Configure Java Development Kit (JDK): Android Studio includes an embedded version of the JDK, but in some cases, you may need to configure it manually if your system uses a separate JDK. Ensure the JDK is correctly set up in the IDE's preferences.

5. Starting a New Project

Once the installation and setup are complete, you're ready to start building Android apps. Android Studio offers a variety of project templates to get started quickly. You can choose a template based on the type of app you want to create (e.g., a basic activity, a navigation drawer, or a full-screen app). You'll also be prompted to choose the app's language (Java or Kotlin), the minimum SDK version, and other configuration details.

Downloading and installing Android Studio is the first step toward becoming an Android app developer. The installation process is straightforward, but it's essential to ensure that your system meets the requirements and that the necessary components, like the Android SDK and emulator, are properly installed. With Android Studio set up, you're now ready to start creating Android applications and exploring the wide range of development tools and features that Android Studio has to offer.

2.2 Configuring the Android SDK and Virtual Devices

After installing Android Studio, one of the most important steps is configuring the Android Software Development Kit (SDK) and setting up Virtual Devices (AVDs). These components are crucial for building and testing your Android applications. The SDK provides the necessary tools and libraries to develop Android apps, while the Virtual Devices allow you to simulate different Android devices and test your apps without needing physical hardware.

This section will guide you through the process of configuring both the Android SDK and Virtual Devices within Android Studio.

1. Understanding the Android SDK

The Android SDK (Software Development Kit) is a collection of tools and libraries that Android developers use to build, test, and debug apps. It includes essential components like the Android platform libraries, SDK tools, Android Emulator, and more.

Android Studio includes the SDK during installation, but you may need to configure it to ensure everything is working correctly.

Key Components of the SDK:

- **SDK Tools**: Includes platform tools like ADB (Android Debug Bridge), SDK Manager, and build tools.
- **Android Platforms**: Different versions of the Android operating system that you can target for app development. For example, Android 10 (API level 29), Android 11 (API level 30), and so on.
- **System Images**: The images required to run Android Emulators, simulating different devices, screen sizes, and Android versions.
- **Android Support Libraries**: Libraries such as Jetpack that provide backward compatibility and additional functionality for app development.

2. Configuring the Android SDK in Android Studio

When you first install Android Studio, the SDK is automatically downloaded and installed. However, in some cases, you may need to configure it manually or update the SDK to ensure you have the latest tools and platform components.

Steps to Configure the SDK:

Open Android Studio: Launch Android Studio, and from the welcome screen, click on Configure (located in the lower right corner of the window). Then select SDK Manager from the dropdown menu. You can also access the SDK Manager from within Android Studio by navigating to File > Settings > Appearance & Behavior > System Settings > Android SDK.

SDK Manager Overview: The SDK Manager window will display a list of installed SDK components, including the SDK tools, platforms, and system images. Here you can manage which versions of the SDK and tools are installed or updated.

Selecting SDK Components: In the SDK Manager, you'll see tabs for:

- **SDK Platforms**: This section shows the different Android versions available. Check the boxes next to the versions you want to install or use. You can install the latest Android API levels or specific older versions if you need to support multiple Android versions.
- **SDK Tools**: Here, you can install or update important SDK tools like the Android SDK Build-Tools, Android Emulator, and platform tools. These tools help with app building, debugging, and emulation.
- **SDK Update Sites**: This tab allows you to manage additional SDK repositories if needed.

Install or Update SDK Components: After selecting the platforms and tools you need, click OK to start the installation or update process. Android Studio will download and install the components. You may be prompted to restart Android Studio once the installation is complete.

Verifying SDK Installation: To ensure that the SDK is correctly installed, you can check if everything is working by opening a new project in Android Studio and running it on a physical device or emulator.

3. Setting Up Virtual Devices (AVDs)

Android Virtual Devices (AVDs) allow you to simulate various Android devices on your computer. These virtual devices are invaluable for testing your apps on different screen sizes, resolutions, and Android versions, especially if you don't have access to physical devices.

Steps to Set Up a Virtual Device:

Open AVD Manager: In Android Studio, open the AVD Manager by clicking on the Tools menu at the top and selecting AVD Manager. You can also open the AVD Manager by clicking on the AVD icon in the toolbar (a phone-like icon).

Create a New Virtual Device:

- Click on the Create Virtual Device button in the AVD Manager.
- A dialog will appear where you can select the type of device you want to emulate. You can choose from a range of pre-configured devices, such as Nexus, Pixel, or other popular Android phones and tablets. You can even simulate wearables and other non-phone devices.

Choose Device Configuration: After selecting a device model, you'll be prompted to select the system image (the Android version) you want the virtual device to run. You can select from a variety of Android versions, including the latest stable release or older versions. If the system image for the selected Android version is not yet downloaded, you can download it at this point.

Configuring the Device Settings:

- **Device**: You can choose from a list of predefined device configurations, such as screen size, resolution, and density. You can even add custom configurations to meet your specific testing needs.
- **Graphics**: You can choose between Software or Hardware graphics acceleration for your virtual device. Hardware acceleration provides faster emulation, but it requires support for hardware acceleration on your machine (for example, Intel HAXM for Windows or Hypervisor Framework for macOS). If your machine doesn't support hardware acceleration, you can use software graphics, but it may be slower.
- **Memory and Storage**: You can configure the RAM, internal storage, and SD card size for the virtual device. If you need more space for your app's data, adjust the storage settings accordingly.

Finalizing AVD Configuration: After configuring the settings for your virtual device, click Finish to create the AVD. The new virtual device will now appear in the AVD Manager.

Launching the Virtual Device: To launch the AVD, simply click the Play button (a green triangle) next to the device in the AVD Manager. The emulator will start, and the virtual device will boot up. Depending on your system, it might take a few moments for the emulator to launch.

4. Running and Testing Your App on Virtual Devices

Once your AVD is set up, you can begin running and testing your Android applications on it.

Steps to Run Your App:

Start a New Project or Open an Existing One: Open your Android project in Android Studio or create a new one by selecting Start a New Android Studio Project.

Choose a Device to Run the App: After you've written your code, click the Run button (a green play icon) located in the toolbar of Android Studio. Android Studio will ask you to select a device to run the app. You can choose the AVD you just created or a physical device (if connected to your computer).

Running the App on the Emulator: If you select the emulator, Android Studio will automatically start the virtual device (if it isn't already running) and install the app. The app will launch on the virtual device, and you can begin interacting with it to test its functionality.

Debugging and Performance Monitoring: Android Studio provides real-time tools to monitor performance and debug your app. Use the Android Monitor tab to view logs, monitor CPU and memory usage, and identify issues with your app's performance. You can also debug your app using breakpoints and step through your code.

5. Managing Virtual Devices

The AVD Manager allows you to manage your virtual devices. You can:

- **Edit a Device**: Click the pencil icon next to any AVD to modify its settings.
- **Delete a Device**: Click the trash can icon next to an AVD to remove it from your system.
- **Wipe Data**: If you want to clear app data from the virtual device, you can use the "Wipe Data" option in the AVD Manager.
- **Launch a Device**: You can start the virtual device by clicking the Play icon.

Configuring the Android SDK and setting up Virtual Devices in Android Studio is a crucial step for any Android developer. With the SDK tools, you gain access to everything necessary for app development, while Virtual Devices provide a convenient and cost-effective way to test your apps on multiple devices and Android versions. By following these steps, you ensure that your development environment is properly configured, enabling you to start building, testing, and deploying Android apps.

2.3 Exploring Android Studio's Interface

Android Studio is a powerful and feature-rich IDE designed specifically for Android development. Understanding its interface is crucial to becoming proficient in developing Android apps. Android Studio's interface is designed to streamline your workflow, providing easy access to tools for coding, testing, debugging, and deploying your Android applications. This section explores the key elements of Android Studio's interface, helping you navigate the IDE efficiently and utilize its features to their fullest potential.

1. The Welcome Screen

When you first launch Android Studio, you're greeted by the Welcome Screen. This screen provides you with a variety of options to start or manage your projects.

- **Start a New Android Studio Project**: This option allows you to create a new Android project, where you can specify the app's name, programming language (Java or Kotlin), template, and minimum SDK version.
- **Open an Existing Android Studio Project**: This option lets you open an already existing project, either locally or from version control (like Git).
- **Check out Sample Code**: If you want to explore some sample Android projects, this option lets you browse through different templates and examples provided by Android Studio.
- **Import Project**: If you have a project in another IDE or a different Android project, you can import it into Android Studio.
- **Configure**: From here, you can access the settings of Android Studio, such as the SDK Manager, AVD Manager, and other configuration options.

Once you open or create a project, you'll be directed to the main interface.

2. Main Window

The main window of Android Studio is where you will spend most of your time writing code, building your app, and managing your project. It consists of several key sections that allow you to easily interact with your app's files, resources, and tools.

2.1 The Toolbar

The Toolbar is located at the top of the screen and provides easy access to common actions and commands. Some of the most important features of the toolbar include:

- **Run Button (Green Play Icon):** Used to compile and run your app on a selected device or emulator.
- **Debug Button (Bug Icon):** Starts the app in debug mode, allowing you to step through code and inspect variables to diagnose issues.
- **Sync Project with Gradle Files**: This button ensures your project is synchronized with its configuration files (e.g., build.gradle).

- **Search and Navigation**: The toolbar contains a search box that helps you quickly navigate to files, classes, methods, or symbols in your project.
- **Build Button**: Compiles your code and resources, ensuring everything is up-to-date before running or testing the app.

2.2 The Project View (Left Sidebar)

The Project View is a crucial part of Android Studio. It displays the structure of your app, showing all your project files in a tree format. This view helps you navigate between different directories and files in your project, including source code, resources, and configuration files. The Project View can be customized to display files in different ways, depending on your needs.

- **Android View**: The default view for Android projects. It groups your app's components like java source code, res resources, and manifest file into a clear, organized structure.
- **Project View**: Displays your project in a file system format (i.e., directories and files as they are in your system).
- **Packages View**: Shows your project organized by Java or Kotlin package structure.

2.3 Code Editor (Center Panel)

The Code Editor is where you write and modify your code. It's the most important area of Android Studio, allowing you to interact with your source code, layout files, and more.

- **Syntax Highlighting**: Android Studio automatically highlights syntax to make it easier to read code and spot errors.
- **Code Suggestions and Auto-completion**: As you type, Android Studio provides code suggestions and completions to speed up your coding process.
- **Refactoring Tools**: Android Studio offers advanced refactoring tools that let you safely rename variables, classes, and methods or restructure your code with a few clicks.
- **Code Navigation**: You can navigate between classes, methods, or variables quickly using features like Ctrl+Click (Windows/Linux) or Cmd+Click (Mac).
- **Multiple Tabs**: The editor allows you to open multiple files simultaneously in tabs for easy switching between them.
- **Linter and Error Highlighting**: The editor highlights syntax errors, warnings, and other issues in your code in real time, making it easier to detect and fix problems as you write.

2.4 The Design Editor (For Layout Files)

When working with layout files (XML), the Design Editor is a key feature. It provides a visual interface for building UIs in Android applications, allowing you to drag and drop UI components onto a screen.

- **Text Editor**: In addition to the Design Editor, you can directly edit the XML code to create the layout manually.
- **Preview**: You can see a live preview of how your layout will look on different screen sizes, resolutions, and orientations.
- **Component Palette**: A sidebar on the left that contains all the UI elements (buttons, text fields, images, etc.) that you can drag into your layout.
- **Attributes Panel**: Displays the properties of the selected UI component, allowing you to modify its attributes, such as size, color, margins, etc.

2.5 The Navigation Bar (Top of the Editor)

The Navigation Bar sits just below the toolbar and provides an easy way to navigate between the different components and files in your project. It shows your current file's location within the project structure and allows you to quickly open other files, folders, or classes.

- **Breadcrumb Navigation**: This helps you track your position in the project hierarchy. You can click on any section of the breadcrumb trail to jump to that section.
- **Quick File Navigation**: You can search for and navigate to any file within your project using the navigation bar.

3. Tool Windows (Right Sidebar)

The right sidebar in Android Studio contains multiple Tool Windows that help you interact with your project in different ways. These windows can be accessed via the buttons at the bottom of the screen or through the View > Tool Windows menu.

3.1 Build Output

The Build Output window displays the output of the Gradle build process, showing detailed information about the build, including success or error messages. If you encounter build errors, this is where you'll find the specific error messages that help you debug your issues.

3.2 Logcat

The Logcat window displays system logs and messages generated by your app. It's an essential tool for debugging, as it shows all runtime logs, including error messages, warnings, and system information. You can filter logs by tag, severity level, or process to focus on relevant information.

3.3 Profiler

The Profiler tool lets you monitor your app's performance, such as CPU usage, memory consumption, and network activity. This is crucial for optimizing the performance of your app, identifying memory leaks, and ensuring smooth operation.

3.4 Terminal

The Terminal window provides a built-in command-line interface directly inside Android Studio. You can run commands, scripts, and version control commands (e.g., Git) without leaving the IDE.

3.5 Version Control (VCS)

If you're working with version control, the Version Control tool window provides an interface to manage your source code repository. You can commit changes, pull updates, resolve conflicts, and push updates directly from within Android Studio.

4. Status Bar (Bottom of the Window)

At the bottom of Android Studio, the Status Bar provides helpful information about your project, build process, and environment.

- **Build Progress**: Displays the progress of your app's build and whether the build was successful or failed.
- **Sync Status**: Shows the status of your project's sync with Gradle, indicating whether everything is up to date.
- **Device Information**: If you have a device connected or an emulator running, the status bar will display details about the device, such as its name and version.

Android Studio's interface is designed to provide a seamless and efficient development experience. By familiarizing yourself with the key sections of the IDE — the toolbar, project view, code editor, design editor, and various tool windows — you'll be able to navigate Android Studio with ease and leverage its full potential for building Android applications. As you get more accustomed to the layout and features, you'll find that Android Studio becomes a powerful ally in your development workflow, streamlining the process of creating high-quality Android apps.

2.4 Using Physical Devices for Testing

Testing your Android app on a physical device is an essential part of the development process. While emulators are useful for preliminary testing, real-world testing on actual devices offers insights into performance, compatibility, and user experience that emulators cannot replicate. This section walks you through the steps for setting up a physical device for testing, ensuring your app runs as intended across various hardware configurations.

1. Why Use Physical Devices for Testing?

Testing on physical devices provides several advantages:

- **Real-World Performance**: You can evaluate how your app performs under real-world conditions, including hardware limitations, network connectivity, and battery constraints.
- **Hardware Features**: Testing on physical devices allows you to access device-specific features such as cameras, sensors (e.g., accelerometer, gyroscope), and biometric authentication.
- **User Experience**: Physical testing reveals how users will interact with your app, including touch responsiveness, gestures, and screen transitions.
- **Device-Specific Bugs**: Different manufacturers implement Android differently, and testing on physical devices helps identify device-specific issues.

2. Setting Up Your Physical Device

Before you can test your app on a physical device, you need to configure it to communicate with Android Studio.

2.1 Enable Developer Options

- Open the Settings app on your Android device.
- Navigate to About Phone (the exact path may vary by manufacturer).
- Find the Build Number and tap it repeatedly (usually 7 times) until you see a message indicating that you are now a developer.
- Return to the main Settings menu, and you'll see a new option called Developer Options.

2.2 Enable USB Debugging

- Open Developer Options in the Settings app.
- Locate and enable USB Debugging.
- Confirm the prompt asking if you want to allow USB debugging.

2.3 Install Necessary USB Drivers

For Windows users, you may need to install OEM-specific USB drivers for your device to connect it to your computer properly. Check the manufacturer's website for the appropriate drivers. Mac and Linux users typically don't require additional drivers.

3. Connecting Your Device to Android Studio

3.1 Connect via USB

- Use a USB cable to connect your Android device to your computer.
- If prompted on your device, choose the File Transfer (MTP) or USB Debugging option from the notification panel.

3.2 Authorize Your Computer

When you connect your device to your computer for the first time, a prompt will appear on your device asking you to authorize the computer. Tap Allow or OK to grant access.

3.3 Verify Device Connection

- Open Android Studio and navigate to the Device Manager (available from the toolbar or menu).
- Your device should appear in the list of connected devices. If it doesn't, try the following:
- Ensure USB Debugging is enabled.
- Check the USB cable and port.

- Restart Android Studio or your device.

4. Running Your App on a Physical Device

Once your device is connected and recognized by Android Studio, you can run your app on it.

- Open your project in Android Studio.
- Click the Run button (green play icon) in the toolbar.
- In the Select Deployment Target window, select your physical device from the list.
- Click OK to build and install the app on your device.

The app will launch automatically on your device once the installation is complete.

5. Wireless Debugging (Optional)

If you prefer to test without a USB connection, Android Studio supports wireless debugging on devices running Android 11 or later.

5.1 Enable Wireless Debugging

- Go to Developer Options on your device.
- Enable Wireless Debugging.

Pair your device with your computer using a pairing code provided in the Wireless Debugging settings.

5.2 Connect in Android Studio

- Open the Device Manager in Android Studio.
- Click the Pair Using Wi-Fi option.
- Enter the pairing code from your device to establish a connection.

This setup allows you to debug your app wirelessly, which is especially useful when testing scenarios that involve movement or device independence.

6. Common Issues and Troubleshooting

6.1 Device Not Recognized

- **Check USB Cable/Port**: Use a data-capable USB cable and try different ports.
- **Reinstall Drivers**: Ensure the correct USB drivers are installed for your device.
- **Reauthorize Device**: Disconnect and reconnect the device, ensuring you allow USB debugging access.

6.2 App Not Installing or Launching

- **Check Storage Space**: Ensure the device has enough storage for the app.
- **Compatibility Issues**: Verify that your app's target SDK version matches the device's Android version.

6.3 Wireless Debugging Fails

- **Check Network**: Ensure your computer and device are on the same Wi-Fi network.
- **Re-pair Devices**: Restart the pairing process if the connection fails.

7. Best Practices for Physical Device Testing

- **Test on Multiple Devices**: Android devices come in a variety of sizes, resolutions, and hardware configurations. Test your app on a diverse set of devices to ensure broad compatibility.
- **Test Real-World Scenarios**: Evaluate your app in conditions similar to what users will experience, such as varying network speeds, low battery, or background app activity.
- **Regularly Update Devices**: Keep your testing devices updated with the latest software and security patches.
- **Document Bugs**: Record any issues you encounter during physical testing and fix them promptly to ensure a polished app.

Using physical devices for testing is an indispensable part of the Android development process. By configuring and connecting your device to Android Studio, you gain access to a more authentic testing environment that replicates the experience of end users. This step ensures that your app is not only functional but also optimized for the wide range of Android devices available in the market. As you progress, incorporating physical device testing into your workflow will help you deliver apps that perform seamlessly and meet user expectations.

2.5 Troubleshooting Common Installation Issues

Setting up your development environment is a crucial first step in Android app development, but sometimes things don't go as planned. From installation hiccups to connectivity problems, these challenges can be frustrating but are often simple to resolve. This section provides a detailed guide to troubleshooting common issues you may encounter when installing Android Studio, configuring the SDK, or connecting devices.

1. Android Studio Installation Issues

1.1 Problem: Installer Fails to Launch

Cause: Missing or incompatible Java Development Kit (JDK) installation.

Solution:

- Ensure you have the correct JDK version installed (recommended: OpenJDK 11 or later).
- Check your system's PATH environment variable to include the JDK's bin directory.

1.2 Problem: Installation Freezes or Crashes

Cause: Insufficient system resources or antivirus interference.

Solution:

- Close other resource-intensive applications to free up memory.
- Temporarily disable antivirus or firewall software that might block the installer.

1.3 Problem: Android Studio Won't Start After Installation

Cause: Graphics driver compatibility or corrupted files.

Solution:

- Update your graphics drivers.
- Delete the Android Studio configuration folder (typically located in your user directory) and reinstall the application.

2. Android SDK Issues

2.1 Problem: SDK Not Found

Cause: SDK path not properly configured.

Solution:

- Open Android Studio and navigate to File > Settings > Appearance & Behavior > System Settings > Android SDK.
- Verify the SDK installation directory or click Edit to specify the correct path.

2.2 Problem: SDK Tools Fail to Download
Cause: Network issues or proxy settings.

Solution:

- Check your internet connection and ensure Android Studio has access.
- Configure proxy settings in Android Studio under File > Settings > Appearance & Behavior > System Settings > HTTP Proxy if you are on a restricted network.

3. Emulator Problems

3.1 Problem: Emulator Fails to Start

Cause: Hardware acceleration is disabled or incompatible CPU.

Solution:

- Enable Intel HAXM or AMD Hypervisor for hardware acceleration (Windows/Mac).
- On Windows, ensure Virtualization Technology is enabled in your BIOS/UEFI settings.

3.2 Problem: Emulator Freezes or Runs Slowly

Cause: Low system resources or incorrect configuration.

Solution:

- Allocate more RAM and CPU cores to the emulator in the AVD Manager.

- Reduce screen resolution or select a device image with lower specifications.

4. Device Connectivity Issues

4.1 Problem: Device Not Detected by Android Studio

Cause: USB debugging not enabled or missing drivers.

Solution:

- Ensure USB Debugging is enabled on your Android device (via Developer Options).
- Install the appropriate USB drivers for your device manufacturer.

4.2 Problem: Device Listed as "Unauthorized"

Cause: USB debugging authorization not granted.

Solution:

- Disconnect and reconnect the device to your computer.
- When prompted on your device, grant debugging authorization.

4.3 Problem: Wireless Debugging Doesn't Work

Cause: Network mismatch or pairing issues.

Solution:

- Ensure your computer and device are connected to the same Wi-Fi network.
- Restart the pairing process in Android Studio.

5. Gradle Sync Errors

5.1 Problem: Gradle Fails to Sync

Cause: Network timeout or incorrect Gradle version.

Solution:

- Check your internet connection and retry the sync.
- Open File > Project Structure > Project, and ensure the correct Gradle version is specified.
- Use an offline Gradle build by enabling Offline Mode in File > Settings > Gradle.

5.2 Problem: Dependency Resolution Issues

Cause: Missing or outdated dependencies.

Solution:

- Update the dependencies in your build.gradle file to the latest versions.
- Click Sync Now to reload and download dependencies.

6. Configuration Problems

6.1 Problem: Incorrect JDK Path

Cause: Misconfigured JDK settings.

Solution:

- Open File > Project Structure > SDK Location in Android Studio.
- Verify or update the JDK path to point to the correct directory.

6.2 Problem: AVD Configuration Errors

Cause: Unsupported device settings.

Solution:

- Recreate the AVD with compatible settings (e.g., reducing RAM allocation for low-resource systems).
- Select a stable system image for your virtual device (e.g., Android 11 or Android 12).

7. Log Analysis for Debugging

When issues arise, analyzing logs can help identify the root cause:

View IDE Logs:

Navigate to Help > Show Log in Explorer/Finder to access Android Studio logs.

View Emulator Logs:

Open the emulator's extended controls and navigate to the Logcat tab for real-time logs.

Use Logcat in Android Studio:

Open the Logcat pane in Android Studio to view app-specific logs during testing.

8. Tips for Avoiding Future Issues

Keep Your Tools Updated:

Regularly update Android Studio, SDK tools, and Gradle to the latest versions.

Follow Official Documentation:

Refer to the official Android Developer documentation for installation guides and troubleshooting tips.

Join Developer Communities:

Participate in forums like StackOverflow and Android developer groups to seek solutions from experienced developers.

Troubleshooting installation issues can seem daunting, but with systematic approaches and attention to detail, most problems can be resolved quickly. Whether it's configuring your SDK, resolving Gradle sync errors, or connecting physical devices, understanding these common issues equips you with the confidence to overcome hurdles and focus on building amazing Android apps. By addressing these challenges early, you ensure a smoother development experience and lay a solid foundation for success in your Android development journey.

3. Understanding Android Architecture

A solid understanding of Android's architecture is crucial for building efficient and scalable apps. In this chapter, you will explore the fundamental structure of the Android platform, including its layered architecture and core components. By understanding how different elements of the system interact, from Activities and Services to the Android Manifest file and Gradle build system, you will gain the knowledge needed to design apps that are both powerful and maintainable. This chapter serves as a foundation for mastering Android app development.

3.1 Overview of Android's Layered Architecture

Android's architecture is a carefully designed layered stack that ensures efficiency, scalability, and modularity for app development. This architecture consists of several layers, each serving a specific purpose, from hardware interaction to user interface management. By understanding this layered approach, developers can better grasp how Android operates and how its components interact to deliver a seamless experience for users.

1. The Layered Structure of Android

Android's architecture is organized into five main layers:

- Linux Kernel
- Hardware Abstraction Layer (HAL)
- Android Runtime (ART)
- Native C/C++ Libraries
- Application Framework
- Applications

Each layer builds upon the functionality of the layer below it, creating a robust and flexible ecosystem.

2. Linux Kernel

At the foundation of Android's architecture lies the Linux Kernel, which provides the following:

- **Hardware Abstraction**: Acts as a bridge between hardware and software, managing drivers for components like display, camera, and sensors.
- **Resource Management**: Handles tasks such as memory management, process scheduling, and power management.
- **Security**: Provides features like user permissions, secure data storage, and encrypted communication.

The Linux Kernel ensures Android's compatibility with a wide range of devices, enabling seamless integration across manufacturers.

3. Hardware Abstraction Layer (HAL)

The HAL serves as a modular interface between the hardware drivers (managed by the Linux Kernel) and the Android system. Key features include:

- **Device-Specific Interfaces**: HAL components are customized to allow Android to communicate with specific hardware without requiring changes to the higher layers.
- **Extensibility**: Enables manufacturers to introduce new hardware features without disrupting the Android core.

For example, the HAL allows Android to utilize camera hardware, audio systems, and Bluetooth devices efficiently.

4. Android Runtime (ART)

The Android Runtime (ART) is responsible for executing Android applications and includes the following:

- **Just-In-Time (JIT) Compilation**: Optimizes app performance by compiling frequently used code at runtime.
- **Ahead-Of-Time (AOT) Compilation**: Precompiles apps during installation to improve startup times and reduce runtime overhead.
- **Garbage Collection**: Manages memory allocation and deallocation, ensuring efficient memory use and preventing leaks.

ART replaced the older Dalvik Virtual Machine, offering better performance and support for modern features.

5. Native C/C++ Libraries

Android relies on a suite of native libraries, written in C/C++, to provide essential functionality:

- **Graphics and Media**: Libraries like OpenGL ES and Media Framework support high-performance rendering and multimedia processing.
- **Database Management**: SQLite enables efficient local data storage for apps.
- **Web Rendering**: WebKit powers web-based content display within applications.

These libraries provide developers with advanced tools to build feature-rich, high-performance apps.

6. Application Framework

The Application Framework is the cornerstone of Android's architecture for developers, offering APIs to interact with system features and manage app behavior. Key components include:

- **Activity Manager**: Controls app lifecycle and navigation.
- **Content Providers**: Facilitate data sharing between apps.
- **Resource Manager**: Manages app resources like layouts, strings, and images.
- **Notification Manager**: Allows apps to display notifications to users.

This layer ensures consistency and simplicity for developers building Android apps.

7. Applications

At the top of the stack are Applications, including:

- Pre-installed system apps like Phone, Messages, and Settings.
- Third-party apps installed by users from the Google Play Store or other sources.

These applications interact with the underlying layers through the Application Framework, providing a seamless and intuitive experience for end-users.

8. Inter-Layer Communication

Each layer of Android's architecture communicates with adjacent layers using well-defined interfaces:

- The Application Framework interacts with native libraries and ART for execution.
- ART relies on the HAL and Linux Kernel for hardware access and system management.
- HAL modules abstract hardware complexities for the kernel.

This modularity ensures that changes in one layer have minimal impact on others, making Android a highly adaptable platform.

9. Benefits of Android's Layered Architecture

The layered design of Android offers several advantages:

- **Modularity**: Developers and manufacturers can update or replace specific components without disrupting the entire system.
- **Scalability**: Android can scale across a wide range of devices, from low-end phones to high-performance tablets.
- **Security**: Each layer has built-in security features, enhancing overall platform integrity.
- **Ease of Development**: The Application Framework abstracts complexities, allowing developers to focus on app functionality.

Android's layered architecture is a testament to its design philosophy of modularity and efficiency. By separating concerns across layers, Android achieves a balance between flexibility and performance, enabling developers to create powerful apps while ensuring compatibility across diverse hardware. Understanding this architecture not only empowers developers to build better applications but also equips them to troubleshoot and optimize their apps effectively.

3.2 Core Android Components Explained

Android applications are built upon four core components, each serving a unique purpose in the application lifecycle and user interaction model. Understanding these components is essential for creating robust and efficient apps. This section explores Activities, Services, Broadcast Receivers, and Content Providers, highlighting their roles, interactions, and practical applications.

1. Activities: The Building Blocks of User Interfaces

An Activity represents a single screen with a user interface, serving as the entry point for user interactions in an Android application. Each activity typically corresponds to a specific task or feature within the app.

Lifecycle Management:

Activities follow a well-defined lifecycle managed by Android, including states such as onCreate(), onStart(), onPause(), and onDestroy(). This lifecycle ensures proper resource allocation and user experience consistency.

Example:

In a messaging app, activities might include a login screen, a contact list, and a chat interface.

Navigation:

Developers use intents to transition between activities, enabling seamless navigation.

2. Services: Background Operations

A Service is a component designed to perform long-running operations in the background, independent of the user interface. Services are ideal for tasks that need to continue running even when the user is not actively interacting with the app.

Types of Services:

- **Foreground Services**: Display a persistent notification (e.g., music players).
- **Background Services**: Perform tasks without user awareness (e.g., syncing data).
- **Bound Services**: Provide a client-server interface for interaction between components.

Lifecycle Management:

Services operate through lifecycle methods like onStartCommand(), onBind(), and onDestroy().

Example:

In a weather app, a service might fetch weather updates periodically in the background.

3. Broadcast Receivers: Responding to System Events

A Broadcast Receiver allows applications to respond to system-wide or app-specific events. Broadcasts are sent when significant system events occur, such as a change in network connectivity, device boot completion, or an incoming SMS.

Two Types of Broadcasts:

- **System Broadcasts**: Sent by the Android OS (e.g., battery low, connectivity change).
- **Custom Broadcasts**: Sent by applications to communicate between components.

Example:

A fitness app might use a broadcast receiver to detect when the device's battery is low and pause background activities to conserve energy.

Registration Methods:

- **Manifest Declaration**: Static, long-term receivers declared in the AndroidManifest.xml.
- **Dynamic Registration**: Temporary receivers registered during runtime for specific tasks.

4. Content Providers: Data Sharing and Management

A Content Provider enables applications to manage and share structured data securely. Content providers act as an intermediary for accessing data stored in databases, files, or external storage.

Role:

They allow apps to read and write data using standardized queries, making data accessible to other apps with proper permissions.

Examples of System Content Providers:

- **ContactsProvider**: Provides access to the user's contacts.

- **MediaStore**: Manages multimedia files like images, videos, and audio.

Custom Content Providers:

Developers can create their own providers to expose app-specific data to other applications.

Example:

A calendar app might use a content provider to share event data with other apps, such as reminders or scheduling assistants.

5. Interaction Between Components

The core components don't operate in isolation—they interact through a mechanism called intents, which act as messengers between components.

- **Explicit Intents**: Directly specify the target component. For example, transitioning from one activity to another.
- **Implicit Intents**: Describe the action to be performed, allowing the system to find the appropriate component. For example, opening a URL using the default web browser.

6. Importance of Core Components

Understanding the core Android components helps developers design applications that are modular, efficient, and aligned with Android's design principles. These components offer the flexibility to create diverse app experiences, from simple single-screen apps to complex, multi-functional applications.

The core components of Android—Activities, Services, Broadcast Receivers, and Content Providers—form the backbone of app development. Mastery of these elements empowers developers to create apps that are responsive, resource-efficient, and highly interactive. By leveraging their unique functionalities and understanding their interplay, developers can build applications that meet the demands of modern users while adhering to Android's best practices.

3.3 Understanding the Android Manifest File

The Android Manifest File is a crucial component in every Android application. It acts as the central configuration file that informs the Android operating system about the app's structure, capabilities, and requirements. Understanding the role and structure of this file is essential for developers, as it directly impacts how the application behaves and interacts with the system and users.

1. What Is the Android Manifest File?

The Android Manifest file, named AndroidManifest.xml, is an XML document located in the root directory of an Android project. It defines the app's essential information, including:

- The app's package name, which serves as its unique identifier.
- Components such as activities, services, broadcast receivers, and content providers.
- Permissions the app needs, like internet access or location services.
- Hardware and software requirements for compatibility with devices.

2. Key Elements of the Manifest File

The Android Manifest contains several key elements that outline the app's structure and functionality:

2.1 <manifest> Element

- The root element of the file.
- Contains the package name, which uniquely identifies the app on the Play Store and devices.

Example:

```
<manifest xmlns:android="http://schemas.android.com/apk/res/android"
    package="com.example.myapp">
</manifest>
```

2.2 <application> Element

- Encloses all app-level configurations and components.
- Defines icons, themes, and app components like activities, services, and receivers.

Example:

```
<application
    android:icon="@mipmap/ic_launcher"
    android:label="@string/app_name"
    android:theme="@style/AppTheme">
</application>
```

2.3 <activity> Element

- Specifies each Activity in the app, including the entry point (main activity).

Example:

```
<activity android:name=".MainActivity">
    <intent-filter>
        <action android:name="android.intent.action.MAIN" />
        <category android:name="android.intent.category.LAUNCHER" />
    </intent-filter>
</activity>
```

2.4 <uses-permission> Element

Declares permissions the app needs, such as camera access or internet connectivity.

Example:

```
<uses-permission android:name="android.permission.INTERNET" />
```

2.5 <uses-feature> Element

Specifies hardware or software features the app requires or uses.

Example:

```
<uses-feature android:name="android.hardware.camera" android:required="true" />
```

2.6 <service> and <receiver> Elements

Declare background components like Services and Broadcast Receivers.

Example (Service):

<service android:name=".MyService" />

3. Importance of the Manifest File

The Manifest file is vital for the following reasons:

- **Component Declaration**: It lists all the components in the app, making them discoverable by the system.
- **Security and Permissions**: It ensures apps only access system resources with explicit permission.
- **Compatibility**: Declares hardware and software requirements, ensuring the app runs only on compatible devices.
- **System Integration**: The file registers app components with the system, enabling functionalities like receiving broadcasts or launching activities.

4. Best Practices for Managing the Manifest File

Minimize Permissions:

Request only the permissions necessary for app functionality to enhance user trust and security.

Use Logical Naming Conventions:

Keep activity, service, and receiver names intuitive and aligned with their functions.

Optimize Feature Declarations:

Specify hardware features with <uses-feature> to improve compatibility filtering in the Play Store.

Maintain a Clean Structure:

Use comments and formatting to make the file readable and maintainable.

Versioning:

Update the versionCode and versionName attributes to reflect changes in app releases.

5. Example of a Full Android Manifest File

Here's a sample Manifest file for a simple Android app:

```xml
<manifest xmlns:android="http://schemas.android.com/apk/res/android"
    package="com.example.myapp">

    <!-- App Permissions -->
    <uses-permission android:name="android.permission.INTERNET" />
    <uses-permission android:name="android.permission.ACCESS_FINE_LOCATION"
/>

    <!-- App Compatibility -->
    <uses-sdk android:minSdkVersion="21" android:targetSdkVersion="33" />
    <uses-feature android:name="android.hardware.location.gps" android:required="true"
/>

    <application
        android:icon="@mipmap/ic_launcher"
        android:label="@string/app_name"
        android:theme="@style/AppTheme">

        <!-- Main Activity -->
        <activity android:name=".MainActivity">
            <intent-filter>
                <action android:name="android.intent.action.MAIN" />
                <category android:name="android.intent.category.LAUNCHER" />
            </intent-filter>
        </activity>

        <!-- Service Declaration -->
        <service android:name=".MyBackgroundService" />

        <!-- Broadcast Receiver -->
        <receiver android:name=".MyBroadcastReceiver" />

    </application>
</manifest>
```

6. Common Errors and Troubleshooting Tips

Invalid Namespace Declaration:

Ensure the root <manifest> element includes the correct namespace:

xmlns:android="http://schemas.android.com/apk/res/android".

Unregistered Components:

Always declare new activities, services, and receivers in the Manifest.

Permissions Mismanagement:

Avoid requesting unnecessary permissions, as it can lead to app rejection during Play Store review.

Incorrect Package Name:

Ensure the package name matches the one used in the code and during app signing.

The Android Manifest file is much more than a configuration file—it is the heart of an Android application. It defines how the app integrates with the system, declares its capabilities, and ensures compatibility with user devices. By mastering the Manifest file, developers can streamline app behavior, improve user experience, and adhere to best practices in Android development.

3.4 The Role of Gradle in Android Projects

Gradle is an advanced build automation tool that plays a central role in Android development. It orchestrates the process of building, testing, and deploying Android applications. By combining flexibility, efficiency, and scalability, Gradle empowers developers to manage complex projects with ease. Understanding Gradle's role is essential for mastering Android development workflows.

1. What Is Gradle?

Gradle is a build system designed to automate the assembly of software. It is used in Android projects to:

- Compile code.
- Package resources.
- Manage dependencies.
- Perform testing and build variants.

Gradle leverages a domain-specific language (DSL) based on Groovy or Kotlin to define and execute build processes. This approach enables developers to describe tasks declaratively while also writing custom logic where necessary.

2. Gradle in the Android Ecosystem

Gradle is tightly integrated into the Android development environment. The Android Gradle Plugin (AGP) provides specialized tools and configurations to handle Android-specific tasks, such as managing APK files, optimizing resources, and signing apps for deployment.

Project-Level Gradle File (build.gradle):

Located in the root directory, this file manages global configurations like repository settings and dependencies shared across modules.

Module-Level Gradle File (build.gradle):

Found in each module, this file contains configurations specific to that module, such as app dependencies, build types, and compile options.

3. Key Roles of Gradle in Android Projects

3.1 Dependency Management

Gradle simplifies managing external libraries and tools by automatically downloading and integrating them into a project.

Dependencies are declared in the dependencies block, specifying the library and version.

Example:

```
dependencies {
    implementation 'com.google.android.material:material:1.9.0'
    implementation 'com.squareup.retrofit2:retrofit:2.9.0'
}
```

Gradle ensures compatibility and resolves version conflicts, saving developers from manual dependency management.

3.2 Build Variants and Flavors

Gradle enables the creation of different build variants to support various configurations like free or paid versions, debug and release builds, or region-specific apps.

Build Types: Define configurations for different stages of development.

Example:

```
buildTypes {
    debug {
        applicationIdSuffix ".debug"
        versionNameSuffix "-DEBUG"
    }
    release {
        minifyEnabled true
        proguardFiles getDefaultProguardFile('proguard-android-optimize.txt'), 'proguard-rules.pro'
    }
}
```

Product Flavors: Allow developers to create multiple versions of an app with unique features or branding.

Example:

```
productFlavors {
    free {
        applicationId "com.example.app.free"
    }
    paid {
        applicationId "com.example.app.paid"
```

```
    }
}
```

3.3 Resource and Code Optimization

Gradle handles resource shrinking, obfuscation, and optimization to reduce app size and improve performance.

ProGuard and R8: Gradle integrates these tools to remove unused code, rename variables, and compress resources during release builds.

Resource Shrinking: Automatically removes unused resources from the APK.

Example:

```
buildTypes {
   release {
      shrinkResources true
      minifyEnabled true
   }
}
```

3.4 Automated Tasks

Gradle supports task automation for repetitive processes like testing, lint checks, and generating documentation.

Example:

```
task customTask {
   doLast {
      println 'Running custom Gradle task!'
   }
}
```

Developers can run automated tasks using the Gradle wrapper or Android Studio's interface.

3.5 Continuous Integration (CI)

Gradle integrates seamlessly with CI tools like Jenkins, GitHub Actions, and GitLab CI/CD to enable automated builds, testing, and deployment pipelines.

4. How Gradle Improves Development Efficiency

Incremental Builds:

Gradle only rebuilds parts of the project that have changed, significantly reducing build times.

Caching:

By reusing outputs from previous builds, Gradle ensures faster development cycles.

Parallel Execution:

Gradle can execute independent tasks in parallel, leveraging multi-core processors.

5. Common Gradle Commands

Build the Project:

./gradlew build

Clean the Project:

./gradlew clean

Run a Specific Task:

./gradlew assembleDebug

List Available Tasks:

./gradlew tasks

6. Best Practices for Using Gradle

Keep Dependencies Updated:

Regularly review and update library versions to benefit from bug fixes and performance improvements.

Minimize Dependency Bloat:

Avoid adding unnecessary libraries to keep the build process lightweight.

Leverage Gradle Properties:

Store sensitive data like API keys in a gradle.properties file instead of hardcoding them.

Use Build Variants Effectively:

Optimize resources and features based on target environments or audiences.

Enable Build Performance Tools:

Use Gradle's built-in performance profiling tools to identify and resolve bottlenecks.

7. Challenges and Troubleshooting Gradle

Slow Builds:

Solution: Use the Gradle daemon and parallel execution options to speed up builds.

Dependency Conflicts:

Solution: Use the dependencyInsight command to identify and resolve version conflicts.

Debugging Build Failures:

Solution: Gradle provides detailed error logs and stack traces to pinpoint issues.

Gradle is a cornerstone of Android development, handling every aspect of the build process with precision and scalability. From managing dependencies to optimizing resources and creating customized builds, Gradle streamlines development workflows and ensures high-quality app delivery. By mastering Gradle's features and adhering to best practices, developers can maximize productivity and create efficient, maintainable Android projects.

3.5 Lifecycle Management in Activities and Fragments

Lifecycle management is one of the most critical concepts in Android development. Activities and Fragments, as core components of an app, have distinct lifecycles that dictate their behavior, resource allocation, and interaction with users. Understanding and effectively managing these lifecycles ensures that your app remains responsive, efficient, and free from resource leaks.

1. The Lifecycle of an Activity

An Activity represents a single screen in an application and interacts with the user. The Activity lifecycle is managed by the Android operating system and consists of several key stages:

onCreate():

- Called when the Activity is first created.
- Used for initializing the UI, setting up bindings, and configuring the environment.

Example:

```
override fun onCreate(savedInstanceState: Bundle?) {
    super.onCreate(savedInstanceState)
    setContentView(R.layout.activity_main)
}
```

onStart():

- Invoked when the Activity becomes visible to the user.
- The Activity is not yet interactive.

onResume():

- Called when the Activity starts interacting with the user.
- This is where the Activity enters the foreground and is fully active.

onPause():

- Invoked when the Activity is partially obscured by another, such as during a pop-up or navigation to another Activity.

- Typically used to pause ongoing tasks like animations or video playback.

onStop():

- Called when the Activity is no longer visible to the user.
- Resources like sensors and network connections are often released here.

onRestart():

- Invoked when the Activity is returning to the foreground after being stopped.

onDestroy():

- Called when the Activity is being destroyed, either by the system or explicitly by the developer.

Lifecycle Diagram for an Activity:

The lifecycle can be visualized as a flow of transitions, from creation to destruction, highlighting entry and exit points at each stage.

2. The Lifecycle of a Fragment

Fragments are reusable portions of the user interface that can be hosted within an Activity. They have their own lifecycle that interacts with the host Activity's lifecycle.

onAttach():

- Called when the Fragment is associated with its host Activity.
- Use this stage to access the Activity context.

onCreate():

- Invoked when the Fragment is being created.
- Used for initializing data that the Fragment retains during its lifecycle.

onCreateView():

- Called to inflate the Fragment's layout.
- The method returns the root View object for the Fragment's UI.

Example:

```kotlin
override fun onCreateView(
    inflater: LayoutInflater, container: ViewGroup?,
    savedInstanceState: Bundle?
): View? {
    return inflater.inflate(R.layout.fragment_layout, container, false)
}
```

onActivityCreated():

- Called when the Fragment's host Activity has completed its onCreate() phase.
- Use this stage to finalize setup that requires access to the Activity.

onStart():

The Fragment becomes visible to the user.

onResume():

The Fragment becomes active and interactive.

onPause():

Invoked when the Fragment is partially obscured, similar to onPause() in an Activity.

onStop():

The Fragment is no longer visible.

onDestroyView():

Called when the Fragment's view hierarchy is being removed.

onDestroy():

The Fragment is being destroyed, and resources are released.

onDetach():

Invoked when the Fragment is detached from its host Activity.

3. Importance of Proper Lifecycle Management

Avoiding Resource Leaks:

Activities and Fragments often allocate resources like threads, listeners, or sensors. Failing to release these during onPause(), onStop(), or onDestroy() can lead to memory leaks and performance degradation.

Maintaining Responsiveness:

By pausing or stopping heavy tasks during onPause() or onStop(), your app remains smooth and responsive.

Saving User State:

Use onSaveInstanceState() to preserve user data across configuration changes like screen rotations.

Example:

```
override fun onSaveInstanceState(outState: Bundle) {
    super.onSaveInstanceState(outState)
    outState.putString("key", "value")
}
```

Handling Configuration Changes:

Activities and Fragments are often recreated during events like screen rotations or language changes. Lifecycle-aware coding ensures that these transitions are seamless.

4. Lifecycle-Aware Components

Android Jetpack provides lifecycle-aware components, such as ViewModel and LiveData, to simplify lifecycle management.

ViewModel: Retains UI-related data during configuration changes without directly relying on Activity or Fragment lifecycles.

Example:

val viewModel: MyViewModel by viewModels()

LiveData: Observes data changes and updates the UI in a lifecycle-aware manner.

Example:

```
viewModel.data.observe(this, Observer { data ->
    // Update UI
})
```

5. Common Pitfalls in Lifecycle Management

Improper Resource Handling:

- Forgetting to unregister listeners or stop tasks can lead to resource leaks.
- Example: Always unregister a sensor in onPause() to prevent battery drain.

UI Updates After Destruction:

- Attempting to update the UI when the Activity or Fragment is no longer in the foreground causes crashes.
- Solution: Use lifecycle-aware components like LiveData.

Overlooking Configuration Changes:

- Not accounting for lifecycle interruptions during configuration changes can lead to data loss or crashes.

6. Tools for Lifecycle Debugging and Management

Logcat:

Use Logcat in Android Studio to track lifecycle method calls.

Example:

```
override fun onPause() {
```

```
    super.onPause()
    Log.d("Lifecycle", "onPause called")
}
```

Android Profiler:

Monitor app performance and detect memory leaks caused by improper lifecycle management.

LeakCanary:

A powerful tool to identify memory leaks related to lifecycle mismanagement.

Lifecycle management in Activities and Fragments is a cornerstone of efficient Android development. By understanding the various lifecycle stages, employing best practices, and leveraging lifecycle-aware components, developers can build responsive and robust applications. Proper handling of resources and user state ensures that apps not only perform well but also deliver seamless user experiences.

4. Kotlin Basics for Android Developers

Kotlin has quickly become the preferred language for Android development due to its concise syntax, powerful features, and seamless interoperability with Java. In this chapter, you'll dive into the basics of Kotlin, learning its key syntax, data types, and essential programming concepts. With Kotlin's modern features like null safety, type inference, and extension functions, you'll discover how it enhances your ability to write clean, efficient, and robust Android applications. This chapter is designed to give you a solid foundation in Kotlin, preparing you to leverage it fully in your Android development projects.

4.1 Setting Up Kotlin for Android Projects

Kotlin has rapidly become the preferred language for Android development, offering concise syntax, enhanced safety features, and seamless interoperability with Java. Setting up Kotlin for your Android projects is a straightforward process thanks to its native integration with Android Studio. In this section, we'll walk you through the steps to configure Kotlin for your Android projects and ensure an efficient development environment.

1. Why Choose Kotlin for Android Development?

Before diving into the setup process, it's essential to understand why Kotlin is a great choice for Android:

- **Conciseness**: Reduces boilerplate code compared to Java.
- **Null Safety**: Eliminates common null pointer exceptions with nullable and non-nullable types.
- **Interoperability**: Works seamlessly with existing Java codebases.
- **Modern Features**: Includes advanced features like coroutines for asynchronous programming and extension functions for cleaner code.

2. Enabling Kotlin in Android Studio

Android Studio, the official IDE for Android development, provides built-in support for Kotlin, making it simple to enable Kotlin in new or existing projects.

For New Projects:

- Launch Android Studio and click on New Project.
- In the "Create New Project" wizard, select a project template (e.g., Empty Activity).
- Ensure the Language dropdown is set to Kotlin in the project setup screen.
- Complete the setup and click Finish.
- Kotlin-specific dependencies and settings will be automatically configured.

For Existing Projects:

If you're migrating an existing Java project:

- Open your project in Android Studio.
- Navigate to Tools > Kotlin > Configure Kotlin in Project.
- Select the desired module and click OK to add Kotlin dependencies.
- Android Studio will update the build.gradle files to include Kotlin support.

3. Configuring Build Files

To use Kotlin, your project's Gradle build files need to include Kotlin-specific configurations.

Module-Level build.gradle:

Add the Kotlin plugin:

```
plugins {
    id 'com.android.application'
    id 'org.jetbrains.kotlin.android'
}
```

Ensure Kotlin standard library dependency is included:

```
dependencies {
    implementation "org.jetbrains.kotlin:kotlin-stdlib:$kotlin_version"
}
```

Project-Level build.gradle:

Define the Kotlin version:

```
buildscript {
    ext.kotlin_version = "1.8.0" // Replace with the latest version
    dependencies {
        classpath "org.jetbrains.kotlin:kotlin-gradle-plugin:$kotlin_version"
    }
}
```

4. Verifying Kotlin Setup

After configuring your project, it's essential to verify that Kotlin is correctly set up:

Add a Kotlin File:

- Right-click on a package in your project.
- Select New > Kotlin File/Class and create a MainActivity.kt file.

Write Sample Code:

```
package com.example.kotlinsetup

import androidx.appcompat.app.AppCompatActivity
import android.os.Bundle

class MainActivity : AppCompatActivity() {
    override fun onCreate(savedInstanceState: Bundle?) {
        super.onCreate(savedInstanceState)
        setContentView(R.layout.activity_main)
    }
}
```

Run the App:

Ensure the app compiles and runs without issues to confirm Kotlin integration.

5. Troubleshooting Common Issues

Kotlin Plugin Missing:

- If Kotlin options aren't visible, ensure you're using the latest version of Android Studio and that the Kotlin plugin is installed.

- Check under File > Settings > Plugins > Installed and install/update the Kotlin plugin if necessary.

Gradle Sync Errors:

- Gradle sync issues may occur if Kotlin dependencies or plugin versions are outdated.
- Use the Sync Project with Gradle Files option in the toolbar to resolve inconsistencies.

Missing Kotlin Runtime:

- Ensure the Kotlin standard library is included in your build.gradle dependencies.

Code Highlighting Issues:

- Restart Android Studio or perform an Invalidate Caches / Restart operation to resolve IDE-related issues.

6. Tips for Smooth Kotlin Setup

Stay Updated:

- Regularly update Kotlin and Android Studio to access the latest features and performance improvements.

Use Kotlin Extensions:

- Enable Kotlin Android Extensions in Gradle for simplified view binding (deprecated in favor of ViewBinding, but still applicable in legacy projects).

Explore Kotlin-Specific Libraries:

Leverage Kotlin libraries like KTX for concise and idiomatic Android code.

Example:

```
// Example of KTX extensions
val preferences = context.getSharedPreferences("prefs", Context.MODE_PRIVATE)
val editor = preferences.edit()
```

editor.putString("key", "value").apply()

Leverage Online Resources:

- The Kotlin documentation and Android Developers website provide extensive resources for Kotlin-based development.

Setting up Kotlin for Android projects is a crucial step toward modern and efficient app development. With its integration into Android Studio and minimal configuration requirements, Kotlin empowers developers to write cleaner, safer, and more robust code. Once set up, you're well-equipped to harness Kotlin's features and develop apps tailored to the modern user.

4.2 Key Syntax and Features of Kotlin

Kotlin has established itself as a powerful language for Android development, thanks to its clean syntax and feature-rich design. In this section, we'll explore the essential syntax and features that make Kotlin a standout choice for developers. Whether you're transitioning from Java or starting fresh, understanding these core concepts will help you write efficient and idiomatic Kotlin code.

1. Variables and Data Types

Kotlin emphasizes safety and simplicity in declaring variables.

Immutable (val): Use val for variables that should not change.

val name: String = "Biagio"

Mutable (var): Use var for variables that can be reassigned.

var age: Int = 30
age = 31

Type Inference: Kotlin often infers the data type, so explicit declaration is optional.

val isAdult = true // Inferred as Boolean

2. Null Safety

One of Kotlin's hallmark features is its approach to null safety, reducing runtime NullPointerException errors.

Non-Nullable Types: By default, variables cannot be null.

val name: String = "Kotlin" // Cannot be null

Nullable Types: Use ? to declare a nullable variable.

val nullableName: String? = null

Safe Call Operator (?.): Use this to safely access properties or methods of a nullable type.

println(nullableName?.length) // Prints null if nullableName is null

Elvis Operator (?:): Provides a default value if the variable is null.

val length = nullableName?.length ?: 0 // Defaults to 0 if null

3. Functions

Kotlin's functions are concise and expressive, with optional default parameters.

Basic Function:

```
fun greet(name: String): String {
    return "Hello, $name!"
}
```

Single-Expression Function:

```
fun add(a: Int, b: Int) = a + b
```

Default Parameters:

```
fun greet(name: String = "Guest") = "Hello, $name!"
Call it as greet() or greet("Biagio").
```

Higher-Order Functions: Functions can accept other functions as parameters.

```
fun performOperation(a: Int, b: Int, operation: (Int, Int) -> Int): Int {
    return operation(a, b)
}
val result = performOperation(5, 3) { x, y -> x * y }
println(result) // Output: 15
```

4. Classes and Objects

Kotlin supports object-oriented programming with enhancements like primary constructors and data classes.

Basic Class:

```
class Person(val name: String, var age: Int) {
    fun greet() {
        println("Hi, I'm $name and I'm $age years old.")
    }
}
```

Data Classes: Use for storing data with built-in toString, equals, and hashCode methods.

```
data class User(val id: Int, val name: String)
val user = User(1, "Biagio")
println(user) // Output: User(id=1, name=Biagio)
```

Inheritance:

```
open class Animal {
    open fun sound() = "Some sound"
}
class Dog : Animal() {
    override fun sound() = "Bark"
}
```

5. Collections and Loops

Kotlin simplifies working with collections like lists and maps.

Immutable Collections:

```
val fruits = listOf("Apple", "Banana", "Cherry")
```

Mutable Collections:

```
val mutableFruits = mutableListOf("Apple", "Banana")
mutableFruits.add("Cherry")
```

Maps:

```
val map = mapOf("A" to 1, "B" to 2)
```

Loops:

```
for (fruit in fruits) {
    println(fruit)
}
```

6. Extensions and Lambdas

Extension Functions: Add functionality to existing classes without modifying them.

```
fun String.isEmailValid() = contains("@") && contains(".")
println("test@example.com".isEmailValid()) // Output: true
```

Lambda Expressions: Compact syntax for functions.

```
val multiply = { a: Int, b: Int -> a * b }
println(multiply(3, 4)) // Output: 12
```

7. Coroutines for Asynchronous Programming

Kotlin provides coroutines to handle asynchronous tasks in a structured way.

Launching a Coroutine:

```
import kotlinx.coroutines.*

fun main() = runBlocking {
```

```
launch {
    delay(1000L)
    println("World!")
}
println("Hello")
}
```

Output:

```
Hello
World!
```

8. Error Handling

Kotlin supports traditional try-catch blocks with enhanced readability.

Using try-catch:

```
try {
    val result = 10 / 0
} catch (e: ArithmeticException) {
    println("Cannot divide by zero.")
} finally {
    println("Execution finished.")
}
```

9. Interoperability with Java

Kotlin and Java coexist seamlessly in Android projects.

Calling Java from Kotlin:

Java methods and classes are accessible in Kotlin without additional effort.

```
public class JavaClass {
    public static String greet() {
        return "Hello from Java";
    }
}
```

```
val message = JavaClass.greet()
println(message) // Output: Hello from Java
```

Calling Kotlin from Java:

Kotlin classes and functions are accessible from Java with generated static methods when annotated with @JvmStatic.

Kotlin's syntax and features are designed to make development faster, safer, and more enjoyable. From its concise variable declarations to advanced asynchronous programming with coroutines, Kotlin empowers developers to build robust and modern Android applications. Mastering these essentials is the first step toward leveraging Kotlin's full potential in app development.

4.3 Understanding Null Safety and Type Inference

Kotlin is celebrated for its strong focus on code safety and developer productivity. Two key features that embody this ethos are null safety and type inference, which work together to minimize runtime errors and simplify code. This section delves into how these features operate and why they are essential for Android development.

1. Null Safety: Eliminating NullPointerExceptions

The infamous NullPointerException (NPE) has long been a bane for developers, causing applications to crash unexpectedly. Kotlin addresses this by enforcing strict null safety at the language level, ensuring that null-related issues are caught at compile time rather than runtime.

1.1 Non-Nullable and Nullable Types

By default, Kotlin variables are non-nullable, meaning they cannot hold a null value.

Non-Nullable:

```
val name: String = "Kotlin"
name = null // Compilation error: Null cannot be a value of a non-null type
```

Nullable: Use the ? operator to allow a variable to hold a null value.

val nullableName: String? = null

1.2 Safe Calls (?.)

To access properties or methods of a nullable variable, Kotlin uses the safe call operator (?.).

Example:

val length: Int? = nullableName?.length
println(length) // Prints null if nullableName is null

This ensures the program won't crash if nullableName is null, as the safe call gracefully handles the scenario.

1.3 The Elvis Operator (?:)

The Elvis operator provides a default value when a nullable variable is null.

Example:

val length: Int = nullableName?.length ?: 0
println(length) // Prints 0 if nullableName is null

1.4 The !! Operator

Kotlin allows you to explicitly tell the compiler that a variable is not null using the non-null assertion operator (!!). However, this can throw an NPE if the assumption is incorrect, so use it sparingly.

Example:

val length: Int = nullableName!!.length // Throws NPE if nullableName is null

1.5 Safe Casting (as?)

You can safely cast an object to a specific type using as?.

Example:

```
val obj: Any = "Kotlin"
val str: String? = obj as? String // Safe casting
```

If the cast is not possible, str will be null rather than causing a ClassCastException.

2. Type Inference: Reducing Boilerplate Code

Kotlin's type inference system allows the compiler to automatically deduce the type of variables and expressions, significantly reducing the need for explicit type declarations.

2.1 Variable Type Inference

The val and var keywords allow you to declare variables without specifying their types explicitly.

Example:

```
val name = "Kotlin" // Inferred as String
var age = 30       // Inferred as Int
```

Here, the Kotlin compiler infers the type based on the assigned value, making the code cleaner and more concise.

2.2 Function Type Inference

Kotlin can infer the return type of single-expression functions.

Example:

```
fun add(a: Int, b: Int) = a + b // Return type is inferred as Int
```

For functions with multiple expressions, the return type must be explicitly declared.

Example:

```
fun multiply(a: Int, b: Int): Int {
    return a * b
}
```

2.3 Lambda Expressions

Type inference extends to lambda expressions, making them concise and readable.

Example:

val sum = { a: Int, b: Int -> a + b } // Type inferred as (Int, Int) -> Int

3. Benefits of Null Safety and Type Inference

- **Reduced Runtime Errors**: Null safety eliminates the possibility of unexpected NPEs, a common cause of app crashes.
- **Cleaner Code**: Type inference reduces boilerplate, making code more concise and easier to read.
- **Enhanced Readability**: Safe calls and the Elvis operator make null handling explicit and intuitive.
- **Improved Developer Confidence**: Compile-time checks ensure robust code, catching errors early in the development process.

4. Practical Examples in Android Development

4.1 Null Safety with Views

In Android, views retrieved from layouts may return null if they are not found. Kotlin's null safety ensures this is handled gracefully.

Example:

val textView: TextView? = findViewById(R.id.textView)
textView?.text = "Hello, Kotlin!" // Safe call to avoid NPE

4.2 Type Inference in APIs

When working with APIs, Kotlin's type inference simplifies dealing with complex data structures.

Example with Retrofit:

val apiResponse = apiService.getUsers() // Type inferred as Call<List<User>>

4.3 Using Null Safety in Database Operations

Handling nullable values is crucial when querying databases where data might be missing.

Example:

```
val user: User? = database.getUserById(userId)
val username = user?.name ?: "Unknown" // Use Elvis operator for default
```

5. Common Pitfalls and Best Practices

5.1 Avoid Overusing !!:

While the non-null assertion operator (!!) can be tempting, it defeats the purpose of null safety and can lead to crashes. Always handle nullable types with safe calls or the Elvis operator.

5.2 Leverage Type Inference Wisely:

Type inference is powerful but can obscure the code's intent if overused. For example, explicitly declaring return types in public APIs improves clarity.

5.3 Handle Nullable Collections:

When working with collections, ensure null safety is considered for each element.

Example:

```
val names: List<String?> = listOf("Alice", null, "Bob")
val filteredNames = names.filterNotNull() // Removes null elements
```

Null safety and type inference are two of Kotlin's most significant advancements, enabling developers to write safer and more concise code. By minimizing null-related errors and automating type management, Kotlin helps developers focus on building features rather than debugging crashes. Mastering these features is an essential step toward becoming proficient in Kotlin and developing robust Android applications.

4.4 Writing Classes, Functions, and Extensions in Kotlin

Kotlin is a powerful and expressive programming language that makes object-oriented and functional programming more efficient and enjoyable. In this section, we will explore how to write classes, functions, and extension functions in Kotlin—three of the key building blocks for any Android application. Kotlin's syntax allows you to write concise, readable, and maintainable code while still offering advanced features such as extension functions to enhance your work.

1. Writing Classes in Kotlin

Kotlin follows a similar object-oriented approach to Java, but with enhanced syntax and additional features. Writing classes in Kotlin is straightforward, and the language reduces boilerplate code significantly.

1.1 Defining a Basic Class

To define a class in Kotlin, use the class keyword, followed by the class name. Unlike Java, Kotlin supports primary constructors directly in the class header.

Example:

class Person(val name: String, var age: Int)

In this example, Person has two properties: name (immutable) and age (mutable). The constructor parameters are automatically assigned to class properties, so you don't need to explicitly write getters and setters.

1.2 Creating Objects

To create an instance of a class, use the new keyword in Java, but Kotlin omits this, simplifying object creation.

Example:

val person = Person("John", 30)

1.3 Defining Methods in a Class

Methods in Kotlin are declared inside a class using the fun keyword. Kotlin supports both instance methods and companion object methods (which are static in Java).

Example:

```kotlin
class Person(val name: String, var age: Int) {
    fun greet() {
        println("Hello, my name is $name and I am $age years old.")
    }
}
```

In this case, the greet method prints a personalized greeting message for the Person instance.

1.4 Constructors and Initialization

Kotlin allows for both primary and secondary constructors. The primary constructor is part of the class declaration, while secondary constructors are defined within the class body.

Primary Constructor:

```kotlin
class Person(val name: String, var age: Int)
```

Secondary Constructor:

```kotlin
class Person {
    var name: String
    var age: Int

    constructor(name: String, age: Int) {
        this.name = name
        this.age = age
    }
}
```

Kotlin also provides an init block for initialization logic, which is executed whenever an instance of the class is created.

Example:

```kotlin
class Person(val name: String, var age: Int) {
    init {
        println("New person created: $name, $age years old.")
```

```
    }
}
```

2. Writing Functions in Kotlin

Kotlin simplifies the syntax for defining functions compared to Java, and it allows for more expressive code. You can create simple one-liner functions, as well as functions with multiple parameters and return types.

2.1 Declaring Functions

Functions in Kotlin are declared using the fun keyword. You can specify parameters and return types as needed. If no return type is provided, Kotlin assumes the function returns Unit (similar to void in Java).

Example:

```
fun greet(name: String) {
    println("Hello, $name!")
}
```

In this example, the function greet takes one parameter, name, and prints a greeting message.

2.2 Returning Values from Functions

To return a value from a function, simply use the return keyword, followed by the value to be returned. Kotlin allows you to define functions with explicit return types or let the compiler infer the type.

Example with an explicit return type:

```
fun add(a: Int, b: Int): Int {
    return a + b
}
```

Example with inferred return type (simpler version):

```
fun multiply(a: Int, b: Int) = a * b
```

2.3 Default Parameters

Kotlin allows functions to have default values for parameters, which makes them more flexible and reduces the need for overloaded methods.

Example:

```
fun greet(name: String = "Guest") {
    println("Hello, $name!")
}
```

You can call greet() without any parameters, and it will use the default value "Guest". Alternatively, you can pass a custom value.

Example:

```
greet()          // Prints "Hello, Guest!"
greet("Biagio")  // Prints "Hello, Biagio!"
```

2.4 Named Arguments

Kotlin allows you to specify argument names when calling a function, improving code readability, especially for functions with many parameters.

Example:

```
fun createUser(name: String, age: Int) {
    println("User: $name, Age: $age")
}

createUser(age = 25, name = "Biagio")
```

3. Extension Functions

One of Kotlin's most powerful features is its support for extension functions. These allow you to add new methods to existing classes without modifying their source code, making your code more modular and reusable.

3.1 Defining Extension Functions

You can define extension functions by prefixing the function with the class type you are extending. The method will appear as if it is part of the class.

Example:

fun String.lastChar(): Char = this[this.length - 1]

This function extends the String class by adding a method lastChar() to retrieve the last character of the string. Now, you can call lastChar() directly on any String object:

Example usage:

val name = "Kotlin"
println(name.lastChar()) // Output: n

3.2 Extension Functions on Collections

You can also create extension functions for collections. For example, here's a function that checks whether all elements of a list are even numbers:

Example:

```
fun List<Int>.allEven(): Boolean {
    for (number in this) {
        if (number % 2 != 0) return false
    }
    return true
}

val numbers = listOf(2, 4, 6)
println(numbers.allEven())  // Output: true
```

3.3 Extension Properties

Along with extension functions, you can also define extension properties. These allow you to add properties to existing classes, but keep in mind they are just computed properties and cannot store state.

Example:

val String.secondChar: Char
  get() = this[1]

You can then access secondChar like a normal property:

Example usage:

- val word = "Kotlin"
- println(word.secondChar) // Output: o

4. Benefits of Kotlin Classes, Functions, and Extensions

- **Concise Syntax**: Kotlin's syntax is compact, reducing boilerplate code for classes, constructors, and functions.
- **Improved Readability**: The ability to create expressive extension functions and use default parameters enhances code clarity.
- **Null Safety**: Kotlin's null safety features integrate seamlessly with classes and functions, reducing runtime errors.
- **Higher Productivity**: With Kotlin's smart features like type inference, default parameters, and extension functions, developers can focus on business logic rather than boilerplate.

Kotlin's design emphasizes simplicity, conciseness, and developer productivity, making it an ideal language for Android development. Understanding how to write classes, functions, and extensions is essential for any Kotlin developer. These features will not only help you write clean and modular code but also enable you to efficiently work with third-party libraries and Android APIs. As you continue to build your skills in Kotlin, these fundamental concepts will lay the foundation for more complex and sophisticated Android applications.

4.5 Working with Coroutines for Asynchronous Programming

Asynchronous programming is a cornerstone of modern mobile development, especially when building applications that require long-running operations such as network calls, database queries, or intensive computations. Kotlin's solution to this problem is coroutines—a powerful and lightweight way to handle asynchronous tasks without the complexity of traditional callback-based methods. In this section, we'll explore how Kotlin coroutines work, how they simplify asynchronous programming, and how you can use them in Android development to create smooth, responsive applications.

1. Understanding Coroutines in Kotlin

Coroutines are a language feature in Kotlin that allow you to write asynchronous code in a sequential manner, making it easier to read, write, and maintain. They are more efficient than traditional approaches such as threads and callbacks because they don't create new threads for each task. Instead, they run on a single thread and suspend themselves when they need to wait for long-running tasks, allowing other tasks to run in parallel.

1.1 What is a Coroutine?

A coroutine is a lightweight thread that can be paused and resumed at a later time. It enables asynchronous execution without blocking the main thread or using complex callback mechanisms. Coroutines are built on suspending functions—functions that can pause their execution and allow other operations to run while waiting for a result.

2. Setting Up Coroutines in Android

To start using coroutines in your Android projects, you need to include the necessary dependencies in your project's build.gradle file:

2.1 Adding Coroutine Dependencies

First, add the required dependencies for Kotlin coroutines. You can add them to your build.gradle (app-level) file under dependencies:

```
dependencies {
    implementation "org.jetbrains.kotlinx:kotlinx-coroutines-core:1.5.2"
    implementation "org.jetbrains.kotlinx:kotlinx-coroutines-android:1.5.2"
}
```

The kotlinx-coroutines-android dependency allows you to use coroutines in Android-specific code, such as updating the UI thread.

3. Basic Coroutine Usage

Kotlin makes working with coroutines simple and intuitive. The core functionality is based around launching and suspending coroutines.

3.1 Launching a Coroutine

The launch function is used to start a coroutine. In Android, this is typically done in the main thread, but you can launch it in background threads for long-running operations.

Example:

```
GlobalScope.launch {
    // Coroutine code here
    println("This is running in a coroutine!")
}
```

The GlobalScope.launch method starts the coroutine in the global scope, meaning it lives for the duration of the application. While GlobalScope is convenient for quick examples, for real-world apps, you should use lifecycleScope (to tie coroutines to the lifecycle of an activity or fragment) or a ViewModelScope (to tie coroutines to the lifecycle of a ViewModel).

3.2 Suspending Functions

A suspending function is a function that can pause execution and resume later, allowing the coroutine to return control back to the calling code while waiting for some result.

Example:

```
suspend fun fetchDataFromNetwork(): String {
    delay(2000)  // Simulating a long-running operation
    return "Data fetched"
}
```

The delay function is a suspending function that simulates a delay without blocking the thread. It's non-blocking, meaning other coroutines can still run while waiting.

3.3 Calling Suspending Functions

To call a suspending function, you need to use it inside a coroutine. You can do this inside a launch or async block.

Example:

```
GlobalScope.launch {
```

```
    val data = fetchDataFromNetwork()
    println(data)
}
```

Here, fetchDataFromNetwork() will suspend the execution of the coroutine for 2 seconds, then resume and print the data.

4. Using Coroutine Builders: launch vs. async

While both launch and async start coroutines, they differ in terms of the result they return.

4.1 launch: For Fire-and-Forget Tasks

Use launch when you want to start a coroutine but don't need a result. It's typically used for operations like updating the UI, logging data, or handling events.

Example:

```
GlobalScope.launch {
    println("Background task started")
    delay(1000)
    println("Background task completed")
}
```

4.2 async: For Returning a Result

Use async when you need to perform an asynchronous operation and retrieve a result. It returns a Deferred object, which represents a future result that will be computed asynchronously.

Example:

```
val result = GlobalScope.async {
    delay(1000)
    "Fetched Data"
}

println(result.await())  // This will print "Fetched Data" after 1 second
```

In this case, the await method is used to block the calling thread until the result is available, but this does not block the main thread.

5. Coroutine Context and Dispatchers

Kotlin provides dispatchers to control the thread on which the coroutine will run. The most commonly used dispatchers are:

- 5.1 **Dispatchers.Main**: Runs on the main (UI) thread, suitable for updating UI elements.
- 5.2 **Dispatchers.IO**: Optimized for I/O operations, such as reading from a database or network requests.
- 5.3 **Dispatchers.Default**: Used for CPU-intensive tasks, such as computations.
- 5.4 **Dispatchers.Unconfined**: Starts the coroutine in the caller's thread, and only switches when the coroutine suspends.

Example:

```
GlobalScope.launch(Dispatchers.IO) {
   val data = fetchDataFromNetwork()
   withContext(Dispatchers.Main) {
      // Update UI with the fetched data
      println(data)
   }
}
```

In this example, fetchDataFromNetwork() runs in the background on the I/O dispatcher, and once the data is fetched, withContext(Dispatchers.Main) is used to switch back to the main thread for updating the UI.

6. Handling Exceptions in Coroutines

Error handling in coroutines is different from regular code, as exceptions in coroutines are not thrown to the caller. Instead, you need to use structured concurrency to handle exceptions.

6.1 Try-Catch in Coroutines

Just like in traditional programming, you can use try-catch blocks inside coroutines to handle exceptions.

Example:

```
GlobalScope.launch {
    try {
        val data = fetchDataFromNetwork()
        println(data)
    } catch (e: Exception) {
        println("Error: ${e.message}")
    }
}
```

6.2 CoroutineExceptionHandler

You can also use a CoroutineExceptionHandler to handle exceptions globally within a coroutine scope.

Example:

```
val exceptionHandler = CoroutineExceptionHandler { _, exception ->
    println("Caught an exception: ${exception.message}")
}

val job = GlobalScope.launch(exceptionHandler) {
    throw RuntimeException("Test Exception")
}
```

7. Best Practices for Using Coroutines in Android

7.1 Use Lifecycle-Aware Scopes

Instead of using GlobalScope, use lifecycleScope for activities and fragments, and viewModelScope for ViewModels to tie the coroutine lifecycle to the UI lifecycle.

7.2 Avoid Blocking the Main Thread

Always make sure that long-running operations such as network requests or database access are run off the main thread using appropriate dispatchers like Dispatchers.IO.

7.3 Handle Cancellation Properly

Coroutines are cancellable, and you can cancel them if needed to avoid memory leaks or unnecessary operations. Always ensure that coroutines are cancelled when no longer needed.

Kotlin coroutines are an essential tool for modern Android development. They provide a clean, efficient, and less error-prone way to manage asynchronous tasks compared to traditional methods like callbacks and AsyncTask. By using coroutines, you can write more readable, maintainable, and responsive code, which is crucial for delivering smooth user experiences in Android applications. Understanding coroutines, their context, dispatchers, and exception handling will empower you to write better, more efficient Android applications.

Part 2: Designing for the Modern User

In today's competitive app market, user experience (UX) is paramount. Part 2 of this book focuses on designing intuitive, visually appealing, and user-centric Android apps. You'll learn how to create interfaces that not only look great but also function seamlessly across a variety of devices and screen sizes. From understanding Material Design principles to mastering modern UI frameworks like Jetpack Compose, this section equips you with the tools and techniques to design apps that resonate with today's users, offering them both beauty and functionality.

5. Crafting User-Centric Interfaces with XML and Jetpack Compose

Creating an intuitive and engaging user interface is a key component of successful app development. In this chapter, you'll explore two powerful tools for building Android UIs: XML and Jetpack Compose. You'll learn how to design flexible, responsive layouts with XML and take advantage of the modern, declarative approach offered by Jetpack Compose. By understanding both methods, you'll be able to craft user-centric interfaces that deliver seamless, high-quality experiences across all Android devices, while also preparing for the future of Android app design.

5.1 Introduction to XML Layouts and View Hierarchies

In Android development, user interfaces are built using layouts and views. Layouts define the structure of the UI, while views represent individual UI elements such as buttons, text fields, images, and more. The combination of XML layouts and view hierarchies enables developers to create responsive and visually appealing applications. Understanding XML layouts and view hierarchies is crucial for Android developers as it forms the foundation for designing intuitive and user-friendly interfaces.

This section introduces the core concepts of XML layouts and view hierarchies, explaining how they work together to build flexible and dynamic user interfaces in Android applications.

1. XML Layouts in Android

In Android, XML (Extensible Markup Language) is used to define the structure of the user interface. XML layouts consist of a hierarchical arrangement of UI components, written as XML tags. Each layout defines how the UI elements should be organized, where they should appear, and their properties (such as size, color, margin, etc.).

1.1 Structure of an XML Layout File

An XML layout file starts with a root element, usually a ViewGroup (a type of container view that can hold other views). This root element wraps all other UI components (views) inside it.

Example of a simple layout file:

```xml
<?xml version="1.0" encoding="utf-8"?>
<LinearLayout xmlns:android="http://schemas.android.com/apk/res/android"
    android:layout_width="match_parent"
    android:layout_height="match_parent"
    android:orientation="vertical">

    <TextView
        android:id="@+id/helloText"
        android:layout_width="wrap_content"
        android:layout_height="wrap_content"
        android:text="Hello, Android!" />

    <Button
        android:id="@+id/helloButton"
        android:layout_width="wrap_content"
        android:layout_height="wrap_content"
        android:text="Click Me" />

</LinearLayout>
```

In this example:

- The root element is a LinearLayout, which arranges its child elements in a vertical orientation.
- Inside the LinearLayout, there are two views: a TextView and a Button.
- Each view has properties like layout_width, layout_height, and specific attributes like text for the TextView and Button.

2. View Hierarchies in Android

A view hierarchy represents the structure of all the views within a layout, with a clear parent-child relationship between them. The root view is the topmost view in the hierarchy (e.g., LinearLayout, RelativeLayout, or ConstraintLayout), and all other views are nested inside it.

2.1 Parent and Child Views

- Parent views are containers that hold other views, such as LinearLayout, RelativeLayout, and FrameLayout.
- Child views are individual UI elements, such as TextView, Button, ImageView, etc. These are the actual elements the user interacts with.

In a view hierarchy, the relationship between views is typically represented in a tree-like structure:

- The root view is the top node.
- The child views are branches and leaves, representing the UI elements.

The view hierarchy can be as simple or as complex as the app's UI demands. For example, a simple app might have a root view with just a few child views, while a more complex app might have several nested layouts with numerous child views.

3. Types of Layouts (ViewGroups) in Android

Android provides several types of ViewGroup containers that help arrange views in different ways. Each ViewGroup offers a specific layout behavior.

3.1 LinearLayout

LinearLayout arranges its child views in a single direction: either vertically or horizontally. This is useful for simple, sequential UI designs.

Example:

<LinearLayout android:orientation="horizontal">
  <Button android:text="Button 1" />
  <Button android:text="Button 2" />
</LinearLayout>

In this example, both buttons are arranged side by side (horizontally).

3.2 RelativeLayout

RelativeLayout allows child views to be positioned relative to each other, making it ideal for more flexible and complex layouts. You can position views by referring to other views' positions.

Example:

```
<RelativeLayout>
    <TextView android:id="@+id/label" android:text="Label" />
    <Button android:layout_toRightOf="@id/label" android:text="Click Me" />
</RelativeLayout>
```

In this example, the button is positioned to the right of the TextView using the layout_toRightOf attribute.

3.3 ConstraintLayout

ConstraintLayout is a powerful and flexible layout introduced in Android to help create complex UIs without nesting multiple layouts. It allows you to define constraints for each view relative to other views or the parent container.

Example:

```
<androidx.constraintlayout.widget.ConstraintLayout>
    <Button android:id="@+id/button" android:text="Click Me"
        app:layout_constraintTop_toTopOf="parent"
        app:layout_constraintStart_toStartOf="parent" />
</androidx.constraintlayout.widget.ConstraintLayout>
```

This layout places the Button at the top-left corner of its parent using constraints.

3.4 FrameLayout

FrameLayout is a simple layout that allows one child view to be displayed at a time. It's often used to display fragments or a single view within a specific region.

Example:

```
<FrameLayout>
    <ImageView android:src="@drawable/image" />
</FrameLayout>
```

In this example, the ImageView is placed inside the FrameLayout without any complex arrangement.

4. Attributes of Views

Each view in Android can be customized using a variety of attributes that determine its behavior and appearance. Some of the most commonly used attributes include:

4.1 layout_width and layout_height

These attributes define the size of the view. The most common values are:

- **match_parent**: The view will expand to match the size of its parent container.
- **wrap_content**: The view will be sized according to its content.

4.2 padding and margin

- **padding**: Defines the space between the view's content and its edges.
- **margin**: Defines the space around the view, separating it from other views.

4.3 id

Each view can be given a unique identifier using the android:id attribute. This allows views to be referenced programmatically in Java or Kotlin.

4.4 background

The android:background attribute is used to set the background color, image, or drawable resource for the view.

5. Nesting Views and Layout Performance

While it's possible to nest views and layouts to create complex UI designs, excessive nesting can lead to performance issues, particularly with layouts like LinearLayout and RelativeLayout. Deep view hierarchies result in more time spent calculating and rendering the UI, which can negatively impact the app's responsiveness.

5.1 Optimizing View Hierarchy with ConstraintLayout

To avoid the pitfalls of deeply nested layouts, it's recommended to use ConstraintLayout for complex UI designs. By reducing nesting and relying on constraints for positioning, you can greatly improve the performance of your app.

6. Best Practices for Designing Layouts

6.1 Use a Single Root View

Android layouts should have a single root ViewGroup element, which helps avoid unnecessary view hierarchies and ensures that the layout is efficient.

6.2 Minimize Nesting

Whenever possible, reduce the depth of the view hierarchy by using ConstraintLayout or other flat layouts. Too many nested layouts can lead to slower rendering and worse performance.

6.3 Maintain Responsive Layouts

Design your layouts to be responsive across different screen sizes and resolutions. Use attributes like dp (density-independent pixels) and sp (scale-independent pixels) for layout dimensions and text size to ensure consistency across devices.

XML layouts and view hierarchies are fundamental concepts in Android development, allowing you to define how your app's user interface is structured. By mastering layouts like LinearLayout, RelativeLayout, and ConstraintLayout, and understanding how views are nested within a hierarchy, you can create flexible, responsive, and performance-optimized UIs. The knowledge of these concepts is essential for developing polished Android applications that offer great user experiences across a wide range of devices.

5.2 Creating Dynamic UIs with Jetpack Compose

Jetpack Compose is a modern, fully declarative UI toolkit for building Android applications. Unlike the traditional XML-based UI design, Jetpack Compose allows developers to build UIs using Kotlin code, offering a more intuitive, flexible, and dynamic approach to designing Android apps. In this section, we'll dive into the process of creating dynamic UIs with Jetpack Compose, exploring its advantages, key concepts, and how to use it effectively in your Android projects.

1. What is Jetpack Compose?

Jetpack Compose is a UI toolkit developed by Google for Android that enables developers to design UIs using a declarative approach. Instead of defining the structure of the UI using XML, Jetpack Compose allows you to build UIs directly in Kotlin code, which simplifies the development process and makes the UI code more readable and maintainable.

1.1 Key Features of Jetpack Compose:

- **Declarative Syntax**: You describe what the UI should look like in different states, rather than how to update the UI in response to state changes.
- **Integration with Kotlin**: Jetpack Compose works seamlessly with Kotlin, leveraging its language features like type safety and null safety.
- **Reactivity**: The UI updates automatically in response to state changes, without requiring explicit calls to update the UI.
- **Simplified UI Code**: Jetpack Compose reduces boilerplate code compared to traditional XML-based UIs.

2. Setting Up Jetpack Compose in Your Project

To start using Jetpack Compose in your Android project, you'll need to ensure that your project is configured correctly to support it. Here's how to get started:

2.1 Add Compose Dependencies:

In your build.gradle file, include the necessary dependencies for Jetpack Compose:

```
android {
  compileSdkVersion 33

  defaultConfig {
    minSdkVersion 21
    targetSdkVersion 33
  }

  buildFeatures {
    compose true
  }

  composeOptions {
    kotlinCompilerExtensionVersion '1.3.2'
    kotlinCompilerVersion '1.6.10'
  }
```

```
dependencies {
    implementation "androidx.compose.ui:ui:1.3.0"
    implementation "androidx.compose.material:material:1.3.0"
    implementation "androidx.compose.ui:ui-tooling-preview:1.3.0"
    implementation "androidx.lifecycle:lifecycle-runtime-ktx:2.4.0"
    implementation "androidx.activity:activity-compose:1.3.1"
  }
}
```

This setup includes the core UI, Material Design, and tools for building and previewing Compose-based UIs.

3. Building a Basic UI with Jetpack Compose

With Jetpack Compose, creating UIs becomes a simple and direct task. Let's start by building a basic UI with Compose:

3.1 Creating a Simple Button and Text UI:

```
import androidx.compose.material.Button
import androidx.compose.material.Text
import androidx.compose.runtime.Composable
import androidx.compose.ui.tooling.preview.Preview

@Composable
fun SimpleUI() {
  Button(onClick = { /* Handle button click */ }) {
    Text("Click Me")
  }
}

@Preview(showBackground = true)
@Composable
fun PreviewSimpleUI() {
  SimpleUI()
}
```

In this example:

- @Composable is an annotation that marks a function as part of the UI that can be composed into a layout.
- Button and Text are Compose UI components (also known as composables) that define UI elements.
- The @Preview annotation lets you preview the composable function directly in the Android Studio preview window.

4. Dynamic UI Components with State Management

One of the primary advantages of Jetpack Compose is its ability to manage dynamic UI elements that respond to changes in the application's state. Jetpack Compose makes it easy to update the UI when the state changes, eliminating the need for manual UI updates.

4.1 **Using State with Jetpack Compose**: Jetpack Compose provides a simple way to manage state within a composable function using the remember and mutableStateOf functions.

Example of dynamic text that updates when a button is clicked:

```
import androidx.compose.material.Button
import androidx.compose.material.Text
import androidx.compose.runtime.Composable
import androidx.compose.runtime.remember
import androidx.compose.runtime.mutableStateOf

@Composable
fun DynamicTextUI() {
    // State to hold the text
    val count = remember { mutableStateOf(0) }

    Button(onClick = { count.value++ }) {
        Text("Click me to update count: ${count.value}")
    }
}
```

In this example:

- remember { mutableStateOf(0) } creates a mutable state variable that holds the current count value.

- When the button is clicked, the count.value++ increments the count, and the Text composable automatically updates to reflect the new state.

4.2 State and Recomposition: When the state changes, Jetpack Compose automatically triggers a recomposition of the UI components that are dependent on that state. This ensures that only the necessary parts of the UI are re-rendered, improving performance.

5. Layouts in Jetpack Compose

Just as in XML layouts, Jetpack Compose provides various composables for arranging UI elements in different ways. The most commonly used layout composables include:

5.1 Column and Row:

- **Column**: Arranges UI elements vertically.
- **Row**: Arranges UI elements horizontally.

Example using Column and Row:

```
@Composable
fun ColumnAndRowExample() {
    Column {
        Text("Item 1")
        Text("Item 2")
        Row {
            Text("Item 3")
            Text("Item 4")
        }
    }
}
```

5.2 Box: The Box composable is used to stack UI elements on top of each other, allowing you to overlap views. It's often used for backgrounds, overlays, and positioning elements relative to each other.

```
@Composable
fun BoxExample() {
    Box {
        Text("Text at the bottom")
        Text("Text on top", modifier = Modifier.align(Alignment.Center))
```

```
    }
}
```

In this example, the second Text is placed in the center of the Box, overlaying the first Text.

6. Lists and Lazy Loading

For dynamic content that involves large data sets, Jetpack Compose provides powerful tools for rendering lists efficiently. LazyColumn and LazyRow are composables designed to display lists of items in a memory-efficient manner by rendering only the items that are currently visible on the screen.

6.1 LazyColumn Example:

```
import androidx.compose.foundation.lazy.LazyColumn
import androidx.compose.material.Text

@Composable
fun LazyListExample() {
    LazyColumn {
        items(100) { index ->
            Text("Item #$index")
        }
    }
}
```

In this example, only the visible items in the LazyColumn are rendered, which significantly improves performance when dealing with large data sets.

7. Theming and Styling in Jetpack Compose

Jetpack Compose allows you to apply consistent styles and themes to your UI using the Material Design components, or your own custom styles.

7.1 **Applying Material Theme**: Jetpack Compose has built-in support for Material Design components, allowing you to apply consistent styles across your app.

```
import androidx.compose.material.MaterialTheme
import androidx.compose.material.Text
```

```
import androidx.compose.runtime.Composable

@Composable
fun ThemedText() {
  MaterialTheme {
     Text("This is themed text")
  }
}
```

You can also customize the theme using colors, typography, and shapes to match your app's branding and design guidelines.

8. Benefits of Using Jetpack Compose

8.1 Reduced Boilerplate Code:

By removing the need for XML, Jetpack Compose reduces the amount of boilerplate code needed to create complex UIs, resulting in faster development and easier maintenance.

8.2 Improved Performance:

Jetpack Compose uses a smart recomposition strategy that only re-renders the parts of the UI that need to be updated. This is much more efficient than the traditional view system, where the entire layout often needs to be re-drawn.

8.3 Flexibility and Power:

Compose offers full flexibility in designing UIs. The declarative approach makes it easier to create dynamic and interactive UIs with much less effort compared to the traditional Android views.

Jetpack Compose marks a significant shift in Android development by offering a simpler, more powerful way to build user interfaces. Its declarative, Kotlin-based approach enables developers to create dynamic, responsive UIs with less boilerplate code and greater flexibility. By embracing Jetpack Compose, you can streamline your Android development process and create modern, efficient apps with ease. Whether you're building a simple app or a complex one, Compose is an excellent tool for creating intuitive and engaging user experiences.

5.3 Using ConstraintLayout for Complex Layouts

ConstraintLayout is one of the most powerful and flexible layout managers available in Android, designed to simplify complex UI designs without requiring deep nesting of layouts. It allows developers to create complex, responsive user interfaces by defining relationships between UI elements through constraints, instead of relying on traditional LinearLayout or RelativeLayout which can lead to deep, inefficient view hierarchies.

This section explores how to use ConstraintLayout for creating dynamic and complex layouts, detailing its key features, how to set up constraints, and the benefits it offers over traditional layout managers.

1. What is ConstraintLayout?

ConstraintLayout is a ViewGroup that allows you to position and size widgets based on constraints relative to other widgets or the parent container. Rather than manually specifying pixel-based positions or relying on layout rules like wrap_content and match_parent, ConstraintLayout enables you to set constraints that describe how views should behave in relation to each other.

The core advantage of ConstraintLayout is that it eliminates the need for deeply nested layouts, improving both performance and readability. You can create complex UIs with fewer nested views, which leads to faster rendering and reduced memory usage.

2. Key Features of ConstraintLayout

2.1 Flexible Positioning and Sizing

ConstraintLayout provides extensive flexibility in defining how a view should be positioned within the layout, with options for:

- **Horizontal and Vertical Constraints**: Position views relative to each other or to the parent layout.
- **Bias**: Allows you to offset a view from the center or edges along either axis.
- **Chains**: Enable you to group views together to control their alignment and spacing.

2.2 No Nested Layouts Required

Instead of using multiple nested LinearLayouts or RelativeLayouts, you can handle all positioning directly in a single ConstraintLayout. This minimizes the complexity and improves the layout's performance by reducing unnecessary view hierarchy levels.

2.3 Responsive Design Support

ConstraintLayout helps you create UIs that adjust and scale smoothly across different screen sizes and orientations. You can set relative dimensions and margins, making the app more responsive to various device types and screen configurations.

3. Basic Components of ConstraintLayout

3.1 Constraints

Constraints define how a view is positioned relative to other views or the parent container. There are two types of constraints:

- **Layout Constraints**: Define the positioning of views relative to the parent layout (top, bottom, left, right, etc.).
- **View Constraints**: Define the relationships between different views within the layout (e.g., aligning one view to another).

3.2 Guidelines

Guidelines are invisible lines that help in positioning views with respect to the layout. You can use them as reference points to ensure consistent spacing across multiple views. They help in centering, aligning, or distributing elements in a responsive way.

3.3 Chains

Chains are a powerful feature of ConstraintLayout that allows you to group views together and control their alignment and distribution along an axis. A chain can be either:

- **Packed Chain**: Aligns views tightly together.
- **Spread Chain**: Spaces views evenly within a defined range.

3.4 Barriers

A Barrier is a special type of constraint that automatically adjusts its position based on the size of the views it's constrained to. It's useful for creating layouts where you want a view to be aligned to the largest or smallest view in a group.

4. Setting Up a Basic ConstraintLayout

Let's walk through creating a simple UI using ConstraintLayout:

```xml
<?xml version="1.0" encoding="utf-8"?>
<androidx.constraintlayout.widget.ConstraintLayout
xmlns:android="http://schemas.android.com/apk/res/android"
    xmlns:app="http://schemas.android.com/apk/res-auto"
    xmlns:tools="http://schemas.android.com/tools"
    android:layout_width="match_parent"
    android:layout_height="match_parent">

    <!-- TextView with constraints -->
    <TextView
        android:id="@+id/label"
        android:layout_width="wrap_content"
        android:layout_height="wrap_content"
        android:text="Hello, ConstraintLayout!"
        app:layout_constraintTop_toTopOf="parent"
        app:layout_constraintStart_toStartOf="parent"
        app:layout_constraintEnd_toEndOf="parent"
        app:layout_constraintHorizontal_bias="0.5" />

    <!-- Button with constraints -->
    <Button
        android:id="@+id/button"
        android:layout_width="wrap_content"
        android:layout_height="wrap_content"
        android:text="Click Me"
        app:layout_constraintTop_toBottomOf="@id/label"
        app:layout_constraintStart_toStartOf="parent"
        app:layout_constraintEnd_toEndOf="parent"
        app:layout_constraintHorizontal_bias="0.5" />

</androidx.constraintlayout.widget.ConstraintLayout>
```

In this example:

- The TextView is centered horizontally at the top of the parent layout using constraints like layout_constraintTop_toTopOf, layout_constraintStart_toStartOf, and layout_constraintEnd_toEndOf.
- The Button is placed directly below the TextView, and similarly constrained to be centered horizontally.

This layout is simple but demonstrates the power of ConstraintLayout in eliminating the need for nesting. By defining the constraints between the parent and child views, you can control their positioning with minimal code.

5. Advanced Techniques with ConstraintLayout

5.1 Using Chains for Complex Layouts

Chains allow you to arrange views in a horizontal or vertical sequence with flexible alignment and spacing. For example, if you want to create a series of buttons that are spaced evenly across the screen, you can use a horizontal chain.

```
<androidx.constraintlayout.widget.ConstraintLayout
xmlns:android="http://schemas.android.com/apk/res/android"
   android:layout_width="match_parent"
   android:layout_height="wrap_content">

   <!-- Buttons in a horizontal chain -->
   <Button
      android:id="@+id/button1"
      android:text="Button 1"
      app:layout_constraintStart_toStartOf="parent"
      app:layout_constraintTop_toTopOf="parent"
      app:layout_constraintEnd_toStartOf="@+id/button2" />

   <Button
      android:id="@+id/button2"
      android:text="Button 2"
      app:layout_constraintStart_toEndOf="@+id/button1"
      app:layout_constraintTop_toTopOf="parent"
      app:layout_constraintEnd_toStartOf="@+id/button3" />
```

```
<Button
    android:id="@+id/button3"
    android:text="Button 3"
    app:layout_constraintStart_toEndOf="@+id/button2"
    app:layout_constraintTop_toTopOf="parent"
    app:layout_constraintEnd_toEndOf="parent" />
```

```
</androidx.constraintlayout.widget.ConstraintLayout>
```

This layout ensures the three buttons are arranged side by side, spaced evenly.

5.2 Using Barriers for Adaptive Layouts

A Barrier is useful when the layout needs to adapt to the size of a view dynamically. It's often used when aligning elements based on the size of other views.

```
<androidx.constraintlayout.widget.ConstraintLayout
xmlns:android="http://schemas.android.com/apk/res/android"
    android:layout_width="match_parent"
    android:layout_height="match_parent">

    <!-- Text views with different lengths of text -->
    <TextView
        android:id="@+id/textView1"
        android:text="Short text"
        android:layout_width="wrap_content"
        android:layout_height="wrap_content"
        app:layout_constraintTop_toTopOf="parent" />

    <TextView
        android:id="@+id/textView2"
        android:text="A much longer piece of text"
        android:layout_width="wrap_content"
        android:layout_height="wrap_content"
        app:layout_constraintTop_toTopOf="parent" />

    <!-- Barrier that adjusts according to the largest text -->
    <androidx.constraintlayout.widget.Barrier
        android:id="@+id/barrier"
        app:constraint_referencedIds="textView1, textView2"
```

app:layout_constraintTop_toBottomOf="@id/textView2" />

</androidx.constraintlayout.widget.ConstraintLayout>

Here, the Barrier adjusts its position based on the largest text view (TextView2), ensuring that the subsequent elements can align properly relative to it.

6. Optimizing Layouts with ConstraintLayout

6.1 Avoiding Over-Constraining

While ConstraintLayout is powerful, it's essential to ensure that your views have the minimum required constraints. Over-constraint (or excessive relationships) can lead to more complexity than needed, potentially reducing the layout's flexibility and performance.

6.2 Using Percentages for Responsive Design

ConstraintLayout allows you to define layout dimensions as percentages, making it easier to build responsive designs that adjust based on screen size. For example, you can set a button's width to 50% of the screen width:

```
<Button
    android:id="@+id/button"
    android:layout_width="0dp"
    android:layout_height="wrap_content"
    app:layout_constraintWidth_percent="0.5"
    android:text="Responsive Button" />
```

This button will take up half of the screen's width, adjusting automatically on different devices.

ConstraintLayout provides a robust and efficient way to build complex UIs without excessive nesting or complicated layouts. By using constraints, chains, barriers, and guidelines, you can create responsive, flexible, and highly customizable user interfaces that look great on all screen sizes. Whether you're building simple views or sophisticated layouts, ConstraintLayout offers all the tools you need to create modern Android UIs efficiently.

5.4 Managing Resources: Strings, Colors, and Dimensions

In Android development, managing resources effectively is a critical aspect of creating maintainable, scalable, and adaptable applications. Android allows developers to externalize resources such as strings, colors, and dimensions, enabling them to manage UI and behavior across multiple devices and configurations easily. By defining these resources separately from the application code, developers can ensure that their apps are more flexible, internationalized, and easier to update.

In this section, we will explore how to manage and utilize key resources like strings, colors, and dimensions in your Android app, explaining the best practices and tools available to streamline development and ensure consistent app design.

1. Strings: Storing Text Resources

Strings are an essential part of any Android app, whether it's displaying button labels, text fields, or messages. Instead of hardcoding text directly into your layouts or Java/Kotlin files, it's best practice to define strings in resource files. This not only makes the app easier to translate but also simplifies the management of UI text.

1.1 Defining Strings in strings.xml

The most common way to store strings is by placing them in the strings.xml file, which resides in the res/values/ directory. Here's an example:

```
<resources>
    <string name="app_name">My Android App</string>
    <string name="hello_message">Welcome to the App!</string>
    <string name="button_submit">Submit</string>
</resources>
```

By storing text this way, you can refer to strings in your layout files or code without hardcoding values. For instance:

In XML layout files:

```
<TextView
    android:id="@+id/welcomeText"
    android:layout_width="wrap_content"
    android:layout_height="wrap_content"
```

android:text="@string/hello_message" />

In Kotlin or Java code:

val message = getString(R.string.hello_message)

This approach makes your app more maintainable, especially when you need to update text or add support for other languages.

1.2 Supporting Multiple Languages

One significant advantage of using strings.xml is the ability to create different resource files for various languages. For instance, to support French and Spanish, you would create strings.xml files in directories such as res/values-fr/ for French and res/values-es/ for Spanish. When the app runs, Android automatically loads the appropriate string file based on the device's language settings.

2. Colors: Defining and Managing Color Resources

Colors are an important part of any UI design, and like strings, they should be stored in a separate resource file for consistency and ease of management. This allows for centralized color control, making it easier to change the app's color scheme without diving into individual layout files.

2.1 Defining Colors in colors.xml

To define colors, you create a colors.xml file inside the res/values/ directory. Here's an example of defining color resources:

```
<resources>
   <color name="primary_color">#FF6200EE</color>
   <color name="secondary_color">#FF03DAC5</color>
   <color name="text_color">#000000</color>
</resources>
```

You can then reference these colors in your layout files or code:

In XML layout files:

<TextView

```
android:layout_width="wrap_content"
android:layout_height="wrap_content"
android:text="Hello World!"
android:textColor="@color/text_color" />
```

In Kotlin or Java code:

```
val textColor = ContextCompat.getColor(this, R.color.text_color)
```

2.2 Using Color Resources for Themes

Another advantage of defining colors as resources is their use in custom themes. Android allows you to create a consistent design by defining a set of colors in the app's theme (styles.xml), such as for primary and secondary colors, text, and background. For example:

```xml
<resources>
  <style name="AppTheme" parent="Theme.MaterialComponents.DayNight">
    <item name="colorPrimary">@color/primary_color</item>
    <item name="colorSecondary">@color/secondary_color</item>
  </style>
</resources>
```

By applying this theme, all components that rely on these color attributes will automatically inherit the app's design.

3. Dimensions: Defining and Using Size Resources

Dimensions refer to values related to size or spacing, such as margins, padding, text sizes, and element dimensions. Managing dimensions in XML ensures consistency and allows for flexible scaling across different screen sizes and resolutions.

3.1 Defining Dimensions in dimens.xml

Dimensions are defined in a dimens.xml file, which also resides in the res/values/ directory. Here's an example:

```xml
<resources>
  <dimen name="text_size_large">18sp</dimen>
  <dimen name="text_size_medium">14sp</dimen>
```

```
    <dimen name="margin_standard">16dp</dimen>
    <dimen name="padding_standard">12dp</dimen>
</resources>
```

By using dimension resources, you can ensure that elements in your app adhere to a consistent design, and make it easier to adjust sizes globally.

3.2 Using Dimensions in Layouts

Just like colors and strings, dimensions are referenced in your layout files:

```
<TextView
    android:id="@+id/welcomeText"
    android:layout_width="wrap_content"
    android:layout_height="wrap_content"
    android:textSize="@dimen/text_size_large"
    android:layout_marginTop="@dimen/margin_standard" />
```

3.3 Adapting Dimensions for Different Screen Densities

Android supports different screen densities, and defining dimensions in dp (density-independent pixels) ensures that UI elements appear consistently across devices. However, for more fine-tuned control, Android allows you to define alternative resource files for different screen densities, such as values-mdpi/, values-hdpi/, and values-xhdpi/, allowing you to adjust dimensions for specific screen types.

3.4 Supporting Multiple Screen Sizes

In addition to screen density, Android supports different screen sizes and form factors (e.g., phones, tablets, foldable devices). To handle different screen sizes, you can create different dimension resource files in res/values-sw600dp/, res/values-sw720dp/, etc., ensuring that your app looks great on all devices.

For example, you might use larger padding or text sizes for tablet devices, while keeping smaller sizes for phones:

```
<resources>
    <dimen name="padding_standard">24dp</dimen> <!-- Tablet version -->
</resources>
```

4. Best Practices for Managing Resources

4.1 Organizing Resources Effectively

When your app starts to grow, organizing resources into clear and concise categories becomes essential. Group related resources together (e.g., keep all text-related strings in one file, and all color-related resources in another). This makes it easier to maintain and update them over time.

4.2 Using Resource Qualifiers for Different Configurations

Android allows you to create resource qualifiers, which enable you to define different resources based on the device's configuration (e.g., language, screen size, density). For instance, by creating different folders for different languages (res/values-es/ for Spanish), screen sizes (res/values-sw600dp/ for tablets), or themes (dark mode and light mode), you can provide customized resources based on the context.

4.3 Avoiding Hardcoding

It's a common practice to avoid hardcoding values directly into your layouts or code. Hardcoding strings, colors, or dimensions limits the flexibility of your app. Externalizing these resources into XML files gives you more control, reduces redundancy, and makes your app more adaptable in the future.

Managing resources such as strings, colors, and dimensions effectively is essential for developing scalable, adaptable, and user-friendly Android applications. By externalizing these resources, you simplify app maintenance, make your app more internationalized, and improve design consistency across different devices. Whether you're managing text, colors, or dimensions, leveraging Android's resource system ensures a more flexible, responsive, and high-quality app that stands the test of time.

5.5 Responsive Design for Multiple Screen Sizes

Responsive design is a key concept in modern Android development, ensuring that your app adapts smoothly to a wide range of screen sizes, resolutions, and form factors. With the diversity of devices in the Android ecosystem — including phones, tablets, foldable devices, and even large screen TVs — it's crucial to design your app in a way that it provides a consistent and user-friendly experience across all these devices.

In this section, we'll explore the principles and techniques for designing Android apps that are responsive, ensuring they look great and function properly on a variety of screen sizes and aspect ratios.

1. Understanding Screen Sizes and Densities

Android devices come in a wide variety of screen sizes and densities, and it's important to understand the difference between them in order to create a responsive design. Screen size refers to the physical dimensions of the display (e.g., 5.5 inches or 10 inches), while screen density measures how many pixels fit into a given physical area, which affects how crisp images and UI elements appear.

1.1 Screen Sizes

Android categorizes screens into different size buckets based on their physical size and usable screen area. These buckets include:

- **Small** (typically low-end phones)
- **Normal** (average-size phones)
- **Large** (larger phones and small tablets)
- **Xlarge** (tablets, large displays)

1.2 Screen Density

Screen density (DPI - dots per inch) measures how many pixels fit into a given area of the screen. The main categories are:

- **ldpi** (low density, 120 dpi)
- **mdpi** (medium density, 160 dpi)
- **hdpi** (high density, 240 dpi)
- **xhdpi** (extra-high density, 320 dpi)
- **xxhdpi** (extra-extra-high density, 480 dpi)
- **xxxhdpi** (extra-extra-extra-high density, 640 dpi)

In Android, resources such as images and layouts are optimized for these different screen densities, ensuring that they look crisp and appropriately sized.

2. Using Density-Independent Pixels (dp) and Scalable Pixels (sp)

One of the core principles for responsive design is using density-independent pixels (dp) and scalable pixels (sp) to define dimensions, padding, and font sizes.

- **dp** (density-independent pixels) is a unit of measurement that helps ensure UI elements maintain consistent physical sizes across different screen densities.
- **sp** (scale-independent pixels) is similar to dp but also takes into account the user's font size preference, ensuring that text remains legible for users with different accessibility settings.

By using dp and sp, you can ensure that your app's UI will look consistent, regardless of the screen size or density. For example:

```
<TextView
    android:layout_width="wrap_content"
    android:layout_height="wrap_content"
    android:text="Hello, World!"
    android:textSize="16sp" />
```

3. Layouts for Different Screen Sizes

To create responsive UIs, Android provides various tools and techniques that allow developers to adjust the layout for different screen sizes. By defining alternative layouts, you can provide a customized experience depending on the size of the device.

3.1 Using Layout Resource Folders

Android allows developers to create different layouts for different screen sizes by placing them in resource directories with appropriate qualifiers. For example:

- res/layout/ – Default layout for most devices.
- res/layout-sw600dp/ – Layout for devices with a screen width of 600dp or more (typically tablets).
- res/layout-sw720dp/ – Layout for larger tablets or devices with wider screens.

By defining multiple layouts in different directories, Android will automatically choose the most appropriate layout depending on the device's screen size. For example:

```
<TextView
    android:layout_width="wrap_content"
    android:layout_height="wrap_content"
```

```
android:text="Welcome to our app!"
android:textSize="@dimen/text_size_large" />
```

For larger screen sizes, you could have a different layout with a different arrangement of UI elements, or use larger font sizes or padding.

3.2 Use of ConstraintLayout for Flexible UIs

ConstraintLayout is a versatile layout manager that makes it easy to create responsive UIs that adjust to various screen sizes. It enables you to position and size UI elements relative to each other, making your layouts flexible and adaptable.

By using ConstraintLayout, you can avoid specifying exact pixel values and instead define relationships between elements. This means that elements can automatically adjust their position and size based on the screen size or orientation. For example, you can have a ConstraintLayout that adjusts the placement of elements when switching between portrait and landscape orientations.

```
<androidx.constraintlayout.widget.ConstraintLayout
    android:layout_width="match_parent"
    android:layout_height="match_parent">

    <TextView
        android:id="@+id/textView"
        android:layout_width="wrap_content"
        android:layout_height="wrap_content"
        android:text="Responsive Design!"
        app:layout_constraintTop_toTopOf="parent"
        app:layout_constraintStart_toStartOf="parent" />
</androidx.constraintlayout.widget.ConstraintLayout>
```

4. Managing Orientation Changes

When the device's orientation changes from portrait to landscape (or vice versa), the layout should adapt to ensure a seamless user experience. Android automatically reuses the existing layout, but sometimes a different layout is necessary for landscape or portrait modes.

4.1 Using Orientation-Specific Layouts

You can define different layouts for portrait and landscape orientations by creating separate resource folders for each, such as res/layout/ for portrait and res/layout-land/ for landscape. For example, you might use a LinearLayout for portrait mode and a GridLayout for landscape mode to display a different UI structure.

4.2 Avoiding Configuration Changes

If you want to preserve certain state information (e.g., user input) during orientation changes, you can either use onSaveInstanceState() to save data or lock the orientation with android:screenOrientation="landscape" in the manifest (though the latter may negatively affect the user experience).

5. Testing Responsiveness Across Devices

Testing your app across a wide range of devices and screen sizes is critical to ensure your app's responsiveness. Android Studio provides various tools to help with this:

5.1 Device Emulator

The Android Emulator in Android Studio allows you to simulate different devices with various screen sizes, resolutions, and Android versions. By running your app in the emulator, you can test how it behaves on a range of devices before testing it on actual hardware.

5.2 Real Device Testing

In addition to using emulators, it's important to test your app on real devices with different screen sizes and resolutions. This provides more accurate feedback regarding how your app performs in real-world conditions.

6. Best Practices for Responsive Design

6.1 Prioritize Content

Responsive design isn't just about fitting everything onto the screen; it's about making the most important content easily accessible. Always prioritize the most critical information and features for each screen size.

6.2 Use Flexible Layouts and Scalable Images

Using flexible layouts like ConstraintLayout, along with scalable images (i.e., vector images or @drawable resources) ensures that your app's design adapts to various screen sizes and densities.

6.3 Consider Touch Targets

For smaller screens, ensure that interactive elements (buttons, icons, etc.) are large enough to be easily tapped. The Android design guidelines recommend a minimum touch target size of 48dp x 48dp.

6.4 Test on a Range of Devices

To ensure your app performs well across all screen sizes and form factors, test it on various devices (phones, tablets, foldables, etc.). This helps ensure that your app offers a consistent user experience no matter what device it's used on.

Responsive design is a crucial element in Android app development, ensuring that your app provides a seamless and engaging experience on a variety of devices with different screen sizes, densities, and orientations. By leveraging Android's layout managers, resource folders, and best practices, you can create apps that look and function well on any device. Testing and adapting for multiple screen sizes will help ensure that your app delivers the best possible experience for your users.

6. Material Design Principles

Material Design is Google's design language, offering a set of guidelines that help create visually appealing and consistent user interfaces across Android apps. In this chapter, you'll learn the core principles of Material Design, including how to use color, typography, spacing, and layout to enhance the user experience. You'll also discover how to incorporate elements like motion, elevation, and responsiveness into your designs to make your apps feel intuitive and immersive. By mastering these principles, you'll be able to create apps that not only look great but also provide a smooth, unified experience for users.

6.1 Understanding Material Design Guidelines

Material Design is a comprehensive design system developed by Google to create visually appealing, intuitive, and consistent user experiences across all Android applications. Launched in 2014, it emphasizes clean, simple layouts, effective use of color, and subtle animations that guide users without overwhelming them. Material Design focuses on unifying the user experience, ensuring consistency across devices and platforms while also accommodating unique device capabilities.

In this section, we will explore the core principles and components of Material Design, explain how to implement its guidelines effectively, and discuss how it shapes the overall look and feel of modern Android apps.

1. Core Principles of Material Design

Material Design is built around a few key principles that guide the visual and interaction design of Android apps:

1.1 Material as Metaphor

Material Design draws inspiration from real-world materials, using paper, ink, and physical surfaces as metaphors to create a tangible sense of depth. The concept of "material" suggests that elements within an app have weight, texture, and movement. These elements can be arranged, stacked, and layered, mimicking how objects interact in the physical world. Shadows, grids, and elevations are used to convey this metaphor visually, creating a sense of hierarchy and focus.

1.2 Bold, Graphic, Intentional

Material Design encourages designers to use bold, strong visuals and colors with clear, meaningful typography and iconography. This principle emphasizes clarity and simplicity, ensuring that design elements serve their purpose and enhance the user experience. It also promotes visual hierarchy, making sure that each UI element clearly communicates its importance in the overall layout.

1.3 Motion Provides Meaning

Motion in Material Design is not just for decoration but serves as a functional aspect of user interactions. Transitions, animations, and gestures are used to indicate changes in the UI or transitions between screens. The goal is to make navigation intuitive by providing visual cues that indicate where an element is moving, how it's behaving, and when something has been successfully completed.

1.4 Adaptive Design

Material Design is adaptable, designed to work seamlessly across various screen sizes, form factors, and platforms. It scales easily from mobile devices to tablets, foldable screens, and even wearables, ensuring a consistent experience no matter the context. The guidelines prioritize flexible layouts and responsive elements that can adjust to different screen sizes.

2. Key Components of Material Design

Material Design breaks down the UI into essential components and guidelines that allow developers and designers to create cohesive and consistent user interfaces.

2.1 Color

Color plays a pivotal role in Material Design by guiding user interactions and providing emphasis. The guidelines suggest using a primary and secondary color palette for your app, while also considering how color affects accessibility. Material Design encourages a vibrant, dynamic color scheme, balanced with ample use of whitespace to maintain clarity. It also suggests using "color contrasts" for legibility and accessibility, especially for text and background.

2.2 Typography

Typography in Material Design is focused on legibility and clarity. The guidelines advocate for a consistent type system with scalable text sizes that adjust to different screen sizes and densities. Material Design promotes the use of sans-serif fonts such as Roboto (the default font for Android) and Noto, ensuring easy reading and modern appeal. It also emphasizes text hierarchy, with clear distinctions between headers, body text, and captions.

2.3 Iconography

Icons are an integral part of Material Design, used to simplify and clarify the user interface. Material Design advocates for a set of geometric, consistent icons that convey meaning with simplicity. The guidelines emphasize clarity, meaning, and consistency, with icons being visually aligned with the app's overall aesthetic. They are often used in conjunction with text labels to provide more intuitive navigation and reduce the cognitive load on users.

2.4 Layout and Spacing

Material Design introduces a responsive grid system, allowing developers to organize elements efficiently while keeping a clean and structured layout. By following the 8dp grid, developers can ensure consistency in the spacing between elements, creating a balanced, polished user interface. This system helps ensure that elements are properly aligned and maintain proportional spacing, regardless of the screen size.

2.5 Components

Material Design includes a range of pre-designed components, such as buttons, cards, text fields, navigation drawers, and dialogs, that developers can use to create consistent and functional user interfaces. These components are customizable but maintain a uniform style, ensuring a cohesive look and feel across the app.

- **Buttons**: Use bold, clear buttons that stand out for actions. There are different button types, such as raised, flat, and outlined, each serving different purposes.
- **Cards**: Cards are used to group content, such as images or text, in a visually engaging and organized way. They use shadows and elevation to suggest depth.
- **Navigation Drawer**: A sliding menu that allows for easy access to various sections of the app, offering smooth transitions and interactions.

2.6 Elevation and Shadows

Elevation and shadows are key to creating the sense of depth and interaction within Material Design. The guidelines use elevation to indicate the priority or importance of UI elements. Elements with higher elevation typically stand out more, drawing the user's attention. Shadows are used to give a sense of layering, making the interface feel more intuitive and grounded in reality.

2.7 Feedback and Interaction

Material Design emphasizes the importance of providing clear feedback to users to communicate the outcome of their actions. This can be achieved through animations, transitions, or visual indicators (e.g., changing button colors or showing loading spinners). Interactive elements should respond to user gestures and taps to enhance the feeling of control and responsiveness.

3. Implementing Material Design in Android Apps

To implement Material Design in Android apps, Google provides the Material Components for Android library, which includes the necessary components and themes to integrate Material Design principles into your app easily.

3.1 Material Components Library

The Material Components library provides UI components such as buttons, sliders, snackbars, and tabs that adhere to the Material Design principles. Developers can integrate these components into their apps using a simple Gradle dependency:

implementation 'com.google.android.material:material:1.4.0'

These components are customizable and can be easily adapted to match the app's color scheme and overall design.

3.2 Material Theme and Styling

Android apps can adopt the Material Design theme to ensure that their UI elements, such as buttons, text fields, and dialogs, adhere to Material guidelines. This is done by setting the app's theme to a Material Components theme in the styles.xml file:

<style name="AppTheme"
parent="Theme.MaterialComponents.DayNight.DarkActionBar">
    <!-- Customize your theme -->

</style>

You can also customize individual components, such as changing button shapes, text styles, and color schemes, to fit the app's brand and design preferences.

4. Best Practices for Material Design Implementation

4.1 Consistency Across Platforms

Material Design is not limited to Android; it extends to web and iOS platforms as well. By adhering to Material Design guidelines, you can ensure that your app provides a consistent experience across multiple platforms, helping users feel familiar with the app regardless of the device they use.

4.2 Focus on Usability

While Material Design emphasizes aesthetics, usability should always be the top priority. Ensure that the elements you design are functional and provide a smooth, intuitive user experience. This means keeping navigation clear, buttons easily tappable, and ensuring that actions are easily reversible (e.g., through confirmation dialogs or undo options).

4.3 Accessibility Considerations

Material Design encourages designers to consider accessibility when designing apps. This includes ensuring that colors have sufficient contrast for users with visual impairments and providing support for screen readers. Material Design also suggests using larger touch targets for buttons and other interactive elements to ensure ease of use for all users.

Material Design is a comprehensive design system that helps create consistent, visually appealing, and user-friendly Android applications. By following its principles and guidelines, you can ensure your app maintains a cohesive, intuitive, and functional design across various devices and screen sizes. Whether you're implementing Material Design components, customizing themes, or focusing on user interaction, adhering to these guidelines will help deliver a seamless and engaging experience for users.

6.2 Applying Themes and Styles in Android Apps

In Android development, themes and styles play a crucial role in controlling the visual appearance of an app. By defining themes and styles, you can ensure a consistent and polished user interface throughout your application. Themes and styles in Android are powerful tools that allow developers to customize the appearance of UI components and enforce consistency, ensuring that the app maintains a unified look and feel.

In this section, we will explore the concepts of themes and styles, how they work in Android, and how to apply them to your app to create an aesthetically pleasing and cohesive user experience.

1. What Are Themes and Styles in Android?

1.1 Styles

A style in Android is a collection of properties that define the visual appearance of a UI element. These properties can include attributes such as color, size, margins, padding, text style, background, and much more. Styles are applied to individual UI elements, allowing developers to define the appearance of views like buttons, text fields, and labels. For instance, you might create a style for buttons that specifies a specific text color, background, and padding.

Example of a style for a button:

```
<style name="CustomButtonStyle">
    <item name="android:background">@drawable/button_background</item>
    <item name="android:textColor">#FFFFFF</item>
    <item name="android:textSize">16sp</item>
    <item name="android:padding">10dp</item>
</style>
```

In this case, the style is applied to customize the look of a button by changing its background, text color, text size, and padding.

1.2 Themes

A theme in Android is a collection of styles that apply globally to an entire app or specific parts of it. It acts as a base styling mechanism for all UI elements in an app. Themes are typically set at the application level and define the overall look and feel, including default colors, fonts, and other visual properties. While styles apply to individual components, themes apply broadly to all views in the app, providing a unified and consistent appearance across the entire interface.

Themes are often used to enforce a color palette and typography across all screens of an app. Themes are particularly useful for maintaining consistent branding and a cohesive look, especially when you want to apply the same styling to many different UI elements (buttons, text fields, navigation bars, etc.).

Example of applying a theme in the styles.xml file:

```
<style name="AppTheme"
parent="Theme.MaterialComponents.DayNight.DarkActionBar">
   <item name="colorPrimary">@color/colorPrimary</item>
   <item name="colorPrimaryDark">@color/colorPrimaryDark</item>
   <item name="colorAccent">@color/colorAccent</item>
   <item name="android:textColor">@color/textColor</item>
</style>
```

In this example, the AppTheme applies a Material Components theme that uses primary and accent colors, as well as a custom text color.

2. Defining and Applying Styles in Android

2.1 Creating Styles

In Android, styles are defined in the res/values/styles.xml file. You can define multiple styles for different UI elements and reuse them to ensure consistency. For instance, you may define different styles for various types of buttons (e.g., primary, secondary, or disabled buttons).

Example of defining a custom style for a button:

```
<resources>
   <style name="PrimaryButton">
     <item
name="android:background">@drawable/primary_button_background</item>
     <item name="android:textColor">@android:color/white</item>
     <item name="android:textSize">14sp</item>
     <item name="android:padding">12dp</item>
   </style>
```

</resources>

In this example, the PrimaryButton style customizes the background, text color, text size, and padding of buttons.

2.2 Applying Styles to UI Elements

Once you define a style, you can apply it to a UI element using the style attribute within the XML layout files. For instance, you can apply the PrimaryButton style to a Button element in the activity_main.xml layout file:

```
<Button
    android:id="@+id/primary_button"
    style="@style/PrimaryButton"
    android:text="Click Me"
    android:layout_width="wrap_content"
    android:layout_height="wrap_content"/>
```

This approach ensures that all buttons styled with PrimaryButton will have the same visual properties, making your code more maintainable and consistent.

3. Defining and Applying Themes in Android

3.1 Creating Themes

Themes are defined in the res/values/styles.xml file as well, but unlike styles, themes typically control the appearance of the entire app or specific activities. When creating a theme, you can either extend an existing theme (e.g., Theme.MaterialComponents) or create a custom one.

Example of a simple custom theme:

```
<resources>
    <style name="AppTheme"
parent="Theme.MaterialComponents.DayNight.DarkActionBar">
        <item name="colorPrimary">@color/colorPrimary</item>
        <item name="colorPrimaryDark">@color/colorPrimaryDark</item>
        <item name="colorAccent">@color/colorAccent</item>
    </style>
</resources>
```

In this example, the custom theme AppTheme extends Theme.MaterialComponents.DayNight.DarkActionBar, which is a Material theme that adapts based on the device's light/dark mode setting. The theme applies custom primary, primary dark, and accent colors defined in the colors.xml file.

3.2 Applying Themes to Activities and the Application

Once a theme is defined, it can be applied at two levels:

At the application level: By setting the theme in the AndroidManifest.xml file, you can apply it to the entire app.

```
<application
    android:theme="@style/AppTheme">

    ...
</application>
```

At the activity level: You can also apply a theme to a specific activity within the app by specifying the theme in the activity tag in the AndroidManifest.xml file:

```
<activity
    android:name=".MainActivity"
    android:theme="@style/CustomActivityTheme">

    ...
</activity>
```

This allows different activities within the same app to have distinct appearances while maintaining overall consistency across the app.

4. Customizing Themes and Styles for Dark Mode

4.1 Supporting Dark Mode

One of the significant benefits of Android's theme system is the ability to adapt your app for Dark Mode. Android 10 introduced system-wide dark theme support, and Material Design guidelines emphasize the use of dark mode to reduce eye strain and conserve battery life.

To support dark mode, you can create separate resource values for light and dark themes. This allows your app to automatically switch between light and dark themes based on the user's system-wide setting.

Example of defining a light and dark theme:

```xml
<!-- Light theme -->
<style name="AppTheme.Light" parent="Theme.MaterialComponents.Light">
    <item name="colorPrimary">@color/light_primary</item>
    <item name="colorPrimaryDark">@color/light_primary_dark</item>
    <item name="colorAccent">@color/light_accent</item>
</style>

<!-- Dark theme -->
<style name="AppTheme.Dark" parent="Theme.MaterialComponents.DayNight">
    <item name="colorPrimary">@color/dark_primary</item>
    <item name="colorPrimaryDark">@color/dark_primary_dark</item>
    <item name="colorAccent">@color/dark_accent</item>
</style>
```

By setting the theme to Theme.MaterialComponents.DayNight, Android will automatically apply the correct theme based on the user's system preference (light or dark).

5. Best Practices for Using Themes and Styles

5.1 Consistency

Themes and styles ensure that UI elements have a consistent appearance across different screens and activities. By defining common styles and applying themes, you can maintain visual consistency, which contributes to a more polished and professional app design.

5.2 Customization and Flexibility

While Material Design components provide pre-defined styles and themes, don't hesitate to customize them to match your app's branding and design. The goal is to strike a balance between adhering to the design guidelines and creating a unique visual identity for your app.

5.3 Use Proper Naming Conventions

Maintain clear and descriptive names for your themes and styles to make your code more readable and easier to manage. For example, name button styles like PrimaryButtonStyle, SecondaryButtonStyle, and theme names like AppThemeLight, AppThemeDark, etc.

Themes and styles are powerful tools for creating visually consistent, cohesive, and user-friendly Android applications. By leveraging these features, you can simplify the management of visual elements and improve the overall user experience. Whether you're creating custom buttons, defining global themes, or supporting dark mode, understanding and applying themes and styles will help you craft a polished, professional Android app.

6.3 Creating Custom Components with Material Design

Material Design offers a robust set of pre-built UI components that help developers create clean, modern, and user-friendly Android apps. However, in some cases, you may need to create custom components to meet specific design requirements or to give your app a unique visual identity. Custom components are highly customizable and can adhere to Material Design principles, ensuring that they blend seamlessly into the overall design system while providing the flexibility needed for unique functionality.

In this section, we will explore how to create custom components using Material Design principles. We will cover the basic structure of custom components, how to apply Material Design's visual aesthetics to them, and how to implement them in your app.

1. What are Custom Components?

Custom components are UI elements that are not part of the pre-defined Material Design components but still conform to Material Design guidelines in terms of style, behavior, and user experience. These components are typically created when the standard set of components does not meet the specific needs of your app.

For example, you might want to create a custom button that includes both text and an image, or a custom card view with unique animation effects. These components can be tailored to suit your app's functionality while maintaining the same polished look and feel as the built-in Material Design elements.

2. Key Principles for Custom Components

When designing custom components, it's crucial to ensure that they align with the Material Design principles of clarity, simplicity, and accessibility. Here are some of the key guidelines to follow:

2.1 Maintain Consistency

Your custom components should align with the general design language of Material Design. This includes maintaining appropriate elevation, shadows, typography, color schemes, and spacing. Using Material Design's style components, like buttons or cards, as a reference for creating custom elements will help you maintain a cohesive and polished look throughout your app.

2.2 Focus on User Interaction

Material Design emphasizes the importance of feedback and interactivity. When creating custom components, make sure they respond well to user actions, such as touches, swipes, and long presses. Provide visual cues, such as color changes, ripples, or animations, that indicate the element has been interacted with.

2.3 Accessibility

Custom components should be designed with accessibility in mind. This means ensuring that they are usable for people with disabilities, such as those who rely on screen readers or have limited mobility. You should consider appropriate touch target sizes, provide text alternatives (e.g., content descriptions), and ensure that all interactive elements can be accessed via assistive technologies.

2.4 Responsiveness

Your custom components should scale well on different screen sizes and densities. They should adapt seamlessly to small and large devices, landscape and portrait orientations, and varying screen resolutions. Using flexible layouts and responsive design practices will ensure that the components remain functional and attractive across multiple device types.

3. Creating Custom Components

There are various ways to create custom components in Android. The approach depends on the type of component you want to create. Below are some of the most common methods for creating custom components while adhering to Material Design principles.

3.1 Custom Button with Image and Text

A custom button is one of the most frequently needed UI components in Android development. You may want to combine an icon with text or add an animated effect to a standard button. Here's how you can create a custom button that follows Material Design's emphasis on clarity and interaction:

Step 1: Define the Button in XML

```xml
<Button
    android:id="@+id/customButton"
    style="@style/CustomMaterialButton"
    android:layout_width="wrap_content"
    android:layout_height="wrap_content"
    android:text="Click Me"
    android:drawableLeft="@drawable/ic_example_icon"
    android:layout_margin="16dp"/>
```

Step 2: Create the Style for the Button in styles.xml

```xml
<style name="CustomMaterialButton">
    <item name="android:background">@drawable/button_background</item>
    <item name="android:textColor">#FFFFFF</item>
    <item name="android:textSize">14sp</item>
    <item name="android:padding">10dp</item>
    <item name="android:elevation">2dp</item>
</style>
```

Step 3: Add Background Drawable in res/drawable/button_background.xml

```xml
<shape xmlns:android="http://schemas.android.com/apk/res/android">
    <solid android:color="#6200EE"/>
    <corners android:radius="8dp"/>
    <elevation android:value="4dp"/>
</shape>
```

This custom button combines text and an icon, uses an elevation effect to provide depth, and applies a consistent color scheme that adheres to Material Design's principles.

3.2 Custom Card View with Animation

Card views are a popular way to display content in a structured, visually appealing format. You may want to create a custom card that includes additional animations, like expanding or collapsing the card when clicked.

Step 1: Define the Card View in XML

```xml
<androidx.cardview.widget.CardView
    android:id="@+id/customCardView"
    android:layout_width="match_parent"
    android:layout_height="wrap_content"
    android:layout_margin="16dp"
    app:cardCornerRadius="10dp"
    app:cardElevation="5dp"
    android:clickable="true"
    android:focusable="true">

    <LinearLayout
        android:layout_width="match_parent"
        android:layout_height="wrap_content"
        android:orientation="vertical"
        android:padding="16dp">

        <TextView
            android:id="@+id/cardTitle"
            android:layout_width="wrap_content"
            android:layout_height="wrap_content"
            android:text="Card Title"
            android:textSize="18sp"
            android:textColor="@android:color/black" />

        <TextView
            android:id="@+id/cardDescription"
            android:layout_width="wrap_content"
            android:layout_height="wrap_content"
            android:text="Description goes here"
            android:textSize="14sp"
            android:textColor="@android:color/darker_gray" />
    </LinearLayout>
```

</androidx.cardview.widget.CardView>

Step 2: Add Click Animation Using Code

You can apply animations such as a rotation or scale effect when the card is clicked to give users visual feedback:

```
cardView.setOnClickListener(v -> {
    // Scale the card on click
    ObjectAnimator scaleX = ObjectAnimator.ofFloat(cardView, "scaleX", 1f, 0.95f, 1f);
    ObjectAnimator scaleY = ObjectAnimator.ofFloat(cardView, "scaleY", 1f, 0.95f, 1f);
    AnimatorSet animatorSet = new AnimatorSet();
    animatorSet.playTogether(scaleX, scaleY);
    animatorSet.setDuration(300);
    animatorSet.start();
});
```

In this example, when the card is clicked, it briefly scales down and then back up, providing an interactive animation that's both responsive and visually engaging.

4. Using Material Components for Customization

While creating custom components from scratch is an essential skill, you can also leverage Material Components to enhance your custom elements. Material Components for Android includes a rich set of UI components such as buttons, cards, chips, text fields, and more, all of which can be easily customized.

For instance, to customize a MaterialButton, you can apply a custom style:

```
<com.google.android.material.button.MaterialButton
    android:id="@+id/customMaterialButton"
    android:layout_width="wrap_content"
    android:layout_height="wrap_content"
    android:text="Custom Button"
    style="@style/CustomButtonStyle"/>
```

The MaterialButton already includes some Material Design principles like ripple effects and accessibility features, so customizing it with your own background, text styles, and elevation can help create a unique but consistent user experience.

5. Best Practices for Custom Components

5.1 Consistency with Material Design Principles

Custom components should still adhere to Material Design principles such as clear visual hierarchy, consistent use of color, responsive interaction, and intuitive design. Keep the user experience consistent across all components to avoid confusion.

5.2 Reusability

When designing custom components, aim for reusability. This means making components modular, easy to integrate into other screens, and adaptable to different situations. For example, avoid hard-coding specific content into your custom components; instead, use parameters or data binding to make them flexible.

5.3 Maintain Accessibility

Always ensure that your custom components are accessible. This includes providing proper content descriptions, ensuring appropriate contrast ratios for text and background colors, and making sure the components are fully navigable via screen readers and other accessibility tools.

5.4 Performance Considerations

Custom components can sometimes introduce performance bottlenecks, especially if they involve complex animations or nested layouts. Always test your components for performance issues and optimize them when necessary by reducing overdraw, simplifying layouts, or using efficient animations.

Creating custom components with Material Design principles allows developers to build unique, branded UI elements while still maintaining a cohesive and professional appearance. By adhering to Material Design's core principles—such as clarity, accessibility, and responsiveness—you can design custom components that provide a seamless and engaging user experience. Whether you're creating custom buttons, cards, or interactive animations, the goal is to ensure consistency, performance, and usability across your app while giving it a distinct, tailored feel.

6.4 Enhancing Usability with Motion and Animation

Motion and animation are powerful tools that can enhance the usability and aesthetic appeal of your Android applications. When done correctly, they can significantly improve the user experience by providing visual feedback, guiding the user's attention, and making the interface feel more responsive and dynamic. In Material Design, motion is not only about making the app visually appealing but also about making interactions more intuitive and creating a sense of continuity within the user interface.

In this section, we will explore how to integrate motion and animation into your app to enhance usability. We will discuss the principles behind motion design in Android, how to implement different types of animations, and best practices to create smooth, user-friendly interactions that contribute to the overall user experience.

1. The Role of Motion in Material Design

In Material Design, motion plays a critical role in creating a natural, seamless flow between interactions. Material Design uses motion to ensure that users are always aware of what is happening within the app, providing them with clear feedback and enhancing their understanding of how elements move and interact within the interface. The role of motion can be broken down into several key aspects:

1.1 Visual Feedback:

When users interact with elements such as buttons, icons, or menus, motion provides them with feedback that confirms their action. For example, a button may ripple when pressed, or a menu may smoothly slide in and out. This feedback helps users feel that their actions are acknowledged and provides clarity on what is happening next.

1.2 Transitions Between States:

Motion can help guide users between different states of the app. For instance, when transitioning from one screen to another, an animated transition can make the experience feel more fluid and less jarring. It also helps users understand the relationship between different elements on the screen and how they fit together in the broader flow of the app.

1.3 Emphasis and Focus:

Motion can draw attention to important actions, notifications, or updates. For example, a small notification icon may animate to signal new content or updates, or a specific button may pulse to highlight a call to action. This directs the user's focus toward the most important interactions.

2. Types of Animations in Android

There are several types of animations you can implement in Android apps, each serving different purposes in terms of enhancing usability and improving user experience. Here are the main types:

2.1 View Animations

View animations are the most basic type of animations in Android and allow you to animate properties such as translation, rotation, scaling, and opacity. View animations can be applied using the Animation class and are most useful for simple UI changes, such as moving elements on the screen or fading them in and out.

- **Translation Animation**: Moving views across the screen.
- **Rotation Animation**: Spinning a view around its center point.
- **Scale Animation**: Increasing or decreasing the size of a view.
- **Alpha Animation**: Changing the transparency of a view.

Example:

```
TranslateAnimation translateAnimation = new TranslateAnimation(0, 200, 0, 0);
translateAnimation.setDuration(500);
view.startAnimation(translateAnimation);
```

2.2 Property Animations (ObjectAnimator)

Property animations provide more flexibility and are a more powerful way to animate objects. They allow you to animate the properties of any object, including views, and can be combined to create more complex animations. With the ObjectAnimator class, you can animate a wide variety of properties such as position, rotation, and color. These animations can also be chained together to create intricate animations.

Example:

```
ObjectAnimator animation = ObjectAnimator.ofFloat(view, "translationX", 0f, 200f);
animation.setDuration(500);
animation.start();
```

2.3 MotionLayout

MotionLayout is a powerful layout manager that enables complex, coordinated animations between different UI states. It provides a way to transition between layouts and animate views as they move and change position. MotionLayout allows you to visually design and control transitions between two different layout states in a declarative manner using XML, making it a great tool for animations with larger and more complex UI changes.

Example:

```xml
<MotionLayout
    xmlns:app="http://schemas.android.com/apk/res-auto"
    android:id="@+id/motionLayout"
    android:layout_width="match_parent"
    android:layout_height="match_parent"
    app:layoutDescription="@xml/scene_transition">

    <Button
        android:id="@+id/button"
        android:layout_width="wrap_content"
        android:layout_height="wrap_content"
        android:text="Tap Me"
        android:layout_centerInParent="true" />
</MotionLayout>
```

2.4 Shared Element Transitions

Shared element transitions are animations used when transitioning between different activities or fragments. They provide a visual continuity by animating the movement of shared elements (like an image or text) from one screen to the next, making the transition feel more natural and cohesive.

Example:

```java
ActivityOptionsCompat options =
ActivityOptionsCompat.makeSceneTransitionAnimation(activity, sharedView,
"transition_name");
startActivity(intent, options.toBundle());
```

3. Best Practices for Using Motion and Animation

While motion and animation can significantly enhance the user experience, it's important to use them strategically and thoughtfully. Poorly executed animations can distract, confuse, or frustrate users, so it's essential to follow best practices for creating effective animations.

3.1 Keep Animations Smooth and Lightweight

Animations should be smooth, lightweight, and not overused. Complex or excessive animations can lead to performance issues, especially on lower-end devices. Keep animations simple, and use them only when they serve a clear purpose, such as providing feedback or guiding user interactions.

3.2 Provide Instant Feedback

Users expect immediate feedback when interacting with elements on the screen. Ensure that your animations respond quickly and efficiently to user actions. For example, when a user clicks a button, the button should immediately animate with a ripple effect to provide instant feedback.

3.3 Focus on Intuitiveness

Animations should help users understand how to interact with the app. For instance, if a menu slides in from the side, it should be clear that it is interactive. Avoid confusing or overly complex animations that may make it difficult for users to understand how to navigate through the app.

3.4 Use Consistent Animation Styles

Consistency in animation helps establish a cohesive experience. If you use a specific animation style (such as a button ripple effect), ensure that it is applied consistently across your app. This consistency reinforces the design language and helps users feel more comfortable interacting with your app.

3.5 Respect User Preferences

Some users may prefer minimal motion due to personal preferences or accessibility needs. You should respect these preferences and provide a way to reduce or disable animations if necessary. Android offers a system-wide setting that allows users to reduce or turn off animations.

You can check this setting and adjust your app accordingly:

```
if (Settings.Global.getFloat(getContentResolver(),
    Settings.Global.ANIMATOR_DURATION_SCALE, 1) == 0) {
    // Disable animations
}
```

Motion and animation are key to making your Android app more engaging and intuitive, aligning with Material Design principles. By incorporating thoughtful animations, you can guide users through interactions, improve usability, and make the app feel more responsive and dynamic. However, it's important to strike a balance—animations should enhance the user experience, not detract from it. By following best practices and using the appropriate types of animations for specific tasks, you can create a visually appealing and user-friendly app that both delights and informs your users.

6.5 Dark Mode and Adaptive UI Design

Dark Mode is one of the most significant trends in modern app design, offering users an alternative to the traditional light-themed interface. Not only does it provide a visually appealing experience, but it can also reduce eye strain in low-light environments and help conserve battery life on OLED screens. Adaptive UI design, on the other hand, focuses on creating a flexible interface that adjusts seamlessly to different themes, screen sizes, orientations, and other device conditions.

In this section, we will explore how to implement Dark Mode in your Android app and how to build adaptive UIs that adjust to various environments, ensuring a consistent, user-friendly experience across a wide range of devices and use cases.

1. Introduction to Dark Mode in Android

Dark Mode is a system-wide theme that uses darker colors for UI elements, making it easier on the eyes, especially in low-light settings. Android introduced official support for Dark Mode in Android 10, allowing developers to design apps that respect the user's system-wide theme preferences.

Enabling Dark Mode can be particularly beneficial for users who spend extended periods of time using their devices in dim environments or those who prefer a darker aesthetic. It also plays a role in reducing battery consumption, particularly on OLED displays, where darker pixels consume less power.

2. Implementing Dark Mode in Your Android App

To implement Dark Mode in your Android app, you need to ensure that your app's UI automatically switches between light and dark themes based on the system settings or user preferences. Below are the steps to enable Dark Mode in your app.

2.1 Support for System-Wide Dark Mode

Android provides a simple way to enable Dark Mode support by using themes that automatically switch based on the system's setting. To do this, you need to define both light and dark themes in your res/values and res/values-night directories:

Step 1: Define Light and Dark Themes

res/values/styles.xml (Light Mode):

```xml
<resources>
    <style name="AppTheme"
parent="Theme.MaterialComponents.DayNight.NoActionBar">
        <item name="colorPrimary">@color/colorPrimary</item>
        <item name="colorPrimaryDark">@color/colorPrimaryDark</item>
        <item name="colorAccent">@color/colorAccent</item>
        <!-- Add other theme attributes here -->
    </style>
</resources>
```

res/values-night/styles.xml (Dark Mode):

```xml
<resources>
    <style name="AppTheme"
parent="Theme.MaterialComponents.DayNight.NoActionBar">
        <item name="colorPrimary">@color/colorPrimaryDark</item>
        <item name="colorPrimaryDark">@color/colorPrimaryLight</item>
        <item name="colorAccent">@color/colorAccentDark</item>
        <!-- Modify the colors for Dark Mode here -->
    </style>
</resources>
```

In the above configuration, you use Theme.MaterialComponents.DayNight as the parent theme, which automatically adjusts based on the system-wide theme preference (light or dark).

Step 2: Ensure Theme Switches Dynamically

When the user switches between Light and Dark Mode in their device settings, Android will automatically adjust the app's theme. However, you can also programmatically set the theme based on user preferences.

To check and set the theme dynamically:

if (isDarkMode()) {

AppCompatDelegate.setDefaultNightMode(AppCompatDelegate.MODE_NIGHT_YES);
} else {

AppCompatDelegate.setDefaultNightMode(AppCompatDelegate.MODE_NIGHT_NO);
}

Here, the isDarkMode() method determines whether the user prefers Dark Mode. You can create a preference screen in your app to allow users to toggle between Light and Dark themes.

3. Adapting UI Elements for Dark Mode

Once Dark Mode is enabled, it's important to adapt your UI elements to make sure they are both functional and aesthetically pleasing. The most critical element to consider is color – both background and foreground elements must be adjusted for contrast to maintain readability.

3.1 Managing Colors in Dark Mode

When designing for Dark Mode, ensure that your app uses appropriate colors that work well in both light and dark settings. Avoid using pure black (#000000) or pure white (#FFFFFF) for backgrounds. Instead, opt for shades of gray for backgrounds and use more vibrant colors for text and primary elements.

For instance:

- Backgrounds in Dark Mode should use shades like #121212 or #2C2C2C.
- Text colors should be light, like #E0E0E0, to provide sufficient contrast.
- Button and accent colors should remain consistent, but you may want to adjust their brightness in Dark Mode to maintain visibility.

Example:

```
<color name="background_color_light">#FFFFFF</color>
<color name="background_color_dark">#121212</color>
<color name="text_color_light">#000000</color>
<color name="text_color_dark">#E0E0E0</color>
```

You can reference these colors in your theme styles:

```
<item name="android:windowBackground">@color/background_color</item>
<item name="android:textColorPrimary">@color/text_color</item>
```

3.2 Icons and Images for Dark Mode

Ensure that your icons and images are visible and stand out against a darker background. For example, if you are using vector images, you should ensure they use the correct color or adjust the icon's color dynamically based on the theme.

You can define specific icon files for light and dark themes:

```
res/drawable/icon_light.xml
res/drawable/icon_dark.xml
```

You can then reference the appropriate icon based on the current theme.

3.3 Dynamic Backgrounds and Gradients

For complex layouts or components with background images, gradients, or patterns, ensure they adapt to both themes. For example, use a gradient background that shifts in tone depending on whether the app is in Light or Dark Mode:

```
<shape xmlns:android="http://schemas.android.com/apk/res/android">
  <gradient
    android:startColor="#E0E0E0"
    android:endColor="#B0B0B0"
```

```
    android:angle="45"/>
</shape>
```

4. Adaptive UI Design for Multiple Devices

Adaptive UI design focuses on making your app look good and work well across different device sizes, screen densities, and orientations. The goal is to ensure that the app layout remains consistent and functional across a wide variety of devices, from smartphones to tablets and foldables.

4.1 Creating Responsive Layouts with ConstraintLayout

One of the most effective tools for adaptive UI design in Android is ConstraintLayout. This layout manager allows you to design complex, responsive layouts that automatically adjust to different screen sizes and orientations.

For example, you can use ConstraintLayout to ensure that your UI components are properly aligned and resized based on available screen space:

```
<androidx.constraintlayout.widget.ConstraintLayout
    android:layout_width="match_parent"
    android:layout_height="match_parent">

    <TextView
        android:id="@+id/title"
        android:layout_width="wrap_content"
        android:layout_height="wrap_content"
        android:text="Hello World"
        app:layout_constraintTop_toTopOf="parent"
        app:layout_constraintLeft_toLeftOf="parent" />
</androidx.constraintlayout.widget.ConstraintLayout>
```

In this example, ConstraintLayout helps ensure that the TextView is positioned correctly regardless of the screen size.

4.2 Supporting Different Screen Sizes and Densities

For adaptive design, you need to create resources for different screen densities and sizes. Android allows you to provide resources for specific screen configurations, such as res/drawable-mdpi, res/drawable-hdpi, and so on for images.

Additionally, you can define layout variations for different screen sizes using resource directories like res/layout-small, res/layout-large, and res/layout-xlarge.

Dark Mode and adaptive UI design are powerful tools to enhance your app's user experience. By implementing Dark Mode, you can cater to users who prefer darker interfaces, reduce eye strain, and conserve battery life. Adaptive UI design ensures that your app looks great and performs well across different screen sizes and device types, creating a seamless experience for users regardless of their device.

By following best practices for both Dark Mode and adaptive layouts, you can build a more inclusive, user-friendly app that provides an optimal experience under various conditions, leading to happier users and improved engagement.

7. Accessibility and Inclusivity in App Design

In today's diverse world, creating apps that are accessible to all users, including those with disabilities, is not just a best practice—it's essential. In this chapter, you'll learn how to design Android apps that are inclusive, ensuring they can be used by individuals with visual, hearing, or motor impairments. From implementing screen readers and accessibility features like TalkBack to designing for a global audience with localization, this chapter teaches you how to make your apps more user-friendly and compliant with accessibility standards. By prioritizing inclusivity, you'll be able to reach a wider audience and create more meaningful experiences for everyone.

7.1 Why Accessibility Matters in Modern Apps

In today's digital world, creating accessible apps is not just a best practice; it's a necessity. Accessibility in mobile apps ensures that users with varying abilities—whether they are visually impaired, hearing impaired, or have motor difficulties—can interact with and navigate your app effectively. As mobile technology becomes more integral to daily life, it's crucial that app developers consider accessibility to ensure that no user is excluded from the digital experience.

The importance of accessibility goes beyond just being a good ethical practice; it also has legal, business, and social implications. In this section, we will explore why accessibility matters in modern apps, highlighting the ethical responsibility, legal requirements, business advantages, and technical considerations for making apps accessible to all users.

1. Ethical Responsibility and Inclusivity

One of the primary reasons accessibility matters is because of the ethical responsibility developers have to ensure their apps are inclusive. The digital divide remains a significant issue, and without proper accessibility features, a large portion of the population is excluded from full participation in digital life.

Inclusion is fundamental to a fair and equal society, and technology should serve everyone, not just those who are able-bodied. By making your app accessible, you're giving users with disabilities the opportunity to access information, services, and entertainment in the same way that others do. It shows social responsibility and an awareness of the challenges faced by those who may have impairments, allowing them to use your app as seamlessly as possible.

2. Legal Requirements and Compliance

In many countries, accessibility is not just a recommendation; it's a legal requirement. Governments worldwide are recognizing the importance of making digital services accessible, and many have put laws and regulations in place to enforce this.

For instance, in the United States, the Americans with Disabilities Act (ADA) requires businesses and developers to make their digital services, including websites and apps, accessible to people with disabilities. Similarly, the European Union's Web Accessibility Directive mandates that public sector websites and mobile applications must comply with accessibility guidelines.

Failure to comply with these regulations can lead to legal consequences, including lawsuits, fines, and a damaged reputation. Therefore, integrating accessibility into your app development process is not just a moral obligation; it's a matter of legal compliance in many regions.

3. Enhancing User Experience for a Larger Audience

While accessibility features directly benefit users with disabilities, they also contribute to an enhanced overall user experience for all users. When you design an app to be accessible, you make it easier to use for everyone. For example:

- **Text-to-speech and screen readers**: Features like text-to-speech not only help visually impaired users but can also be useful for users in situations where they cannot look at their phone screen, such as when driving.
- **High contrast themes**: Dark mode or high contrast color schemes are often appreciated by users in bright sunlight or those who prefer to reduce eye strain, in addition to helping people with visual impairments.
- **Simplified navigation**: Accessibility features such as larger touch targets, gesture-based navigation, and alternative text make apps easier to use for people with motor impairments but also provide a smoother user experience for everyone.

These features improve the usability of your app and can lead to greater user satisfaction, increased retention, and a wider user base.

4. Business Advantages and Market Reach

Accessibility not only impacts the user experience but also has a direct effect on the success of your app in the marketplace. The more accessible your app is, the larger the potential audience becomes. According to the World Health Organization (WHO), over 1 billion people globally live with some form of disability. Ignoring this demographic means missing out on a significant portion of potential users.

Accessibility also helps improve your app's reputation. As users become more aware of the importance of inclusivity, they are more likely to support brands and apps that demonstrate social responsibility. A positive reputation for accessibility can help differentiate your app from competitors, attract more loyal users, and boost your brand's overall image.

By designing with accessibility in mind, you cater not only to individuals with disabilities but also to aging populations, people who may have temporary impairments (e.g., a broken arm), and those in challenging environments (such as bright sunlight or noisy surroundings). This increases your app's marketability and gives you a competitive edge.

5. Meeting Industry Standards and Guidelines

Another reason why accessibility is crucial is that major platforms, such as Android and iOS, have established clear guidelines and standards to help developers build accessible apps. These guidelines provide best practices for ensuring your app works well for users with disabilities, and adhering to them not only improves the quality of your app but also guarantees it integrates seamlessly with the built-in accessibility tools that both platforms offer.

For example, Android provides accessibility features like TalkBack (a screen reader), magnification gestures, and high contrast text, while iOS offers VoiceOver, Switch Control, and other accessibility settings. To ensure that your app works with these built-in features, you must follow the platform-specific accessibility standards.

Both Google and Apple also require apps to meet certain accessibility criteria before they can be published on the Google Play Store or the Apple App Store. By following these guidelines, you make sure that your app meets industry expectations and avoids potential issues with the app review process.

6. Technical Benefits of Building Accessible Apps

Incorporating accessibility into your app development also has technical advantages. For example:

- **Semantic markup**: When you use semantic tags for your UI elements, such as buttons, text fields, and checkboxes, it helps screen readers interpret the app's content correctly. This leads to more structured and maintainable code.
- **Modular design**: Accessibility often encourages developers to break down complex layouts into simpler, smaller components, leading to better code organization and more manageable projects.
- **Error handling and validation**: Accessibility guidelines emphasize clear error messaging, which also improves app usability for all users. For example, when a user enters an invalid form field, accessibility guidelines suggest that the error should be clearly announced via screen readers, as well as visually highlighted on the screen.

By focusing on accessibility during development, developers ensure the app is well-structured, reliable, and user-friendly for a broad range of people, making it more robust in the long run.

Accessibility is an essential aspect of modern app development that goes beyond the needs of users with disabilities. It serves as a critical factor for ethical inclusivity, legal compliance, business success, and market reach. By designing apps that are accessible, you not only meet the needs of a wider audience but also create better user experiences, enhance usability, and ensure long-term sustainability. Furthermore, by aligning with industry standards and building with accessibility in mind, your app is likely to perform better, be more widely adopted, and stand out in a competitive market.

Ultimately, accessibility should be an integral part of your development process from the very beginning—because every user, regardless of their abilities, deserves a seamless, enjoyable app experience.

7.2 Implementing TalkBack and Screen Readers

For individuals who are blind or have low vision, screen readers like TalkBack on Android play an essential role in enabling them to navigate and interact with mobile applications. TalkBack is an accessibility feature built into Android devices that provides spoken feedback for what is displayed on the screen. This allows users to hear descriptions of UI elements, text, and other information, and perform actions through gestures.

Implementing proper support for TalkBack in your app is crucial for making it fully accessible to users who rely on these features. This section will explore how TalkBack works, why it's important, and how to implement it effectively in your app to ensure it meets accessibility guidelines.

1. What is TalkBack?

TalkBack is Android's built-in screen reader, designed for users who are blind or have low vision. It reads aloud the content displayed on the screen and allows users to interact with their device by using gestures. For example, a user can swipe to navigate between elements, double-tap to activate buttons, and swipe up or down to adjust values or scroll through lists.

TalkBack is enabled by default in Android devices, and it's part of the Accessibility Services provided by Android. When TalkBack is turned on, all elements in the UI (such as buttons, text fields, images, and more) should be properly labeled with content descriptions to ensure that the user can understand and interact with them through auditory feedback.

2. The Role of Accessibility Labels

To make your app compatible with TalkBack, you need to provide content descriptions for UI elements. A content description is a textual label that describes an element's purpose or content, which TalkBack reads aloud. For example, an image button should have a content description explaining its function.

In Android, the android:contentDescription attribute is used to provide these labels for elements that require textual descriptions. Here's how you can add a content description to a button:

```
<Button
    android:id="@+id/submit_button"
    android:layout_width="wrap_content"
    android:layout_height="wrap_content"
    android:text="Submit"
    android:contentDescription="Submit your form" />
```

When TalkBack is enabled, it will read out the description "Submit your form" when the user interacts with this button.

Key Points for Effective Content Descriptions:

- **Be clear and concise**: Avoid overly long descriptions. A few words that summarize the action or content are sufficient.
- Avoid repeating information that is already provided visually (e.g., don't say "button" or "image").
- **Provide context**: If the element is part of a complex layout, ensure that the description gives enough information to understand its function in that context (e.g., "Delete item" instead of just "Delete").

3. Supporting Interactive Elements with Accessibility

Beyond content descriptions, interactive elements (buttons, checkboxes, switches, etc.) must also be properly labeled for TalkBack users to know what actions they can perform. For example:

- Buttons should have an action-specific description.
- EditText fields (text input) should indicate the type of data being input (e.g., "Enter your name").
- Checkboxes and switches should indicate whether they are checked or unchecked.

Here's an example for a checkbox:

<CheckBox
    android:id="@+id/agree_checkbox"
    android:layout_width="wrap_content"
    android:layout_height="wrap_content"
    android:text="I agree to the terms and conditions"
    android:contentDescription="I agree to the terms and conditions" />

Additionally, it is important to use the android:checked attribute to reflect the state of checkboxes, switches, and other toggle elements to ensure that TalkBack reads the current state:

<Switch
    android:id="@+id/notifications_switch"
    android:layout_width="wrap_content"
    android:layout_height="wrap_content"
    android:text="Enable notifications"

```
android:checked="true"
android:contentDescription="Enable notifications, currently turned on" />
```

This provides context to TalkBack users, helping them understand the state of elements.

4. Navigating Complex UIs

For more complex layouts, such as forms, lists, and dynamic content, it is essential to structure your UI so that TalkBack can navigate through it in a logical and intuitive order. Here are some tips for enhancing navigation:

Use LinearLayout, RelativeLayout, or ConstraintLayout for layout hierarchy: These layouts help maintain a logical order for TalkBack to follow when reading out the UI.

Use android:importantForAccessibility attribute: This attribute helps you control whether a UI element is ignored by accessibility services. For example, if you have an element that is purely decorative and does not add functional value (such as a non-interactive image), you can set it to importantForAccessibility="no".

```
<ImageView
    android:id="@+id/decorative_image"
    android:layout_width="wrap_content"
    android:layout_height="wrap_content"
    android:src="@drawable/decorative_image"
    android:importantForAccessibility="no" />
```

Grouping related elements: For forms or sections that require multiple inputs, grouping them together using ViewGroup elements can help ensure TalkBack reads them in a natural flow. If necessary, you can also group related elements into a ViewPager or RecyclerView to improve navigation and accessibility.

Custom Views: For custom views, you should make sure that the view is focusable and provides meaningful feedback to TalkBack. For example, custom buttons, sliders, or other interactive components should be properly announced using the setContentDescription method programmatically.

5. Testing with TalkBack

After implementing accessibility features, it's essential to test your app with TalkBack to ensure that it provides a seamless experience for users who rely on screen readers. Testing involves:

- **Enabling TalkBack**: On Android devices, you can enable TalkBack by going to Settings > Accessibility > TalkBack. Alternatively, you can quickly enable it by using a gesture (such as tapping the power button multiple times or accessing the accessibility menu).
- **Navigating through your app**: As you navigate through the app, listen to how TalkBack reads out UI elements and verify that all elements are described correctly.
- **Interacting with controls**: Test interactive elements such as buttons, form fields, and checkboxes to make sure they are properly announced and the app reacts as expected.
- **Regularly using** TalkBack during development and testing ensures your app is accessible and user-friendly for those with visual impairments.

Implementing TalkBack support and ensuring that your app is compatible with screen readers is essential for creating an inclusive experience for all users. Properly labeling UI elements, ensuring logical navigation, and testing with TalkBack are key steps to making your app accessible. By doing so, you not only comply with accessibility standards and legal requirements, but you also provide a better user experience, increase your app's reach, and improve user satisfaction.

Accessibility isn't just about meeting requirements; it's about creating a user-centric experience that benefits everyone, regardless of their abilities. Incorporating TalkBack and other accessibility features into your app is an investment in both social responsibility and app quality.

7.3 Designing for Visual, Motor, and Hearing Impairments

Designing mobile applications to be inclusive and accessible for users with visual, motor, and hearing impairments is an essential part of creating a user-friendly experience for everyone. By considering the unique needs of these groups, developers can ensure that their apps are usable by a diverse audience. In this section, we will discuss how to design Android apps that are accessible to users with these specific impairments, covering key considerations and practical strategies for each type of disability.

1. Designing for Visual Impairments

Visual impairments, ranging from partial vision loss to complete blindness, can present significant challenges for users interacting with mobile apps. However, by implementing several design strategies, you can make your app more usable for users with visual disabilities.

Key Strategies for Visual Impairments:

Content Descriptions: Providing accurate and descriptive content for all interactive elements, including images, buttons, and other UI components, is critical. Use android:contentDescription for images, icons, and buttons to describe their purpose or functionality. This is essential for screen readers like TalkBack to announce the content to users who cannot visually perceive it.

Example:

```
<ImageView
    android:id="@+id/imageView"
    android:layout_width="wrap_content"
    android:layout_height="wrap_content"
    android:src="@drawable/sample_image"
    android:contentDescription="An image of a sunset over the ocean"/>
```

Color Contrast: Many users with visual impairments, such as color blindness or low vision, benefit from high contrast in text and background colors. Ensure that there is sufficient contrast between text and its background (WCAG guidelines suggest a contrast ratio of at least 4.5:1 for normal text and 3:1 for large text).

Text Size and Scaling: Allow users to scale text and UI elements to meet their needs. Android provides the android:textSize attribute for text elements, and users can adjust text size in the device settings. Additionally, you should design your UI to be responsive to text size changes, ensuring that elements do not overlap or break when text is scaled.

Support for Screen Readers: Integrating screen readers, such as Android's TalkBack, ensures that users with low vision or blindness can navigate your app. Ensure all interactive elements are properly labeled with contentDescription and provide clear, meaningful feedback on actions taken by the user.

2. Designing for Motor Impairments

Motor impairments, which can range from limited mobility to full paralysis, affect a user's ability to interact with touchscreens and control devices using precise movements. Designing for motor impairments requires accommodating various forms of input and ensuring that UI elements are easy to navigate and interact with.

Key Strategies for Motor Impairments:

Larger Touch Targets: People with motor impairments may have difficulty interacting with small buttons or UI elements. To address this, make touch targets larger. Android recommends a minimum size of 48x48dp for tappable elements, such as buttons and switches, to ensure they are accessible.

Gestures and Navigation: While touch gestures are the primary mode of input, users with motor impairments may struggle with precise gestures. Offering alternative ways to navigate, such as enabling swipe actions or customizing the gesture sensitivity, can provide a better experience. Consider offering on-screen buttons for key navigation actions and allowing users to customize gestures to suit their needs.

Voice Commands and Voice Control: Implementing voice controls is another way to help users with motor impairments interact with your app. Android's SpeechRecognizer class enables developers to add voice command functionality, allowing users to control your app through spoken commands.

Accessibility Features for Motor Impairments: Android provides several accessibility features, such as Switch Access and Magnification Gestures, which allow users to control their devices with switches, simplified gestures, or through magnification. As a developer, it is important to ensure that your app works well with these features.

Avoiding Complex Multi-Touch Gestures: Avoid relying on complex gestures, such as pinch-to-zoom or multi-finger swipe gestures, which may be difficult for users with limited dexterity. Provide alternative options, such as buttons or slider controls, to perform the same actions.

3. Designing for Hearing Impairments

Hearing impairments, ranging from mild hearing loss to complete deafness, require thoughtful design to ensure that users can still access important audio-based content and notifications. Designing for hearing impairments focuses on providing alternative ways to convey information that is typically provided via sound.

Key Strategies for Hearing Impairments:

Text Alternatives for Audio Content: Any audio content, such as sound effects, voiceovers, or notifications, should be accompanied by text-based alternatives. For instance, if your app provides an audio cue for a successful action, include a visual confirmation (e.g., a message or animation) as well.

Subtitles and Captions: For apps that feature video or multimedia content, always provide captions or subtitles. Captions help users with hearing impairments follow along with video content, and they can also improve the app's usability for users in noisy environments or those who prefer to read.

Visual and Vibration Cues: Ensure that important notifications are not solely conveyed through sound. Provide visual cues (e.g., icons, pop-up messages) and vibration feedback to alert users to important events or changes within the app.

Notification Customization: Allow users to configure the way they receive notifications. For example, users with hearing impairments may prefer vibration or visual cues instead of sounds. Providing this customization in the app's settings can make the app more adaptable.

Accessibility Support for Audio: Many Android devices come with built-in features like Live Transcribe and Sound Amplifier, which can help users with hearing impairments. You should ensure that your app is compatible with these features by offering text-based alternatives or simplifying interaction flows to accommodate them.

4. Cross-Disability Design Considerations

While designing for specific impairments is important, it's also crucial to adopt a holistic approach that considers users with multiple impairments. For example, a user who is both blind and has motor impairments may rely on both voice commands and screen readers to navigate your app. By considering these cross-disability scenarios, you can create an app that serves a broader audience.

Key Cross-Disability Design Tips:

Simplified Navigation: Keep navigation clear and simple. Avoid overly complex or nested menus that may be difficult for users with disabilities to navigate, whether they are using gestures, voice commands, or screen readers.

Customizable UI: Provide customization options, such as the ability to adjust text size, color contrast, or the layout, to allow users to adapt the app to their needs. This approach benefits users with varying abilities and preferences.

Consistent Layout and Structure: Maintain consistency in your app's layout. This is especially important for users with cognitive disabilities, as it helps them become familiar with your app's structure and improves their ability to predict how the app will behave.

Testing with Real Users: The best way to ensure your app is truly accessible to users with visual, motor, and hearing impairments is by testing it with real users from these communities. User feedback is invaluable for identifying areas that need improvement and ensuring that your app provides a seamless experience.

Designing for visual, motor, and hearing impairments is a critical aspect of creating an inclusive app experience. By considering the specific needs of users with these disabilities, you can make your app more accessible and ensure that everyone can interact with it, regardless of their physical or sensory abilities. Providing alternative text descriptions, enabling customizable navigation, supporting voice control, and offering visual or vibration feedback are just a few of the key strategies you can employ to meet these needs.

By adopting these best practices, you not only enhance the user experience but also contribute to a more inclusive digital world. Accessibility should not be an afterthought—it should be an integral part of the development process to ensure that all users have equal access to the features and services your app provides.

7.4 Testing Apps for Accessibility Compliance

Ensuring that your Android app is accessible to users with disabilities is not just a best practice, but often a legal requirement. However, accessibility goes beyond just implementing features like screen readers, large touch targets, or color contrast adjustments—it requires thorough and consistent testing to ensure compliance with accessibility standards. This section will discuss how to test Android apps for accessibility compliance, the tools and techniques available to developers, and how to integrate accessibility testing into your app development process.

1. Why Accessibility Testing Matters

Testing for accessibility ensures that your app is usable by all individuals, regardless of their physical abilities or limitations. Apps that are accessible can reach a broader audience, including people with visual, hearing, and motor impairments. Furthermore, accessibility is becoming an increasing focus for regulatory bodies, meaning non-compliant apps could face legal challenges or be excluded from certain platforms or app stores. Conducting proper accessibility testing helps meet the following goals:

- **Improved User Experience (UX):** Accessibility features, when properly implemented, lead to a smoother experience for all users, not just those with disabilities.
- **Legal Compliance**: Many countries have laws requiring apps to comply with accessibility standards, such as the Americans with Disabilities Act (ADA) in the United States or the Web Content Accessibility Guidelines (WCAG).
- **Wider Reach**: By ensuring your app is accessible, you make it usable for a wider range of users, thus improving the app's market potential and user satisfaction.

2. Accessibility Testing Guidelines

Before diving into the specific tools, it's essential to understand the core guidelines that Android apps need to follow to be considered accessible. These guidelines are primarily based on:

WCAG (Web Content Accessibility Guidelines): Although WCAG is primarily for websites, its principles are also applicable to apps. Key WCAG criteria to follow include:

Text alternatives for non-text content (e.g., images, icons).

- **Contrast**: Ensure text has enough contrast with the background to be legible.
- **Keyboard and Focus Control**: Ensure all interactive elements are focusable and can be interacted with using accessibility tools like screen readers or external keyboards.
- **Accessible Forms**: Label form elements appropriately, and ensure that input fields and buttons are correctly tagged.

Android Accessibility Guidelines: These guidelines are specific to the Android ecosystem and include rules for ensuring that apps work with Android's built-in accessibility features, such as TalkBack (screen reader), magnification gestures, and other assistive technologies.

Some key accessibility rules include:

- **Content Descriptions**: Use android:contentDescription for all interactive elements (e.g., images, buttons, clickable icons).
- **Focus Management**: Ensure that interactive elements receive focus in a logical order, especially when using talk-back, keyboard navigation, or switch access.
- **Error Handling**: Ensure form errors are clearly communicated with accessible labels and messages.

3. Manual Testing for Accessibility Compliance

Manual testing involves navigating your app with assistive technologies and tools to identify accessibility issues. It's one of the most direct ways to ensure your app complies with accessibility standards. Some critical manual testing procedures include:

Testing with Screen Readers: Use TalkBack to navigate through the app as a visually impaired user would. Make sure that all elements are announced appropriately, including their functionality. For instance, when testing a button, TalkBack should read aloud the button's purpose and description. You can enable TalkBack through the accessibility settings on Android devices. Test the app by interacting with buttons, forms, sliders, and any interactive components.

Keyboard Navigation: Some users rely on external keyboards or switch devices for interaction. Test your app's usability with keyboard navigation by using the Accessibility Scanner or the Android Emulator with keyboard input enabled. Check if all focusable elements are reachable and if they can be activated correctly using keyboard shortcuts.

Testing with Color Contrast: Turn off colors and test the contrast between text and its background. Use Android's Color Correction feature or manually check the color contrast ratio to ensure it meets WCAG guidelines. You can also use third-party apps or browser tools like the Color Contrast Analyzer to verify that the contrast is high enough for users with low vision or color blindness.

Testing Touch Targets: Ensure all touch targets (e.g., buttons, clickable elements) are large enough (48x48dp minimum) and are easily tappable for users with motor impairments. This is especially important for users with limited dexterity or who use assistive touch devices.

Testing with Visual Impairments in Mind: Enable features like magnification gestures or high-contrast text to test how your app responds. Ensure that text and icons scale appropriately and that interactive elements are still usable when zoomed in or when colors are adjusted.

4. Automated Accessibility Testing

In addition to manual testing, you can also integrate automated accessibility testing tools into your development process to quickly identify issues. Automated tests can scan for certain accessibility violations, such as missing content descriptions or non-compliant contrast ratios. While automated testing can't catch every issue, it's a great way to cover basic accessibility checks and ensure that you're not missing common errors.

Key Automated Tools for Accessibility Testing:

Android Accessibility Test Framework (A11y Test Framework): Android provides a test framework that can be integrated into your development environment to check for accessibility violations. This tool automatically scans the app to check for common accessibility problems like missing content descriptions, improper focus management, and insufficient contrast.

Google's Accessibility Scanner: This app is designed for Android developers and testers to analyze their apps for potential accessibility issues. The scanner checks the app's layout, structure, and components to recommend improvements. For example, it might suggest adding content descriptions to buttons or making touch targets larger.

Espresso Accessibility Checks: If you are using the Espresso testing framework for UI testing, you can include accessibility checks in your automated tests. Espresso offers features for checking the accessibility of UI elements and can help you find issues like missing content descriptions or improperly ordered focusable elements.

Lighthouse: While primarily a web tool, Lighthouse is also available as a Chrome extension and can audit web-based Android apps or websites for accessibility. It provides detailed reports on issues related to accessibility and suggests improvements. Although it is more tailored to web-based apps, it can still be useful for hybrid apps.

5. Using Android's Accessibility Testing Tools

Accessibility Scanner: This is a tool provided by Google for both users and developers to scan an app for potential accessibility issues. It evaluates elements like button sizes, content descriptions, and color contrast. It can be downloaded from the Google Play Store and integrated into your testing routine.

TalkBack and Switch Access: These tools allow you to test your app's compatibility with Android's accessibility features. Switch Access lets users interact with their devices using switches instead of touch input. TalkBack, on the other hand, reads aloud the text and descriptions of elements, enabling users to navigate the app through gestures and auditory feedback. Testing your app with these features enabled ensures that the app is navigable and usable for users with motor and visual impairments.

6. Continuous Integration of Accessibility Testing

To ensure that accessibility remains a priority throughout the app's lifecycle, integrate accessibility testing into your Continuous Integration (CI) pipeline. By running automated accessibility tests as part of your CI build process, you can quickly identify and fix accessibility issues before they reach the production stage. This ensures that your app is continually meeting accessibility standards as it evolves.

Testing for accessibility compliance is an ongoing process that ensures your app can be used by everyone, regardless of their abilities or disabilities. By using a combination of manual and automated tools, you can identify potential accessibility issues early and ensure your app remains compliant with industry standards such as WCAG. Regular accessibility testing should be integrated into every stage of development, from initial design through to post-launch updates. This approach will not only help you avoid legal challenges but also improve the user experience for a diverse range of people, ultimately making your app more inclusive and accessible to all.

7.5 Globalization and Localization for Diverse Audiences

In today's interconnected world, creating Android apps that cater to a global audience is essential for maximizing your app's reach and success. To ensure that your app is usable and relevant to users from different countries and cultures, it's important to consider globalization and localization. While globalization refers to the process of designing and building an app that can be adapted to different languages and regions, localization focuses on the actual adaptation of content, text, and design to fit a specific locale. This section will explore how to globalize and localize Android apps to provide a seamless experience for diverse audiences.

1. Understanding Globalization vs. Localization

Globalization: Globalization is the process of making your app flexible and capable of adapting to different cultural, regional, and linguistic norms. It ensures that your app is built in such a way that it can easily be localized for different regions and languages without requiring significant changes to the underlying codebase. This includes the use of Unicode for text encoding, designing flexible layouts, and supporting multiple time zones, currencies, and date formats.

Localization: Localization is the actual process of adapting your app for a specific region or language. This involves translating text, adjusting images and icons to be culturally appropriate, ensuring the app adheres to local norms and standards, and customizing content to fit regional preferences.

Globalization makes localization easier, and localization is the final step in creating an app that's tailored for specific users around the world.

2. Preparing Your App for Globalization

To begin the process of globalization, you need to ensure your app is designed in a way that can easily be localized. Here are some key considerations to make your app ready for a global audience:

Use of Unicode for Text Encoding: Ensure that all text used within your app is encoded using Unicode, a standard that allows the representation of text in virtually all human languages. Android supports Unicode out of the box, and by using it, you ensure that text from any language is properly displayed on any device.

Avoid Hard-Coding Strings: Hard-coding strings directly into your app's code can make localization difficult. Instead, store all text, labels, and messages in string resources. This allows for easy translation into different languages without modifying the app's code. Android uses strings.xml files for this purpose.

Support for Different Time Zones and Calendars: Android allows you to adjust time formats to accommodate various regions. Make sure that your app uses the java.util.Date and java.text.SimpleDateFormat classes for handling date and time, as these will automatically adjust to the user's locale and time zone.

Currency, Number Formats, and Units: Different regions use different formats for numbers, currencies, and measurement units (e.g., imperial vs. metric). Android provides built-in classes like java.text.NumberFormat and java.text.CurrencyFormat that adapt based on the user's locale. This helps ensure that your app correctly displays numerical data and currency values according to local conventions.

Flexible Layouts: Designing flexible, responsive layouts is essential for globalization. Some languages, such as Arabic and Hebrew, are written from right to left (RTL), while most languages are left to right (LTR). To ensure that your app works well for both types of writing systems, Android provides a way to handle RTL layout by using the android:supportsRtl="true" attribute in the manifest file. Your app's layout should adapt automatically based on the user's language and locale.

3. Localizing Your Android App

Once your app is globally prepared, the next step is localization. Localization involves translating your app's content and adapting its design for different markets. Here's how you can localize your app effectively:

String Translation: The core of localization involves translating your app's text content into the desired languages. Create separate strings.xml files for each language and region you are targeting. For example, for Spanish, you'd create res/values-es/strings.xml. Each language or region should have its own directory containing translations for strings, button labels, error messages, and other textual content.

Example:

<string name="welcome_message">Bienvenido</string> <!-- Spanish →

Handling Plurals and Gender: Languages often have complex rules for pluralization and gender. Android provides specific resources for handling these cases, such as plurals.xml for plural forms and string resource placeholders for gender-specific content. These resources ensure that your app adapts dynamically to plural and gender variations based on language rules.

Right-to-Left (RTL) Layout Support: As mentioned earlier, certain languages like Arabic and Hebrew are written from right to left. To support RTL languages, Android provides automatic layout mirroring when the android:supportsRtl attribute is set in the manifest. Ensure that all images, buttons, icons, and other UI elements adjust their orientation accordingly. You may need to create RTL-specific versions of some assets (e.g., arrows pointing in different directions).

Customizing for Cultural Preferences: Localization goes beyond just translation. It also involves adjusting the app's content to fit cultural norms, beliefs, and preferences. For example, imagery and color schemes that are acceptable in one country may have different connotations in another. Carefully consider these factors when localizing your app to avoid cultural misunderstandings.

Locale-Specific Content: Certain regions may require unique content or features, such as region-specific holidays, festivals, or local news. Consider providing different content depending on the user's location by dynamically loading region-specific data and updating your app's features accordingly.

4. Testing Your Localized App

Once your app is localized, thorough testing is crucial to ensure it performs well for all users across different regions. Here's how you can approach testing for localization:

Test Different Locales: Use Android's built-in locale testing tools to simulate how your app will behave in different languages and regions. You can change the device's locale settings to test how your app responds to different languages, currencies, and date formats. This ensures that all strings are translated correctly and that the layout adapts as expected.

Check for Text Overflow: Different languages have varying text lengths. For instance, some languages (such as German) may require more space than others (such as English). Ensure that longer strings do not cause text to overflow out of buttons or labels by making the UI flexible and accommodating. Test the app with text in different languages to ensure that no content is cut off or misplaced.

Test with RTL Languages: Ensure that your app behaves correctly when used with RTL languages. Test the UI to check for mirrored layouts and correct text alignment. Check whether UI elements such as buttons, navigation bars, and icons are properly oriented for RTL reading.

Real-World Testing: Whenever possible, involve native speakers and users from the target regions in the testing process. They can provide feedback on translation accuracy, cultural appropriateness, and overall user experience. Their insights can help identify areas where your localization efforts may need refinement.

5. Tools for Globalization and Localization

Android provides several tools and frameworks to help developers with globalization and localization:

Android Studio's Localization Tools: Android Studio offers built-in tools that simplify the localization process. The IDE helps you manage translation files, edit string resources, and generate different versions of your app for various locales.

Google Play Console: The Google Play Console allows you to manage localized versions of your app on the Play Store. You can upload translations and provide localized descriptions, screenshots, and other marketing materials to cater to different regions.

Crowdsourced Translation Platforms: Platforms like Crowdin, Transifex, or OneSky allow you to crowdsource translations for your app. These platforms offer collaboration tools for translators and help ensure that your app's localization is accurate and culturally appropriate.

String Resource Management Tools: Tools like Android's strings.xml management plugin or third-party services like POEditor can help streamline the management of string resources and their translation across multiple languages.

Globalization and localization are crucial for reaching a diverse, international audience. By preparing your app for multiple languages and cultural norms, you can increase its usability and appeal in different markets. Through thoughtful and comprehensive localization, your app can bridge language and cultural barriers, providing a user experience that resonates with a global audience.

Remember that successful globalization and localization require not only accurate translations but also attention to cultural and regional preferences. Always test your app thoroughly in different locales, and make sure to continuously update your translations and regional content to keep your app relevant as it expands into new markets.

Part 3: Advanced Development Techniques

As you progress in your Android development journey, mastering advanced techniques is key to building high-quality, feature-rich apps. Part 3 of this book delves into more sophisticated aspects of Android development, including handling user inputs, integrating APIs, optimizing performance, and working with modern technologies like machine learning and augmented reality. This section will challenge you to go beyond the basics, equipping you with the tools and knowledge to tackle complex app requirements, enhance functionality, and deliver exceptional user experiences.

8. Handling User Inputs and Events

User interaction is at the heart of every Android app, and understanding how to handle inputs and events effectively is crucial for creating intuitive experiences. In this chapter, you'll explore various ways to manage user inputs, including touch gestures, keyboard input, and voice commands. You'll also learn how to handle events such as button clicks, swipes, and long presses, and how to build custom event listeners for more complex interactions. By mastering these techniques, you'll be able to design apps that respond fluidly to user actions and provide a smooth, interactive experience.

8.1 Understanding Input Types: Touch, Keyboard, and Voice

User input is a fundamental aspect of mobile app development, and understanding how to handle different types of input is crucial to creating a seamless and interactive experience for users. In Android development, input comes in various forms, including touch gestures, keyboard interactions, and voice commands. Each of these input types has unique characteristics and challenges, and developers need to implement robust solutions for each type to ensure a smooth, user-friendly experience.

This section will delve into the three primary input types for Android apps—touch, keyboard, and voice—and explore the best practices for handling each input type effectively.

1. Touch Input: The Primary Form of Interaction

Touch input is the most common form of user interaction on Android devices, as most modern smartphones and tablets rely on touchscreens. It encompasses a wide range of gestures, such as taps, swipes, pinches, and long presses, that allow users to interact with apps intuitively. As such, understanding how to detect and respond to different touch events is critical for building interactive and responsive mobile applications.

Touch Events and MotionEvent Class: Android uses the MotionEvent class to handle touch events. Each touch event, whether a tap, swipe, or long press, is captured as a MotionEvent object. This object contains information such as the position of the touch (in terms of x and y coordinates), the type of touch (e.g., ACTION_DOWN, ACTION_UP, ACTION_MOVE), and additional touch properties (e.g., touch pressure or size).

Example:

```kotlin
override fun onTouchEvent(event: MotionEvent): Boolean {
    when (event.action) {
        MotionEvent.ACTION_DOWN -> {
            // Handle the touch down event
        }
        MotionEvent.ACTION_MOVE -> {
            // Handle touch movement
        }
        MotionEvent.ACTION_UP -> {
            // Handle touch release
        }
    }
    return true
}
```

Gestures: Android provides built-in gesture detection through the GestureDetector class, which simplifies the implementation of common gestures such as tap, double-tap, long press, fling, and scroll. The GestureDetector listens for specific gestures and triggers corresponding events.

Example:

```kotlin
val gestureDetector = GestureDetector(context, object :
GestureDetector.SimpleOnGestureListener() {
    override fun onSingleTapConfirmed(e: MotionEvent): Boolean {
        // Handle single tap
        return true
    }
})
override fun onTouchEvent(event: MotionEvent): Boolean {
    return gestureDetector.onTouchEvent(event)
}
```

Multi-Touch and Pinch Gestures: Android supports multi-touch gestures, allowing users to interact with the screen using two or more fingers. Pinch-to-zoom is a typical use case for multi-touch, where users spread or pinch their fingers to zoom in or out. The MotionEvent object provides information on multiple touch points (finger positions), and developers can use this data to implement multi-touch gestures.

2. Keyboard Input: Enhancing Text Input

While touch gestures are ideal for navigation and interaction, text input via the keyboard is essential for tasks that require more detailed data entry, such as login forms, search queries, and chat interfaces. Android provides various tools for handling text input through software keyboards, and it's important to design the app to handle keyboard interactions efficiently.

Soft Keyboard: The Android soft keyboard (on-screen keyboard) automatically appears when users focus on an editable text field, such as an EditText view. The keyboard provides different layouts based on the context, such as a number pad for numeric input or a full QWERTY keyboard for text input.

Input Types and Attributes: Android allows developers to customize the input behavior through the android:inputType attribute in XML or programmatically. For instance, you can specify whether the input field expects a number, email address, password, or text. Using the correct input type ensures that the appropriate keyboard layout is shown and that the input is validated properly.

Example (XML):

```
<EditText
    android:id="@+id/email"
    android:layout_width="match_parent"
    android:layout_height="wrap_content"
    android:inputType="textEmailAddress" />
```

Example (Kotlin):

```
val editText = findViewById<EditText>(R.id.email)
editText.inputType = InputType.TYPE_TEXT_VARIATION_EMAIL_ADDRESS
```

Keyboard Visibility and Handling: One common issue when dealing with keyboard input is that the soft keyboard can obstruct the UI elements. Developers need to manage the keyboard visibility efficiently. You can control whether the keyboard appears or hides programmatically by using the InputMethodManager class.

Example (show keyboard):

```
val imm = getSystemService(Context.INPUT_METHOD_SERVICE) as
InputMethodManager
imm.showSoftInput(editText, InputMethodManager.SHOW_IMPLICIT)
```

Example (hide keyboard):

```
val imm = getSystemService(Context.INPUT_METHOD_SERVICE) as
InputMethodManager
imm.hideSoftInputFromWindow(editText.windowToken, 0)
```

Hardware Keyboards: In addition to the software keyboard, Android devices can also support external hardware keyboards. These keyboards work similarly to desktop keyboards, allowing users to type text or navigate the app via physical keys. To handle hardware keyboard input, developers can listen to key events using the onKey() method, which captures key presses and releases.

Example:

```
override fun onKeyDown(keyCode: Int, event: KeyEvent?): Boolean {
    if (keyCode == KeyEvent.KEYCODE_ENTER) {
        // Handle the "Enter" key press
    }
    return super.onKeyDown(keyCode, event)
}
```

3. Voice Input: Leveraging Speech Recognition

Voice input is an increasingly popular method of interaction on mobile devices, especially with the rise of virtual assistants like Google Assistant. Voice input allows users to interact with apps using natural language commands or dictate text, providing a hands-free experience. Android provides APIs for integrating voice input through speech recognition.

Speech Recognition API: Android provides the SpeechRecognizer class to implement voice recognition in apps. This allows users to speak into the device, and the app can convert their speech into text. You can trigger voice recognition via a button or action and display the recognized text in a field.

Example:

```
val recognizerIntent = Intent(RecognizerIntent.ACTION_RECOGNIZE_SPEECH)
```

```
recognizerIntent.putExtra(RecognizerIntent.EXTRA_LANGUAGE_MODEL,
RecognizerIntent.LANGUAGE_MODEL_FREE_FORM)
startActivityForResult(recognizerIntent, REQUEST_CODE_SPEECH_INPUT)
```

In onActivityResult, you can capture the recognized speech:

```
override fun onActivityResult(requestCode: Int, resultCode: Int, data: Intent?) {
    super.onActivityResult(requestCode, resultCode, data)
    if (requestCode == REQUEST_CODE_SPEECH_INPUT && resultCode ==
Activity.RESULT_OK) {
        val result = data?.getStringArrayListExtra(RecognizerIntent.EXTRA_RESULTS)
        val spokenText = result?.get(0)
        // Display the spoken text or process it
    }
}
```

Voice Commands and Virtual Assistants: For more advanced voice interaction, Android provides integration with virtual assistants like Google Assistant. By integrating with Google's Voice Actions or other third-party assistants, you can enable voice commands to trigger actions within your app, such as launching specific screens, sending messages, or making calls.

Handling Permissions: When using voice input, it's essential to request the necessary permissions to access the device's microphone. You must request the RECORD_AUDIO permission in the app's manifest file and at runtime (for devices running Android 6.0 and above).

Example (Manifest):

```
<uses-permission android:name="android.permission.RECORD_AUDIO"/>
```

4. Best Practices for Handling Multiple Input Types

User Preferences: Some users may prefer one input method over another, so it's important to give them the flexibility to switch between touch, keyboard, or voice. For example, users may prefer voice input for hands-free operation, while others may feel more comfortable typing on a keyboard. Providing multiple input methods increases the app's accessibility and usability.

Responsive UI: When handling multiple types of input, ensure that the app's UI adapts appropriately. For instance, when the keyboard is shown, make sure that input fields are not hidden behind the keyboard. Similarly, when voice input is active, provide clear feedback to the user about what's happening.

Fallback and Accessibility: Always provide fallback options for users who might have limitations in using one input method. If a user is unable to use the touch interface, make sure they can use a keyboard or voice input. Android provides several accessibility features, such as TalkBack, to assist users with disabilities.

Understanding and handling different input types—touch, keyboard, and voice—are essential for developing an interactive and accessible Android app. Each input type offers unique advantages and challenges, and it's crucial to design the app in a way that accommodates the diverse needs and preferences of users. By leveraging Android's input handling capabilities, developers can create an intuitive, engaging experience that allows users to interact with their apps in a manner that feels natural and efficient. Whether users interact via touch, typing, or voice, the goal is to ensure smooth, seamless, and intuitive input handling across all devices.

8.2 Handling Gestures and Multi-Touch Events

Gestures and multi-touch events are essential components of modern mobile applications, enabling users to interact with the app in intuitive and engaging ways. Android devices support a variety of touch interactions, including single-touch gestures (such as taps and swipes) as well as multi-touch events (such as pinch-to-zoom and rotate). Handling these events effectively enhances the user experience, allowing for more dynamic and interactive applications.

This section will explore how to detect and handle different gestures and multi-touch events in Android apps, utilizing built-in classes and methods to create fluid interactions for users.

1. Understanding Gestures in Android

Gestures are predefined movements on the touch screen that trigger specific actions in an app. Android provides a number of ways to capture gestures, from basic taps to complex multi-finger swipes. Recognizing these gestures is essential for creating intuitive and responsive UIs.

Simple Touch Events: The most basic touch event is a tap or press, which can be captured using onTouchEvent() or a gesture detector. These simple interactions form the foundation of gesture-based navigation and actions in apps.

Example of detecting a simple tap:

```
override fun onTouchEvent(event: MotionEvent): Boolean {
    if (event.action == MotionEvent.ACTION_DOWN) {
        // Handle tap (user has touched the screen)
        return true
    }
    return false
}
```

Swipe and Fling Gestures: Android supports swipe gestures (horizontal or vertical) that can trigger actions like navigating between screens or performing a function. The GestureDetector class can be used to detect swipe and fling gestures, offering an easy way to implement these types of interactions.

Example of detecting a swipe gesture with GestureDetector:

```
val gestureDetector = GestureDetector(context, object :
GestureDetector.SimpleOnGestureListener() {
    override fun onScroll(e1: MotionEvent, e2: MotionEvent, distanceX: Float, distanceY:
Float): Boolean {
        // Detect swipe motion
        if (distanceX > 0) {
            // Swipe right
        } else {
            // Swipe left
        }
        return true
    }
})

override fun onTouchEvent(event: MotionEvent): Boolean {
    return gestureDetector.onTouchEvent(event)
}
```

Long Press and Double Tap: The GestureDetector can also handle long press and double-tap gestures. These gestures are commonly used for additional actions, such as showing a context menu or performing a zoom-in action.

Example of detecting a long press:

```
val gestureDetector = GestureDetector(context, object :
GestureDetector.SimpleOnGestureListener() {
    override fun onLongPress(e: MotionEvent) {
        // Handle long press
    }
})
```

Example of detecting a double tap:

```
val gestureDetector = GestureDetector(context, object :
GestureDetector.SimpleOnGestureListener() {
    override fun onDoubleTap(e: MotionEvent): Boolean {
        // Handle double tap
        return true
    }
})
```

2. Multi-Touch Events: Pinch, Rotate, and More

Multi-touch gestures enable more complex interactions such as zooming, rotating, and panning. Android provides native support for multi-touch events, where the system tracks multiple points of contact on the screen simultaneously. The MotionEvent object contains detailed information about each individual touch event, including coordinates and action types (e.g., ACTION_DOWN, ACTION_MOVE, ACTION_UP).

Pinch-to-Zoom: One of the most common multi-touch gestures is pinch-to-zoom, which allows users to zoom in and out by pinching or spreading two fingers on the screen. Android makes it easy to detect these types of gestures by comparing the distance between two touch points and determining if they are getting closer or farther apart.

Example of detecting pinch-to-zoom:

```
private var initialDistance = 0f
```

```kotlin
override fun onTouchEvent(event: MotionEvent): Boolean {
    when (event.actionMasked) {
        MotionEvent.ACTION_POINTER_DOWN -> {
            if (event.pointerCount == 2) {
                initialDistance = distanceBetweenFingers(event)
            }
        }
        MotionEvent.ACTION_MOVE -> {
            if (event.pointerCount == 2) {
                val currentDistance = distanceBetweenFingers(event)
                val scaleFactor = currentDistance / initialDistance
                // Scale the UI or image accordingly
            }
        }
    }
    return true
}

private fun distanceBetweenFingers(event: MotionEvent): Float {
    val x0 = event.getX(0)
    val y0 = event.getY(0)
    val x1 = event.getX(1)
    val y1 = event.getY(1)
    return Math.sqrt(((x1 - x0) * (x1 - x0) + (y1 - y0) * (y1 - y0)).toDouble()).toFloat()
}
```

Rotation: Android also supports rotation gestures, allowing users to rotate objects or images by rotating their fingers on the screen. Like pinch-to-zoom, rotation requires tracking multiple touch points. The MotionEvent class provides the coordinates of each touch point, which can be used to calculate the angle of rotation.

Example of detecting rotation:

```kotlin
private var initialAngle = 0f

override fun onTouchEvent(event: MotionEvent): Boolean {
    if (event.pointerCount == 2) {
        when (event.actionMasked) {
            MotionEvent.ACTION_POINTER_DOWN -> {
                initialAngle = angleBetweenFingers(event)
```

```
        }
        MotionEvent.ACTION_MOVE -> {
            val currentAngle = angleBetweenFingers(event)
            val rotationDelta = currentAngle - initialAngle
            // Apply rotation to object
        }
    }
}
return true
}

private fun angleBetweenFingers(event: MotionEvent): Float {
    val x0 = event.getX(0)
    val y0 = event.getY(0)
    val x1 = event.getX(1)
    val y1 = event.getY(1)
    val deltaX = x1 - x0
    val deltaY = y1 - y0
    return Math.toDegrees(Math.atan2(deltaY.toDouble(), deltaX.toDouble())).toFloat()
}
```

Multi-Touch Panning: In addition to pinch and rotate, Android also supports multi-touch panning, where multiple fingers can be used to move the content around the screen. By tracking the motion of multiple touch points, you can implement drag-and-drop interactions or free-form content movement.

Example of detecting multi-touch panning:

```
private var lastX = 0f
private var lastY = 0f

override fun onTouchEvent(event: MotionEvent): Boolean {
    if (event.pointerCount >= 2) {
        when (event.actionMasked) {
            MotionEvent.ACTION_MOVE -> {
                val deltaX = event.getX(0) - lastX
                val deltaY = event.getY(0) - lastY
                // Pan content or view based on deltaX, deltaY
            }
        }
```

```
    lastX = event.getX(0)
    lastY = event.getY(0)
  }
  return true
}
```

3. Best Practices for Gesture and Multi-Touch Handling

To provide users with a smooth and consistent experience when using gestures and multi-touch events, consider the following best practices:

Consistency: Maintain consistency in how gestures behave across your app. If a swipe gesture triggers a specific action in one part of the app, ensure that the same gesture triggers a similar action throughout the app.

Feedback: Provide immediate visual or haptic feedback when a gesture is detected. For example, when a pinch-to-zoom gesture is used, updating the UI immediately to reflect the zooming action can provide clear feedback to the user.

Edge Cases: Always account for edge cases, such as simultaneous touch events from multiple fingers or rapid, erratic movements. Implement logic to handle gestures that may conflict with other touch events, like distinguishing between a scroll and a swipe.

Testing: Ensure extensive testing of gestures and multi-touch functionality across a variety of devices and screen sizes. Gesture recognition may vary depending on device sensitivity and hardware capabilities, so thorough testing helps ensure a consistent user experience.

Accessibility: Consider accessibility when implementing gestures. Ensure that users with motor disabilities can also interact with your app, either by providing alternatives (such as voice commands) or adjusting the sensitivity of gestures to accommodate different input speeds.

Handling gestures and multi-touch events is an essential skill for Android developers. By utilizing Android's gesture detection tools and understanding multi-touch events, you can create rich, interactive apps that respond intuitively to user input. Whether implementing simple swipes or complex pinch-to-zoom and rotation gestures, the key is to design an app that feels natural and responsive, offering a seamless experience across devices and screen sizes. By mastering gesture and multi-touch handling, you can take your Android development skills to the next level and build dynamic apps that enhance user engagement.

8.3 Building Custom Event Listeners

In Android development, handling user interactions is essential to creating a responsive and intuitive user experience. While Android provides a variety of built-in event listeners (like OnClickListener, OnTouchListener, and OnLongClickListener), there are scenarios where the predefined event listeners may not suffice. This is where custom event listeners come into play.

Custom event listeners allow you to define your own interfaces for handling specific events that are unique to your application. This can help you capture more complex interactions or tailor the behavior of certain components to meet the needs of your app. Whether you need to detect custom gestures, respond to specific touch patterns, or handle other specialized user actions, custom event listeners provide flexibility in how your app responds to user input.

This section will explain how to build and use custom event listeners in Android apps, offering examples and best practices for creating and managing these listeners efficiently.

1. What Are Custom Event Listeners?

A custom event listener is an interface that defines a set of methods for handling specific events or interactions within your app. These events could include custom gestures, drag-and-drop actions, or any other type of user interaction that does not fit within the scope of Android's standard listeners. When a user interacts with a UI element in a way that triggers the event, your custom listener can respond and execute the necessary actions.

Building a custom event listener involves the following steps:

- **Defining an Interface**: Create an interface that contains the methods to handle the event.
- **Implementing the Interface**: Attach the custom listener to the relevant UI element and implement the methods of the interface.
- **Triggering the Event**: In the UI element or interaction code, invoke the appropriate listener methods when the event occurs.

2. Defining a Custom Event Listener Interface

The first step in creating a custom event listener is to define an interface that declares the methods you want to use. For example, let's say you want to create a custom listener to detect when a user has double-tapped an area of the screen.

Here's how you would define the interface:

```
interface OnDoubleTapListener {
    fun onDoubleTap(x: Float, y: Float)
    fun onSingleTap(x: Float, y: Float)
}
```

In this case, the OnDoubleTapListener interface includes two methods: one for handling a double tap (onDoubleTap) and one for a single tap (onSingleTap). Both methods take x and y coordinates as arguments, which represent the position of the tap.

3. Implementing the Custom Listener in Your View

Once you've defined the interface, the next step is to implement the listener in your view or component. You can do this by creating a class or activity that implements the OnDoubleTapListener interface.

For example, let's create a CustomTouchView that detects double-tap events:

```
class CustomTouchView(context: Context, attrs: AttributeSet) : View(context, attrs) {
    private var doubleTapListener: OnDoubleTapListener? = null

    fun setOnDoubleTapListener(listener: OnDoubleTapListener) {
        this.doubleTapListener = listener
    }

    override fun onTouchEvent(event: MotionEvent): Boolean {
        when (event.action) {
            MotionEvent.ACTION_DOWN -> {
                // Capture the x and y coordinates of the first touch
                val x = event.x
                val y = event.y

                // Handle single or double tap
                if (isDoubleTap(event)) {
```

```
                doubleTapListener?.onDoubleTap(x, y)
            } else {
                doubleTapListener?.onSingleTap(x, y)
            }
        }
    }
    return true
}

    private fun isDoubleTap(event: MotionEvent): Boolean {
        // Implement logic to detect double-tap based on timing or distance between
touches
        // This is just a placeholder logic
        return event.eventTime - event.downTime < 300 // 300ms between taps
    }
}
```

In the above code:

- The CustomTouchView class extends View and overrides the onTouchEvent() method to capture user touch interactions.
- The setOnDoubleTapListener() method allows the caller to set a listener for double-tap events.
- The isDoubleTap() method is a placeholder function that implements simple logic to detect a double tap based on the time difference between taps.

4. Attaching the Custom Event Listener

Now that you've created the listener and implemented it within your custom view, the next step is to attach the listener to a specific instance of your view. This is typically done in the Activity or Fragment where the view is used.

For example, in an Activity:

```
class MainActivity : AppCompatActivity() {

    override fun onCreate(savedInstanceState: Bundle?) {
        super.onCreate(savedInstanceState)
        setContentView(R.layout.activity_main)
```

```kotlin
val customTouchView: CustomTouchView = findViewById(R.id.customTouchView)

customTouchView.setOnDoubleTapListener(object : OnDoubleTapListener {
    override fun onDoubleTap(x: Float, y: Float) {
        Toast.makeText(this@MainActivity, "Double Tap Detected at ($x, $y)",
Toast.LENGTH_SHORT).show()
    }

    override fun onSingleTap(x: Float, y: Float) {
        Toast.makeText(this@MainActivity, "Single Tap Detected at ($x, $y)",
Toast.LENGTH_SHORT).show()
    }
})
    }
}
```

In the MainActivity, we retrieve the CustomTouchView from the layout and use the setOnDoubleTapListener() method to set the custom listener. The listener's methods (onDoubleTap and onSingleTap) display a toast message with the touch coordinates when the respective event is detected.

5. Handling Multiple Custom Events

You can also create custom event listeners for more complex interactions. For example, if you're implementing a drag-and-drop feature, you might want to create a listener that handles touch events during a drag operation.

Here's an example of a custom listener for a drag-and-drop operation:

```kotlin
interface OnDragListener {
    fun onDragStart(x: Float, y: Float)
    fun onDragMove(x: Float, y: Float)
    fun onDragEnd(x: Float, y: Float)
}
```

In your custom view:

```kotlin
class DraggableView(context: Context, attrs: AttributeSet) : View(context, attrs) {
    private var dragListener: OnDragListener? = null
```

```kotlin
fun setOnDragListener(listener: OnDragListener) {
    this.dragListener = listener
}

override fun onTouchEvent(event: MotionEvent): Boolean {
    when (event.action) {
        MotionEvent.ACTION_DOWN -> {
            dragListener?.onDragStart(event.x, event.y)
        }
        MotionEvent.ACTION_MOVE -> {
            dragListener?.onDragMove(event.x, event.y)
        }
        MotionEvent.ACTION_UP -> {
            dragListener?.onDragEnd(event.x, event.y)
        }
    }
    return true
}
}
```

In this case, the DraggableView class provides three methods for handling drag events: onDragStart, onDragMove, and onDragEnd. You can use this setup to provide a smooth drag-and-drop experience.

6. Best Practices for Custom Event Listeners

When working with custom event listeners in Android, consider the following best practices:

Separation of Concerns: Keep event listener logic separate from UI logic. For example, use separate listener classes or interfaces to decouple the event handling from the activity or view logic.

Use Weak References: When storing a reference to the listener (especially in long-lived objects like activities or views), use weak references to avoid memory leaks. This ensures that the listener is not holding onto the activity or view longer than necessary.

Efficiency: Custom listeners should be lightweight and efficient. Make sure the event handling logic is fast, especially for frequent events like touch interactions.

Testing: Always thoroughly test custom event listeners, as they can introduce complex logic. Ensure they perform well across different devices and screen sizes.

Building custom event listeners in Android gives you the flexibility to tailor user interactions to your specific app requirements. By defining interfaces that represent custom events and attaching them to views or components, you can handle complex gestures, user actions, and touch interactions efficiently. Whether you're detecting double taps, implementing drag-and-drop functionality, or responding to custom gestures, custom event listeners can enhance the responsiveness and user experience of your app.

8.4 Managing Input Validations and Error Handling

In any Android application, handling user input effectively is crucial for providing a smooth, reliable, and error-free user experience. Validating user input ensures that the data entered into the app is correct and can be processed without causing crashes, data corruption, or unexpected behavior. Additionally, implementing robust error handling mechanisms can help developers catch and address issues before they negatively affect the user experience.

This section explores best practices for managing input validations and error handling in Android apps, ensuring that your application can gracefully handle a variety of input scenarios, including invalid or missing data, and provide meaningful feedback to users.

1. Why Input Validation Matters

Input validation serves several important purposes:

Ensuring Data Integrity: Validating inputs ensures that the data received from users meets the necessary constraints, such as correct format, length, or value ranges.

Preventing Crashes and Bugs: Invalid input or unexpected data can lead to crashes, bugs, or incorrect processing. For example, submitting an empty email field or an invalid date format can cause the app to behave unpredictably.

Improving User Experience: Proper validation can prevent users from submitting invalid or incomplete data, reducing frustration and enhancing their overall experience.

2. Types of Input Validations

There are several types of input validation that developers typically need to implement in their Android applications:

Format Validation: This checks whether the entered input matches a specific format. For example, validating if an email address follows the correct pattern (user@example.com) or if a phone number contains the appropriate number of digits.

Range Validation: This ensures that the user input falls within a defined range of values. For example, checking if the age entered is between 18 and 100, or if the entered number is within a specified range.

Required Fields: This ensures that essential fields, such as name, email, or password, are not left empty. For example, if the user submits a form without entering their name, you should display an error message indicating that the field is required.

Cross-field Validation: This checks if two or more fields are consistent with each other. For instance, in a registration form, validating that the "Password" and "Confirm Password" fields match.

3. Implementing Input Validations in Android

To validate user input in Android, you can use various techniques, such as EditText input filters, TextWatcher for real-time validation, or custom validation methods that check user input when a form is submitted. Below are common approaches for handling input validation:

Using Regular Expressions

For format validation, regular expressions (regex) are a powerful tool. They allow you to specify complex patterns that the input should match, such as checking for a valid email or phone number.

For example, validating an email address with regex:

```
fun isValidEmail(email: String): Boolean {
    val emailPattern = "[a-zA-Z0-9._-]+@[a-zA-Z0-9.-]+\\.[a-zA-Z]{2,}"
    return email.matches(emailPattern.toRegex())
}
```

Here, the isValidEmail() function uses a regex pattern to check if the input email matches a standard email format.

Real-time Validation with TextWatcher

The TextWatcher interface allows you to perform real-time input validation while the user types. It helps you provide immediate feedback, such as showing error messages or disabling form submission until the input is valid.

Here's an example of using TextWatcher to validate an email field:

```
val emailEditText: EditText = findViewById(R.id.emailEditText)

emailEditText.addTextChangedListener(object : TextWatcher {
    override fun beforeTextChanged(charSequence: CharSequence?, start: Int, count: Int, after: Int) {}

    override fun onTextChanged(charSequence: CharSequence?, start: Int, before: Int, count: Int) {}

    override fun afterTextChanged(editable: Editable?) {
        val email = editable.toString()
        if (isValidEmail(email)) {
            emailEditText.error = null  // Clear error if valid
        } else {
            emailEditText.error = "Invalid email format"
        }
    }
})
```

In this example, the email field is continuously validated as the user types, and if the email format is incorrect, an error message is displayed immediately.

Required Field Validation

To ensure that critical fields are not left empty, you can check if the input string is empty or null. Here's an example of validating a name field:

```
fun isValidName(name: String?): Boolean {
    return !name.isNullOrEmpty()
```

```
}
```

When the user tries to submit the form, you can check whether the isValidName() method returns true:

```
if (isValidName(nameEditText.text.toString())) {
    // Proceed with form submission
} else {
    nameEditText.error = "Name is required"
}
```

4. Handling Errors Gracefully

In addition to validating inputs, error handling is equally important for ensuring that the application runs smoothly, even when unexpected issues arise.

Showing Meaningful Error Messages

When a validation fails, it's important to display meaningful error messages to the user. A vague message such as "Invalid input" can confuse users, whereas a specific message like "Please enter a valid email address" gives clear guidance on how to correct the input.

You can use EditText.setError() to display an error message next to the problematic field:

```
if (!isValidEmail(emailEditText.text.toString())) {
    emailEditText.error = "Please enter a valid email address"
} else {
    emailEditText.error = null
}
```

Handling Network Errors and Unexpected Exceptions

While input validation is crucial, network errors and unexpected exceptions should also be handled gracefully. For example, when making network requests (e.g., API calls), always implement error handling to deal with scenarios like no internet connection, server unavailability, or data parsing errors.

You can handle network errors using try-catch blocks, and provide appropriate error messages to the user:

```
try {
    // Make network request
    val response = apiClient.getData()
    // Handle successful response
} catch (e: IOException) {
    // Handle network failure (e.g., no internet connection)
    Toast.makeText(this, "Network error, please check your connection.",
Toast.LENGTH_SHORT).show()
} catch (e: Exception) {
    // Handle unexpected errors
    Toast.makeText(this, "An unexpected error occurred.",
Toast.LENGTH_SHORT).show()
}
```

This ensures that your app does not crash when an error occurs and provides users with helpful feedback.

Validating Server Responses

Once the user input is validated locally, it's important to also validate the responses from external sources, such as a server or database. For instance, after submitting form data, you should check if the server returns a success response or if there are issues that need to be addressed.

5. Best Practices for Managing Input Validation and Error Handling

To ensure that your app provides a seamless and robust user experience, consider the following best practices:

Provide Immediate Feedback: Use TextWatcher or similar techniques to validate inputs in real-time. This reduces user frustration and prevents incorrect data from being submitted.

Keep Error Messages Clear and Specific: Provide users with specific guidance on how to fix errors. Avoid vague error messages and ensure they understand what went wrong.

Validate Inputs at Multiple Levels: Validate inputs both on the client-side (in the app) and server-side (when communicating with an API) to ensure data consistency and security.

Use a Unified Validation Approach: Implement a centralized validation system for consistency. Create helper methods or validation classes to handle common validation tasks.

Gracefully Handle Edge Cases: Ensure that your app can handle edge cases, such as missing input, unexpected server errors, or network failures, without crashing or misbehaving.

Input validation and error handling are critical aspects of Android app development, ensuring that the app functions smoothly and users have a positive experience. By using the proper validation techniques and providing clear error messages, you can help users understand what is expected of them and reduce frustration. Implementing effective error handling ensures that the app can recover gracefully from unexpected issues, whether they are related to network connectivity, invalid input, or system errors. Ultimately, strong input validation and error handling lead to more reliable, user-friendly apps that users can trust and enjoy.

8.5 Integrating Voice Commands with Google Assistant

Voice commands have become an essential feature of modern apps, enabling hands-free interactions and improving the overall user experience. With the rise of voice assistants like Google Assistant, integrating voice control into your Android app can provide users with a seamless and efficient way to interact with your app using simple voice commands.

This section covers how to integrate voice commands with Google Assistant, allowing your users to control your app through voice input, enhance accessibility, and create more intuitive user experiences. By the end of this chapter, you will have a clear understanding of how to implement voice command features in your Android apps using the Google Assistant SDK and related tools.

1. What is Google Assistant and How It Works

Google Assistant is an AI-powered virtual assistant developed by Google, capable of understanding and responding to voice commands. It works by processing speech input, converting it to text, and then interpreting the command or query based on pre-programmed logic and context.

When integrated with Android apps, Google Assistant enables users to interact with your app through natural language commands. These commands can trigger specific actions, such as opening an app, performing a search, or controlling app features, without requiring any manual input.

For example, a voice command like "Open weather app" could open your weather application, or "Play music" could start the music player. Integrating voice commands enhances usability, making your app more accessible and user-friendly.

2. Setting Up Google Assistant Integration

To integrate voice commands with Google Assistant, you need to set up a couple of key components in your Android app. Here's an overview of the steps to get started:

Step 1: Enable Google Assistant and Voice Search

Google Assistant is available on Android devices by default, but you need to ensure that your app is optimized to work with it. You must configure your app to respond to specific voice commands through the Google Assistant.

Ensure that Google Assistant is available on your device: Most modern Android devices come with Google Assistant pre-installed. However, ensure that your app is compatible with devices running Google Assistant.

Enable Voice Search: If you want your app to respond to specific voice queries or commands (such as "Search for recipes"), enable the Google Assistant Voice Search API in your app. You can access Google Assistant's voice search through the Google Assistant SDK.

Step 2: Create a Google Assistant Action

Google Assistant uses actions to trigger specific tasks in your app. Each action corresponds to a specific voice command that users can issue to interact with your app.

To create a custom action for your app, you need to configure the action in the Actions Console. Here's how you can get started:

- Visit the Actions Console (console.actions.google.com).
- Create a new project for your app.

- Define your actions by specifying the voice commands that will trigger them. You can create intents like "open app," "search," or "get weather."
- Configure the responses that Google Assistant should provide when a command is recognized.

Step 3: Implementing the Google Assistant SDK

After configuring the Google Assistant action, you need to implement the Google Assistant SDK in your Android app to handle voice commands.

Google provides an SDK called Google Assistant SDK for Android to facilitate easy integration. This SDK allows your app to communicate with Google Assistant and trigger predefined actions in your app based on voice input.

Here's a basic setup of how you can initialize Google Assistant in your app:

```
// Example code to trigger Google Assistant through an Intent
val assistantIntent = Intent(Intent.ACTION_VOICE_COMMAND)
assistantIntent.putExtra(Intent.EXTRA_VOICE_COMMAND, "Open my app")
startActivity(assistantIntent)
```

This code will allow your app to respond to specific voice input and activate corresponding actions.

3. Voice Command Features and Capabilities

Google Assistant can be used for a variety of voice-based interactions within your app. Some common functionalities that you can integrate include:

Launching Your App via Voice

With proper setup in the Actions Console, users can trigger your app to launch using a voice command, such as "Hey Google, open [App Name]." For this to work, you must define the launch command in your action configuration.

```
// Example code to launch the app using a voice command
val openAppIntent = Intent(Intent.ACTION_MAIN)
openAppIntent.setClassName("com.example.yourapp",
"com.example.yourapp.MainActivity")
startActivity(openAppIntent)
```

Interacting with In-App Features

Google Assistant can also help control specific in-app features via voice commands. For example, users can issue commands to control media playback (like "Play music") or navigate within your app. You can integrate voice commands to start certain actions based on context, like "Show me the weather" or "Play my favorite playlist."

To handle such commands, define specific actions and associate them with triggers in the Actions Console.

Providing Real-Time Feedback

Once a user interacts with the app through voice, providing real-time feedback through Google Assistant is important. For instance, after completing a task like checking the weather, your app could send a spoken response back to the user, confirming the action or providing additional details.

```
// Responding with a simple message after the command
val assistantResponse = "The current temperature is 25°C."
val responseIntent = Intent(Intent.ACTION_VOICE_COMMAND)
responseIntent.putExtra(Intent.EXTRA_VOICE_COMMAND, assistantResponse)
startActivity(responseIntent)
```

4. Testing and Debugging Voice Commands

Once you've integrated Google Assistant with your Android app, testing is crucial to ensure everything functions as expected. Here are some ways to test your voice command integration:

Use the Google Assistant Simulator: You can test voice commands using the Google Assistant simulator in the Actions Console. This tool lets you simulate voice interactions without needing to use a real device.

Test on Real Devices: Once you've simulated commands, test your app on an actual Android device that has Google Assistant enabled. Speak voice commands to check how well your app responds.

Monitor Logs and Analytics: Use Android's built-in logging (e.g., Logcat) and Google Assistant's built-in analytics to monitor the success of voice interactions, identify issues, and fine-tune the functionality.

5. Best Practices for Voice Command Integration

While integrating voice commands into your Android app can enhance usability, there are a few best practices to keep in mind:

Be Clear and Simple: Voice commands should be clear, simple, and easy to remember. Avoid complicated phrasing or multiple commands that may confuse users.

Provide Feedback: Always offer visual or audible feedback when a command is processed, even if it's just a confirmation message like "Opening app" or "Starting playback."

Test Across Different Devices: Voice recognition can vary across different Android devices and versions. Ensure your app works consistently across devices that support Google Assistant.

Enhance Accessibility: By allowing users to control your app using voice, you're making it more accessible for people with disabilities or those who have difficulty interacting with touch interfaces.

Contextual Awareness: Ensure that the commands you integrate are context-aware. For example, commands like "Next" or "Stop" should work only when they make sense in the app's current state.

Integrating voice commands with Google Assistant in Android apps opens up new possibilities for improving user experience, accessibility, and convenience. By allowing users to control your app through voice input, you can enhance its functionality and provide an intuitive interface for a broader audience. With proper setup in the Google Assistant Console, integration with the Google Assistant SDK, and thoughtful design, voice command features can significantly elevate your app's user engagement.

9. Networking and APIs

In today's interconnected world, most mobile apps rely on external data to provide dynamic and up-to-date content. In this chapter, you'll learn how to effectively work with networking and APIs in Android development. You'll explore how to make API calls, handle JSON data, and parse responses using popular libraries like Retrofit. Additionally, you'll dive into securing API communications and managing network operations efficiently to create responsive, reliable apps. Mastering networking and API integration will empower you to build apps that can connect with cloud services, databases, and third-party platforms.

9.1 Introduction to Networking in Android

Networking is a fundamental component of modern mobile applications. Whether your app is pulling data from a remote server, sending user input to a database, or interacting with third-party APIs, understanding how to effectively handle networking in Android is crucial for building dynamic, responsive, and real-time applications. Android provides robust support for networking tasks, allowing developers to retrieve and send data over the internet seamlessly.

In this section, we'll explore the essential aspects of networking in Android, including how to set up network connections, communicate with remote servers, handle various network protocols, and ensure efficient and secure data transmission. This knowledge will lay the foundation for incorporating features like fetching content from APIs, managing real-time interactions, and handling background data synchronization in your app.

1. Networking Basics in Android

At the core of networking in Android, there are several key principles and components you need to understand:

Network Communication: Network communication involves the process of sending and receiving data between your Android app and a server (or any other external system). Android provides several tools for managing network communication, including the HttpURLConnection class and popular libraries such as Retrofit and OkHttp.

HTTP and RESTful APIs: Most modern applications use REST (Representational State Transfer) APIs for communication. REST APIs use HTTP (HyperText Transfer Protocol) to send requests and receive responses in formats like JSON or XML. Networking in Android frequently involves making HTTP requests to REST APIs to send or retrieve data.

Asynchronous Requests: Since network communication can be slow or unreliable, it's essential to handle network requests asynchronously to avoid blocking the user interface (UI). Android uses AsyncTask (deprecated in favor of Kotlin Coroutines or Java's ExecutorService), Volley, and libraries like Retrofit to handle asynchronous communication.

JSON Parsing: Many APIs send data in JSON format, so you need to know how to parse JSON responses into Java/Kotlin objects for use in your app.

Security and Error Handling: Ensuring secure communication (via HTTPS) and gracefully handling errors (like network timeouts or server failures) are essential aspects of networking.

2. Common Networking Tasks in Android

When building an Android application, you'll likely encounter several common networking tasks:

Making HTTP Requests: The most basic networking task is making an HTTP request (GET, POST, PUT, DELETE, etc.) to a remote server. This is typically done to fetch or send data to an API.

Handling JSON Data: JSON is the most widely used format for data exchange. After receiving a JSON response from the server, you need to parse it into Android data structures for further processing.

Uploading Data: Some applications require sending data (such as user input, images, or files) to a server. Handling POST requests and encoding data appropriately (e.g., multipart for file uploads) is a critical skill.

Handling Network Errors: Network issues, such as timeouts, poor connectivity, or server errors, can occur at any time. It's important to handle these scenarios gracefully by providing feedback to the user and retrying failed requests when necessary.

Caching Data: To reduce network calls and improve app performance, you may need to implement caching strategies, storing frequently accessed data locally (e.g., in SQLite databases or SharedPreferences).

3. Key Networking Libraries in Android

Android provides several libraries to streamline networking tasks, making it easier for developers to interact with remote servers and handle data efficiently. Below are the most popular ones:

HttpURLConnection (Native)

The HttpURLConnection class is Android's built-in, low-level API for handling HTTP requests. While it's powerful and flexible, it requires more manual work, such as managing threads and parsing responses.

Example of a simple GET request using HttpURLConnection:

```
val url = URL("https://api.example.com/data")
val connection = url.openConnection() as HttpURLConnection
connection.requestMethod = "GET"
connection.connect()

val responseCode = connection.responseCode
if (responseCode == HttpURLConnection.HTTP_OK) {
    val inputStream = connection.inputStream
    val reader = BufferedReader(InputStreamReader(inputStream))
    val response = StringBuffer()
    reader.forEachLine { response.append(it) }
    reader.close()
    println(response.toString())
} else {
    println("Error: $responseCode")
}
```

Retrofit

Retrofit is a widely-used networking library in Android that simplifies API interactions by abstracting the complexity of raw HTTP requests. It allows developers to define interfaces that represent API endpoints, automatically handling HTTP methods and parsing responses into objects.

A simple example using Retrofit to fetch data from an API:

```kotlin
interface ApiService {
    @GET("data")
    suspend fun getData(): Response<List<DataModel>>
}

val retrofit = Retrofit.Builder()
    .baseUrl("https://api.example.com/")
    .addConverterFactory(GsonConverterFactory.create())
    .build()

val apiService = retrofit.create(ApiService::class.java)
val response = apiService.getData()
```

Retrofit automatically handles the network request asynchronously, parses the JSON response into DataModel objects, and returns it to the calling function.

OkHttp

OkHttp is a powerful and flexible HTTP client that works well with Retrofit. OkHttp is particularly useful for handling network requests, managing connections, caching responses, and retrying failed requests. It offers low-level control over network operations and can be used independently or alongside Retrofit.

Example of making a simple GET request using OkHttp:

```kotlin
val client = OkHttpClient()
val request = Request.Builder()
    .url("https://api.example.com/data")
    .build()

client.newCall(request).enqueue(object : Callback {
    override fun onFailure(call: Call, e: IOException) {
        e.printStackTrace()
    }

    override fun onResponse(call: Call, response: Response) {
        if (response.isSuccessful) {
            val data = response.body?.string()
            println(data)
```

```
    }
  }
})
```

Volley

Volley is an Android-specific library developed by Google for handling network requests. It simplifies the process of making asynchronous network calls, handling image loading, and managing network queues. Volley's strengths lie in handling HTTP requests, image caching, and managing multiple network operations in parallel.

Example of a GET request using Volley:

```
val requestQueue = Volley.newRequestQueue(context)
val stringRequest = StringRequest(Request.Method.GET,
"https://api.example.com/data",
  Response.Listener<String> { response ->
    println(response)
  },
  Response.ErrorListener { error ->
    error.printStackTrace()
  })

requestQueue.add(stringRequest)
```

4. Networking Best Practices

When working with networking in Android, several best practices can help ensure efficient, secure, and maintainable code:

Use Asynchronous Requests: Network operations should always be done on a background thread to avoid blocking the main UI thread, which could lead to UI freezes or ANRs (Application Not Responding).

Use Retrofit or Volley for Ease of Use: For most networking tasks, using libraries like Retrofit or Volley makes it easier to manage HTTP requests, parse responses, and handle errors.

Error Handling: Always handle network errors (e.g., timeouts, no internet connection, server errors) by providing user-friendly feedback. Use retries, backoff strategies, or caching where appropriate.

Secure Data Transmission: Always use HTTPS to encrypt sensitive data during transmission. This ensures that user data remains secure and prevents man-in-the-middle attacks.

Rate Limiting: Some APIs impose rate limits on how many requests you can make in a given period. Implement strategies like request throttling or caching to minimize the number of requests and ensure compliance.

Handle Connectivity Issues: Mobile apps often experience connectivity fluctuations. Always check the device's network status before making requests, and show appropriate error messages when the network is unavailable.

Networking is an integral part of Android app development, enabling your app to interact with external servers, retrieve data, and send user input. By understanding the fundamental concepts of networking in Android, along with the tools and libraries available, you can build robust and efficient apps that offer real-time data, enhance user experience, and function reliably under various network conditions. Whether you're making simple HTTP requests or integrating with complex APIs, mastering networking is essential to building feature-rich Android apps that keep users engaged and satisfied.

9.2 Making API Calls with Retrofit

Retrofit is one of the most popular and powerful libraries for making network requests in Android. It simplifies the process of interacting with REST APIs, parsing responses, and managing HTTP requests. Retrofit abstracts the complexity of managing network communication and allows you to work with APIs seamlessly by mapping HTTP requests to method calls in your code.

In this section, we will walk you through the process of making API calls using Retrofit, including how to configure Retrofit, create service interfaces, handle asynchronous requests, and parse the responses into usable objects.

1. What is Retrofit?

Retrofit is a type-safe HTTP client for Android and Java that simplifies network calls to RESTful APIs. It eliminates the boilerplate code that developers have to write when manually creating HTTP requests. Retrofit uses annotations to define HTTP request methods (GET, POST, PUT, DELETE, etc.) and automatically converts the response into Java or Kotlin objects, which you can easily work with.

Some key features of Retrofit:

- **Simple API definition**: Use Java/Kotlin interfaces and annotations to define the HTTP methods.
- **Automatic JSON parsing**: With built-in converters (e.g., Gson), Retrofit can automatically convert the server's response into an object.
- **Asynchronous calls**: Retrofit supports asynchronous requests out of the box, allowing you to perform network operations without blocking the UI thread.
- **Integration with other libraries**: Retrofit can be used alongside libraries like OkHttp for advanced networking needs and logging.

2. Setting Up Retrofit in Your Android Project

To use Retrofit in your Android app, you need to include it as a dependency. Here's how you can do that:

Add Retrofit dependency: Open your app-level build.gradle file and add Retrofit's dependency:

```
dependencies {
    implementation 'com.squareup.retrofit2:retrofit:2.9.0'
    implementation 'com.squareup.retrofit2:converter-gson:2.9.0' // Gson converter for JSON parsing
    implementation 'com.squareup.okhttp3:logging-interceptor:4.9.0' // For logging network requests (optional)
}
```

Sync the project: After adding the dependencies, sync your project to download and set up the Retrofit library.

3. Define the API Interface

Retrofit works by defining an interface where you declare methods that represent the HTTP request actions (like GET, POST, etc.). The interface will be used to create a Retrofit instance that can execute these API calls.

Here's an example of how to define an API interface:

```
import retrofit2.Call
import retrofit2.http.GET
import retrofit2.http.Path


interface ApiService {
    // Define a GET request to fetch user data from a URL
    @GET("users/{id}")
    fun getUserData(@Path("id") userId: String): Call<User> // Call<User> represents the
response type
}
```

In this example:

- **@GET("users/{id}")**: This annotation specifies that we are making a GET request to the users/{id} endpoint, where {id} is a variable that will be passed as a parameter to the method.
- **Call<User>**: The Call object represents a request that will return a User object once the response is parsed.

4. Create the Retrofit Instance

Now that you have your API interface defined, you need to create an instance of Retrofit that will execute your requests. You also need to specify the base URL of the API.

Here's an example of how to set up Retrofit:

```
import retrofit2.Retrofit
import retrofit2.converter.gson.GsonConverterFactory

class RetrofitInstance {
    companion object {
        private const val BASE_URL = "https://api.example.com/"

        // Create and return Retrofit instance
```

```
fun getRetrofitInstance(): Retrofit {
    return Retrofit.Builder()
        .baseUrl(BASE_URL) // Base URL of the API
        .addConverterFactory(GsonConverterFactory.create()) // Gson converter to
parse the JSON response
        .build()
    }
  }
}
```

- **baseUrl(BASE_URL):** This defines the base URL for your API. All endpoint URLs will be appended to this base URL.
- **addConverterFactory(GsonConverterFactory.create()):** This specifies the converter factory to use. In this case, Gson is used to parse the JSON response into Java objects.

5. Making an API Call

With the Retrofit instance set up and the API interface defined, you can now use Retrofit to make an API call. Retrofit supports both synchronous and asynchronous calls.

Making an Asynchronous Call

In most cases, you want to make an asynchronous call to avoid blocking the main UI thread. This is especially important for network operations. Retrofit provides the enqueue() method to make asynchronous requests.

Here's how to make an asynchronous GET request:

```
// Get an instance of Retrofit
val retrofit = RetrofitInstance.getRetrofitInstance()

// Create an instance of the ApiService interface
val apiService = retrofit.create(ApiService::class.java)

// Make the network call asynchronously
val call = apiService.getUserData("12345") // Pass the user ID parameter

// Enqueue the call and handle the response or failure
call.enqueue(object : Callback<User> {
```

```kotlin
    override fun onResponse(call: Call<User>, response: Response<User>) {
        if (response.isSuccessful) {
            // Handle the successful response
            val user = response.body()
            println("User data: ${user?.name}")
        } else {
            // Handle the error response
            println("Error: ${response.code()}")
        }
    }

    override fun onFailure(call: Call<User>, t: Throwable) {
        // Handle failure (e.g., network issues)
        println("Failed to fetch data: ${t.message}")
    }
})
```

- **enqueue():** This method makes the call asynchronously. When the network response is received, the appropriate callback methods (onResponse() and onFailure()) are called.
- **onResponse():** This method is triggered when the network request is successful. You can access the response data here.
- **onFailure():** This method is triggered when there is a failure, such as a network error or timeout.

Making a Synchronous Call

While asynchronous calls are the preferred method, sometimes you might want to perform synchronous requests, especially when you need to fetch data on a background thread or during startup. Here's how you can make a synchronous call:

```kotlin
val call = apiService.getUserData("12345")
try {
    val response = call.execute() // Executes the request synchronously
    if (response.isSuccessful) {
        val user = response.body()
        println("User data: ${user?.name}")
    } else {
        println("Error: ${response.code()}")
    }
```

```
} catch (e: Exception) {
    println("Request failed: ${e.message}")
}
```

- **execute():** This method performs the request synchronously. It's important to note that execute() must not be called on the main thread, as it will block the UI.

6. Handling Responses and Errors

After making an API call, it's crucial to handle the response and errors properly to ensure a smooth user experience.

- **Successful Response**: If the response is successful, Retrofit will parse the server's response into the appropriate object (in our case, a User object) based on the return type defined in the service interface.
- **Error Handling**: If the request fails or the server returns an error (e.g., 404 Not Found or 500 Internal Server Error), you should handle this gracefully by showing an appropriate message to the user.

Handling API Errors

Retrofit provides several ways to handle errors:

- Check the HTTP status code (e.g., response.code()).
- Handle different types of exceptions (e.g., IOException, SocketTimeoutException) in the onFailure() method.
- For instance, if the response is unsuccessful, you might want to show a message like "Data not found" or "Server error occurred."

Using Retrofit to make API calls in Android simplifies the process of communicating with remote servers and handling responses. With its clear syntax, automatic parsing of JSON data, and seamless asynchronous execution, Retrofit makes it easy to integrate networking into your Android apps. By defining API interfaces, setting up Retrofit instances, and making asynchronous calls, you can build efficient, scalable apps that interact with RESTful services with minimal boilerplate code. With proper error handling and response parsing, Retrofit also helps you provide users with a robust and responsive app experience.

9.3 Handling JSON Parsing and Data Binding

Handling JSON parsing and data binding are crucial steps in Android development when dealing with network responses, especially when interacting with REST APIs. Once you retrieve the data from an API, you need to parse it into a format your app can understand and display, typically through JSON. Data binding allows you to seamlessly connect this parsed data to your UI elements, reducing boilerplate code and ensuring your app responds to data changes dynamically.

In this section, we'll explore how to parse JSON data using popular libraries like Gson and Moshi, and then integrate the parsed data into your Android UI through data binding. By the end, you'll be able to retrieve data from an API, parse it into models, and bind it directly to your user interface with minimal effort.

1. JSON Parsing with Gson

JSON (JavaScript Object Notation) is a lightweight data interchange format commonly used for transmitting data between a server and a web application. Android provides several libraries to handle JSON parsing, with Gson being one of the most popular and efficient ones.

Gson is a Google library for converting Java objects into JSON and vice versa. Retrofit, which we covered in the previous section, uses Gson (or other converters) to automatically parse the response into Java/Kotlin objects.

Setting Up Gson in Android

To use Gson in your Android project, you'll need to add the Gson dependency in your build.gradle file:

```
dependencies {
    implementation 'com.google.code.gson:gson:2.8.8'
}
```

After syncing your project, you can begin using Gson for parsing JSON data.

Parsing JSON Response Using Gson

Here's an example of how to parse a JSON response into a Kotlin object using Gson:

Define a Data Model: First, create a Kotlin data class that corresponds to the structure of the JSON response.

```
data class User(
    val id: Int,
    val name: String,
    val email: String
)
```

Make the API Request: After you've made an API call (using Retrofit, for example), you can parse the JSON response into the User object using Gson:

```
import com.google.gson.Gson
import retrofit2.Call
import retrofit2.Callback
import retrofit2.Response

// Assuming you have an ApiService that fetches user data
val apiService = retrofit.create(ApiService::class.java)
val call = apiService.getUserData("12345")

call.enqueue(object : Callback<User> {
    override fun onResponse(call: Call<User>, response: Response<User>) {
        if (response.isSuccessful) {
            val user = response.body()
            println("User Data: ${user?.name}, ${user?.email}")
        }
    }

    override fun onFailure(call: Call<User>, t: Throwable) {
        println("API call failed: ${t.message}")
    }
})
```

In this example, Retrofit uses Gson to automatically convert the JSON response into a User object based on the data class structure.

Custom Gson Serialization/Deserialization

In some cases, you might need to customize how JSON is parsed. For example, if the API returns JSON with field names that don't match the names in your data model, you can use Gson annotations like @SerializedName to map them correctly:

```
data class User(
    @SerializedName("user_id") val id: Int,
    @SerializedName("user_name") val name: String,
    val email: String
)
```

This way, Gson will correctly map the incoming JSON fields (user_id and user_name) to the properties in the User class (id and name).

2. JSON Parsing with Moshi

Moshi is another popular JSON library for Android that can be used in a similar manner to Gson. It is a modern alternative to Gson with some performance optimizations and support for Kotlin out of the box. Like Gson, Moshi can be integrated with Retrofit for automatic JSON parsing.

Setting Up Moshi in Android

To use Moshi in your Android project, add the following dependencies in your build.gradle file:

```
dependencies {
    implementation 'com.squareup.moshi:moshi:1.13.0'
    implementation 'com.squareup.moshi:moshi-kotlin:1.13.0'
    implementation 'com.squareup.retrofit2:converter-moshi:2.9.0'
}
```

Parsing JSON Response Using Moshi

Define a Data Model: Similar to Gson, define a Kotlin data class for your model.

```
data class User(
    val id: Int,
    val name: String,
    val email: String
)
```

Configure Moshi with Retrofit: Next, configure Retrofit to use Moshi as the converter for JSON parsing.

```
import com.squareup.moshi.Moshi
import com.squareup.moshi.kotlin.reflect.KotlinJsonAdapterFactory
import retrofit2.Retrofit
import retrofit2.converter.moshi.MoshiConverterFactory

val moshi = Moshi.Builder().add(KotlinJsonAdapterFactory()).build()
val retrofit = Retrofit.Builder()
    .baseUrl("https://api.example.com/")
    .addConverterFactory(MoshiConverterFactory.create(moshi))
    .build()
```

Make API Request and Parse with Moshi: After setting up Retrofit with Moshi, the parsing is done automatically in the same way as with Gson.

```
val apiService = retrofit.create(ApiService::class.java)
val call = apiService.getUserData("12345")

call.enqueue(object : Callback<User> {
    override fun onResponse(call: Call<User>, response: Response<User>) {
        if (response.isSuccessful) {
            val user = response.body()
            println("User Data: ${user?.name}, ${user?.email}")
        }
    }

    override fun onFailure(call: Call<User>, t: Throwable) {
        println("API call failed: ${t.message}")
    }
})
```

Moshi automatically handles parsing into your User model in the same way as Gson.

3. Data Binding in Android

Data Binding is an Android framework that enables you to directly bind UI components in the layout to data sources in your app. This eliminates the need for manual UI updates by automatically updating the UI whenever the data changes. Using data binding with network responses allows you to simplify and optimize your UI code.

Setting Up Data Binding

To enable data binding in your Android project, follow these steps:

Enable Data Binding in Gradle: Add the following line inside the android block in your build.gradle file:

```
android {
  ...
  viewBinding {
    enabled = true
  }
}
```

Create the Layout File with Data Binding: In your layout XML file, use the <layout> tag to enable data binding:

```
<layout xmlns:android="http://schemas.android.com/apk/res/android">
  <data>
    <variable
      name="user"
      type="com.example.app.User" />
  </data>

  <LinearLayout
    android:layout_width="match_parent"
    android:layout_height="wrap_content">
    <TextView
      android:id="@+id/userName"
      android:layout_width="wrap_content"
      android:layout_height="wrap_content"
      android:text="@{user.name}" />
  </LinearLayout>
</layout>
```

Here, the @{user.name} syntax binds the TextView to the name property of the user object.

Binding Data to the UI

In your activity or fragment, you can bind the data using the generated binding class.

```
val binding = ActivityMainBinding.inflate(layoutInflater)
setContentView(binding.root)

val user = User(1, "John Doe", "john.doe@example.com")
binding.user = user
```

When the user object changes, the TextView will automatically update, without any need for manual calls to setText().

By combining JSON parsing libraries like Gson or Moshi with Android's data binding system, you can streamline the process of handling network data and binding it directly to the user interface. This approach allows for cleaner, more efficient code, minimizes the need for boilerplate code, and ensures that your app's UI is always in sync with the underlying data. Whether you use Gson for its simplicity or Moshi for its performance and Kotlin support, both libraries integrate seamlessly with Retrofit and Android's data binding architecture, providing a powerful solution for modern Android development.

9.4 Securing API Communications with OAuth and HTTPS

In modern Android development, ensuring secure communication between your app and a backend API is essential. Sensitive user data, such as login credentials, personal information, and payment details, must be protected against malicious attacks and data breaches. OAuth (Open Authorization) and HTTPS (Hypertext Transfer Protocol Secure) are two widely used technologies for securing API communication in Android applications. This section will explore how to implement these security mechanisms to safeguard your app's data and protect user privacy.

1. Understanding HTTPS and Its Importance

HTTPS is the secure version of HTTP, the protocol used for transmitting data over the web. It works by encrypting the data sent between the client (your Android app) and the server, ensuring that sensitive information such as passwords, tokens, or credit card numbers remains private.

How HTTPS Works

HTTPS uses SSL/TLS (Secure Socket Layer / Transport Layer Security) to encrypt communication between the server and the client. SSL/TLS ensures that:

- Data is encrypted so that it cannot be read or modified by third parties.
- The server is authenticated to prevent man-in-the-middle attacks, where an attacker intercepts the data being transmitted.

For an Android app, HTTPS ensures that the connection between the app and the server is secure, preventing any potential eavesdropping or tampering with the data.

Setting Up HTTPS in Android

To use HTTPS in your Android app, the server must have an SSL certificate installed. When making network requests using libraries like Retrofit or OkHttp, HTTPS is automatically handled as long as the API URL begins with https://.

Here's a basic example of how you can make a secure network request using Retrofit:

```
val retrofit = Retrofit.Builder()
    .baseUrl("https://api.example.com/") // Make sure the base URL uses HTTPS
    .addConverterFactory(GsonConverterFactory.create())
    .build()

val apiService = retrofit.create(ApiService::class.java)
```

In this example, the baseUrl begins with https://, ensuring that all requests made through Retrofit will be encrypted using HTTPS.

Pinning SSL Certificates for Added Security

Even though HTTPS encrypts data, it's still possible for an attacker to set up a fake server with an SSL certificate that looks valid. SSL certificate pinning is a technique that allows your Android app to explicitly trust only a specific server's certificate, even if the certificate is technically valid.

You can configure SSL pinning in your app using libraries such as OkHttp:

```
val certificatePinner = CertificatePinner.Builder()
```

```
.add("api.example.com", "sha256/xxxxxxxxxxxxxxxxxxxxxxx")
.build()

val client = OkHttpClient.Builder()
  .certificatePinner(certificatePinner)
  .build()

val retrofit = Retrofit.Builder()
  .baseUrl("https://api.example.com/")
  .client(client)
  .build()
```

By pinning the SSL certificate, the app ensures that only the trusted certificate is used, preventing MITM (Man-in-the-Middle) attacks.

2. Introduction to OAuth for Authentication and Authorization

OAuth is an open standard for access delegation, commonly used for securing API access. OAuth allows users to authorize third-party apps to access their data on a different service (such as Google, Facebook, or Twitter) without sharing their credentials. Instead of storing sensitive login credentials, OAuth uses authorization tokens to grant secure access.

How OAuth Works

OAuth is commonly used in the context of Authorization and Authentication. It works in two main ways:

- **OAuth 2.0**: The most commonly used version of OAuth, it allows third-party applications to request access tokens for accessing a user's data on a server.
- **OAuth Flow**: OAuth works by redirecting users to an authorization server, where they grant access permissions to the app. Once the user grants access, an authorization code is sent back to the app, which then exchanges it for an access token.

Here's a basic flow of OAuth 2.0:

- The user is redirected to the authorization server (for example, Google) and grants permission to the app to access certain data.

- The authorization server redirects the user back to the app with an authorization code.
- The app exchanges the authorization code for an access token.
- The app uses the access token to authenticate API requests on behalf of the user.

OAuth Flow for Mobile Apps

In a mobile app, the OAuth flow typically involves integrating with popular identity providers like Google, Facebook, or GitHub. You'll use OAuth to authenticate users, ensuring that your app does not store passwords and that user sessions are securely managed.

Implementing OAuth with Retrofit

Retrofit, combined with a library like OkHttp or Auth0, can be used to manage OAuth tokens for secure API communication.

Obtain OAuth Tokens: First, authenticate the user with an identity provider and obtain an OAuth token.

Use Token for API Calls: You can use the token in the Authorization header of your API calls to authenticate requests.

Here's an example using Retrofit and an OAuth access token:

```
val retrofit = Retrofit.Builder()
    .baseUrl("https://api.example.com/")
    .client(OkHttpClient.Builder()
        .addInterceptor { chain ->
            val newRequest = chain.request().newBuilder()
                .addHeader("Authorization", "Bearer $accessToken") // Add OAuth token
                .build()
            chain.proceed(newRequest)
        }
        .build())
    .addConverterFactory(GsonConverterFactory.create())
    .build()

val apiService = retrofit.create(ApiService::class.java)
```

In this example, the Authorization header is used to send the OAuth access token with every request to authenticate the user.

3. Refreshing OAuth Tokens

OAuth access tokens are typically short-lived for security reasons, meaning they expire after a certain period. When this happens, the app needs to request a new token using a refresh token.

A refresh token is issued by the authorization server alongside the access token and can be used to obtain a new access token when the old one expires. Here's a simple flow for refreshing OAuth tokens:

- If the access token expires, the app sends a request to the token endpoint with the refresh token.
- The authorization server validates the refresh token and responds with a new access token.
- The app stores and uses the new access token for subsequent requests.

Refreshing Tokens with Retrofit

```kotlin
val retrofit = Retrofit.Builder()
    .baseUrl("https://api.example.com/")
    .client(OkHttpClient.Builder().build())
    .build()

val apiService = retrofit.create(ApiService::class.java)
val call = apiService.refreshToken(refreshToken)

call.enqueue(object : Callback<TokenResponse> {
    override fun onResponse(call: Call<TokenResponse>, response:
Response<TokenResponse>) {
        if (response.isSuccessful) {
            val newAccessToken = response.body()?.accessToken
            // Save the new access token and use it for future requests
        }
    }

    override fun onFailure(call: Call<TokenResponse>, t: Throwable) {
        // Handle failure
```

```
    }
})
```

This ensures that your app can maintain a secure session for the user, even after the access token expires.

Securing API communication with HTTPS and OAuth is essential for protecting user data and ensuring the integrity of your Android app. HTTPS ensures that all data exchanged between your app and the server is encrypted, while OAuth provides a secure, token-based authentication mechanism that avoids the need to store user credentials. By combining both technologies, you can create a robust and secure system for interacting with APIs, ensuring that sensitive information remains safe and that users can trust your app with their data.

9.5 Implementing WebSockets for Real-Time Data

In modern mobile applications, delivering real-time updates to users is essential for providing a responsive and engaging experience. Whether it's for chat apps, live sports scores, financial data, or social media feeds, users expect to receive timely information without needing to refresh their app. WebSockets provide a powerful mechanism for maintaining a constant, open connection between the client (your Android app) and the server, enabling real-time bidirectional communication.

This section explores how to implement WebSockets in Android apps to receive real-time updates from a server.

1. What are WebSockets?

WebSockets are a communication protocol that enables full-duplex (two-way) communication channels over a single, long-lived connection. Unlike traditional HTTP requests, where the client sends a request and waits for a response, WebSockets allow both the client and server to send messages to each other at any time over a single, persistent connection.

Key Features of WebSockets:

- **Persistent connection**: Once a WebSocket connection is established, it remains open, reducing the overhead of repeatedly opening new connections.

- **Low latency**: Since the connection is persistent, there is minimal delay between sending and receiving messages, making WebSockets ideal for real-time data transmission.
- **Efficient communication**: WebSockets minimize the need for excessive polling (repeated requests to the server), saving bandwidth and improving performance.

WebSockets are commonly used in applications that require real-time interactions, such as messaging platforms, online games, and live data feeds.

2. WebSocket Workflow

The WebSocket communication flow is simple:

- **Handshake**: The client sends an HTTP request to the server to initiate the WebSocket connection. This is known as the WebSocket handshake. Once the server accepts the handshake, the protocol switches from HTTP to WebSocket.
- **Communication**: After the handshake, data can be exchanged freely between the client and server without further requests or responses.
- **Closing the Connection**: Either the client or the server can terminate the connection when it's no longer needed. This is done using a specific WebSocket close frame.

The WebSocket protocol enables seamless, low-latency communication between the client and server, making it ideal for applications where real-time data is crucial.

3. Setting Up WebSocket in Android

To implement WebSockets in an Android app, we'll use an external library like OkHttp or Socket.IO. These libraries simplify the process of working with WebSockets and handling events such as connecting, receiving messages, and disconnecting.

Using OkHttp for WebSocket Implementation

OkHttp is a popular HTTP client library that also supports WebSocket communication. Here's how to implement WebSockets in your Android app using OkHttp:

Add the OkHttp Dependency: In your project's build.gradle file, add the OkHttp dependency:

dependencies {

```
    implementation 'com.squareup.okhttp3:okhttp:4.9.0'  // Add OkHttp for WebSocket
support
}
```

Creating a WebSocket Client: Use the OkHttpClient to create a WebSocket client. The client will connect to the server and handle incoming and outgoing messages.

```
val client = OkHttpClient()

val request = Request.Builder()
    .url("wss://example.com/realtime")  // WebSocket URL (note the "wss" for secure
WebSocket)
    .build()

val listener = object : WebSocketListener() {
    override fun onOpen(webSocket: WebSocket, response: Response) {
        super.onOpen(webSocket, response)
        Log.d("WebSocket", "Connection opened")
    }

    override fun onMessage(webSocket: WebSocket, text: String) {
        super.onMessage(webSocket, text)
        // Handle incoming messages
        Log.d("WebSocket", "Received message: $text")
    }

    override fun onFailure(webSocket: WebSocket, t: Throwable, response: Response?)
{
        super.onFailure(webSocket, t, response)
        Log.e("WebSocket", "Connection failed: ${t.message}")
    }

    override fun onClosing(webSocket: WebSocket, code: Int, reason: String) {
        super.onClosing(webSocket, code, reason)
        Log.d("WebSocket", "Connection closing")
    }

    override fun onClosed(webSocket: WebSocket, code: Int, reason: String) {
        super.onClosed(webSocket, code, reason)
        Log.d("WebSocket", "Connection closed")
```

```
    }
}
```

```
// Open the WebSocket connection
client.newWebSocket(request, listener)
```

```
client.dispatcher().executorService().shutdown()  // Important for cleaning up resources
```

In the above code:

- The Request.Builder().url("wss://example.com/realtime") initiates the connection to the WebSocket server.
- The WebSocketListener class handles various events such as connection opening (onOpen), receiving messages (onMessage), and closing the connection (onClosing, onClosed).

Sending Messages: Once the WebSocket connection is established, you can send messages to the server using the send method:

```
webSocket.send("Hello, server!")
```

This allows you to send data in real-time to the server, such as user input or status updates.

Handling Incoming Messages: In the onMessage method, you can process any data that the server sends to your app. For example, in a messaging app, this could be a new chat message:

```
override fun onMessage(webSocket: WebSocket, text: String) {
    // Update the UI with the received message
    runOnUiThread {
        // Handle UI updates here
        messagesAdapter.addMessage(text)
    }
}
```

In this example, the received message is added to the UI in real time, allowing users to see new content as soon as it arrives.

4. Best Practices for WebSocket Usage in Android

To ensure that WebSocket connections work efficiently and reliably in your Android app, follow these best practices:

Handle Connection Lifecycle: Ensure that your WebSocket connection is properly managed by handling various lifecycle events like connection opening, closing, and failure. This ensures that your app can gracefully handle unexpected interruptions.

Reconnection Logic: Implement automatic reconnection mechanisms in case the WebSocket connection drops. This is especially important for mobile networks, where connections might be unreliable.

```
override fun onFailure(webSocket: WebSocket, t: Throwable, response: Response?) {
    super.onFailure(webSocket, t, response)
    Log.e("WebSocket", "Error: ${t.message}, Reconnecting...")
    reconnectWebSocket()  // Reconnect logic here
}
```

Security Considerations: Always use the wss:// (WebSocket Secure) protocol instead of ws:// to encrypt communication and protect sensitive data. This ensures that data exchanged between the client and server remains private and secure.

Message Size Management: Be mindful of the message sizes being sent and received via WebSockets. While WebSockets support large messages, transmitting large data in real-time can lead to performance issues. Consider chunking data if necessary.

Efficient Resource Usage: WebSockets are designed to be long-lived, but it's important to close connections when they're no longer needed. Implement logic to close the WebSocket connection when the user navigates away from the screen or the app goes into the background to conserve resources.

WebSockets provide a powerful tool for implementing real-time, bidirectional communication in Android apps. Whether you're building a messaging app, live data feed, or any other application that requires immediate updates, WebSockets offer an efficient and scalable way to maintain a continuous connection between your app and the server. By using libraries like OkHttp, you can easily integrate WebSocket functionality and handle the connection lifecycle, messaging, and error handling seamlessly.

With proper implementation, WebSockets can greatly enhance the user experience by delivering instantaneous updates, making your app more interactive and engaging.

10. Storing and Managing Data

Efficiently storing and managing data is essential for any Android app that needs to persist user information, settings, or content. In this chapter, you'll explore various data storage options available on Android, from simple SharedPreferences and local databases like SQLite to more advanced solutions like Room and cloud storage. You'll also learn best practices for managing data efficiently, ensuring it remains secure, consistent, and accessible across sessions. By mastering these techniques, you'll be able to build apps that can store, retrieve, and synchronize data seamlessly, providing a smooth and reliable user experience.

10.1 Overview of Local Storage Options

When developing Android apps, one critical aspect to consider is how to handle data storage. While cloud-based storage solutions are valuable for synchronizing and backing up data across devices, there are situations where local storage is essential. Local storage enables your app to function offline or handle data that doesn't need to be constantly synced with the server, providing a faster and more efficient way to store small to medium amounts of data directly on the device.

In Android development, there are several local storage options, each with specific use cases, performance considerations, and advantages. Understanding these options is crucial for selecting the right one based on your app's requirements, such as the type and amount of data being stored, the need for offline capabilities, and the complexity of the data.

1. SharedPreferences

SharedPreferences is a lightweight and easy-to-use storage solution in Android, ideal for storing small amounts of primitive data. This is typically used for app settings, user preferences, or flags that don't require complex data structures. Data is saved in the form of key-value pairs, which makes it highly efficient for storing configuration settings or app-specific preferences.

Key Features:

- Stores key-value pairs (strings, booleans, integers, etc.).
- Ideal for simple data like user preferences, settings, or app configuration.

- Data is stored in XML format in the app's private storage.
- Quick and easy to use for basic needs.

Example Use Case:

- Storing user settings like theme preferences (dark mode vs light mode).
- Tracking if the user has seen a welcome message or tutorial.

Code Example:

```kotlin
// Save data
val sharedPref = context.getSharedPreferences("AppPreferences",
Context.MODE_PRIVATE)
with(sharedPref.edit()) {
   putBoolean("dark_mode", true)
   apply()
}

// Retrieve data
val darkMode = sharedPref.getBoolean("dark_mode", false)
```

SharedPreferences is not suitable for storing large or complex data, such as large lists or objects.

2. SQLite Database

For more complex or structured data, SQLite is the go-to local storage option in Android. SQLite is a relational database management system that allows you to store and retrieve data in tables, similar to how data is stored in traditional relational databases like MySQL or PostgreSQL. It supports SQL queries, which means you can perform complex queries, filters, sorting, and joins on your stored data.

Key Features:

- Full relational database management system.
- Suitable for storing structured data that requires querying and relationships.
- Supports SQL for creating, reading, updating, and deleting (CRUD) operations.
- Stored in a single file within the app's private storage.

Example Use Case:

- Storing a list of contacts with name, phone number, and email.
- Managing inventory or product data in an e-commerce app.

Code Example:

```
val dbHelper = DBHelper(context)
val db = dbHelper.writableDatabase

// Insert data
val values = ContentValues().apply {
    put("name", "John Doe")
    put("phone", "123-456-7890")
}
db.insert("contacts", null, values)

// Query data
val cursor = db.query("contacts", null, null, null, null, null, null)
while (cursor.moveToNext()) {
    val name = cursor.getString(cursor.getColumnIndex("name"))
    val phone = cursor.getString(cursor.getColumnIndex("phone"))
    // Process the data
}
cursor.close()
```

While SQLite is powerful, it can be overkill for simple use cases and involves more boilerplate code than simpler options like SharedPreferences.

3. Room Database

For developers who prefer a more modern and robust way of interacting with SQLite, Room is the official ORM (Object-Relational Mapping) library provided by Google. Room simplifies database operations by allowing you to work with plain Kotlin or Java objects instead of directly dealing with SQL queries. It also provides compile-time verification of SQL queries, which reduces the chances of runtime errors.

Room abstracts away the complexities of managing SQLite directly, making it a great option for larger, more complex apps that still require local storage.

Key Features:

- Built on top of SQLite but abstracts away the complexity.
- Allows you to work with plain Kotlin/Java objects and annotations to define the schema.
- Supports relationships between entities (tables), making it easier to model complex data.
- Provides powerful query methods and compile-time verification of SQL.

Example Use Case:

- A task management app with multiple users, where each task belongs to a specific user and can be marked as complete.
- A financial tracking app that stores transactions and categories.

Code Example:

```
@Entity(tableName = "contacts")
data class Contact(
    @PrimaryKey(autoGenerate = true) val id: Int = 0,
    val name: String,
    val phone: String
)

@Dao
interface ContactDao {
    @Insert
    suspend fun insert(contact: Contact)

    @Query("SELECT * FROM contacts")
    suspend fun getAll(): List<Contact>
}

@Database(entities = [Contact::class], version = 1)
abstract class AppDatabase : RoomDatabase() {
    abstract fun contactDao(): ContactDao
}

// Usage:
val db = Room.databaseBuilder(context, AppDatabase::class.java, "database-
name").build()
```

```
val contactDao = db.contactDao()
contactDao.insert(Contact(name = "John Doe", phone = "123-456-7890"))
```

Room simplifies database management and reduces boilerplate code, making it an ideal choice for most Android apps that need to manage complex data.

4. File Storage

Android also provides File Storage options, which allow you to read and write files directly to the device's storage. This method is useful when dealing with binary data, such as images, videos, or large files that don't fit well into a structured database.

Key Features:

- Allows reading and writing to the device's internal or external storage.
- Suitable for large files like images, PDFs, or JSON files.
- Offers both internal storage (private to the app) and external storage (shared with other apps, depending on permissions).

Example Use Case:

- Saving images or files that the user has uploaded or generated.
- Storing logs or other data that can be reviewed offline.

Code Example:

```
// Writing to a file in internal storage
val file = File(context.filesDir, "data.txt")
file.writeText("Some data to store in a file.")

// Reading from the file
val fileContent = file.readText()
```

While file storage is great for large, unstructured data, it can be less efficient for querying and managing smaller, structured datasets.

5. DataStore (Jetpack)

For developers seeking a modern, flexible alternative to SharedPreferences, DataStore is a newer, asynchronous data storage solution provided by Jetpack. It provides two implementations: Preferences DataStore for key-value pairs and Proto DataStore for structured data using Protocol Buffers.

DataStore is designed to handle data asynchronously, ensuring that it doesn't block the UI thread. It is a more modern and safer option compared to SharedPreferences, especially for applications where you need to store preferences or other small pieces of data.

Key Features:

- Asynchronous, ensuring non-blocking operations.
- Two implementations: Preferences DataStore (key-value pairs) and Proto DataStore (structured data).
- Designed for performance and reliability.
- Provides better error handling than SharedPreferences.

Example Use Case:

- Storing user preferences in a modern, thread-safe manner.
- Storing small amounts of data like authentication tokens.

Code Example:

```
// Preferences DataStore
val dataStore: DataStore<Preferences> = context.createDataStore(name = "settings")

// Write data
suspend fun savePreference(key: String, value: String) {
    dataStore.edit { preferences ->
        preferences[stringPreferencesKey(key)] = value
    }
}

// Read data
val storedValue: Flow<String> = dataStore.data
    .map { preferences ->
        preferences[stringPreferencesKey("user_name")] ?: "Default"
    }
```

DataStore is a great choice when you want modern, secure, and efficient key-value storage.

Choosing the right local storage solution depends on your app's specific requirements. SharedPreferences is ideal for simple key-value pairs, while SQLite and Room are better suited for structured, relational data. File storage is perfect for large binary data, and DataStore offers a modern, asynchronous way to handle smaller pieces of data securely. By understanding the pros and cons of each option, you can make an informed decision on the best storage method for your Android app's needs.

10.2 Using SharedPreferences for Simple Data

In Android app development, SharedPreferences is one of the most commonly used mechanisms for storing simple data locally. It allows you to store small amounts of primitive data in key-value pairs and is especially useful for saving user preferences, app settings, and small amounts of state data that don't need to be stored in a more complex database like SQLite. SharedPreferences provides a straightforward and efficient way to persist user settings across app launches and is typically used for items like user preferences, app configurations, and simple flags (e.g., whether a user has completed a tutorial or enabled dark mode).

This section explains how to use SharedPreferences effectively to store and retrieve simple data within your Android app.

1. Understanding SharedPreferences

SharedPreferences stores data in key-value pairs, where the key is a unique string identifier, and the value is a primitive data type (such as a string, integer, boolean, etc.). The data is stored in an XML file, which is private to the app. This makes SharedPreferences perfect for small data that doesn't require complex querying or relationships.

Key Features of SharedPreferences:

- Stores data in key-value pairs.
- Data is saved in XML format in the app's private storage.
- Simple API for saving and retrieving data.
- Ideal for storing small amounts of data like user settings, app configurations, or simple flags.

- Provides persistent storage across app restarts.

2. How to Use SharedPreferences in Your App

To use SharedPreferences, you need to follow these steps:

- **Access SharedPreferences**: Use the getSharedPreferences() method to access the SharedPreferences instance.
- **Edit SharedPreferences**: Use the SharedPreferences.Editor class to modify the data.
- **Commit or Apply Changes**: Use apply() to save changes asynchronously or commit() for synchronous saving.

Let's explore how you can use SharedPreferences in more detail.

Storing Data in SharedPreferences

To store data in SharedPreferences, you need to access the SharedPreferences object and use the edit() method to modify its contents.

Code Example:

```
// Access SharedPreferences
val sharedPref = getSharedPreferences("AppPreferences", Context.MODE_PRIVATE)

// Get SharedPreferences.Editor to edit data
val editor = sharedPref.edit()

// Add key-value pairs
editor.putString("username", "JohnDoe")    // Storing a string
editor.putInt("userAge", 25)            // Storing an integer
editor.putBoolean("isLoggedIn", true)      // Storing a boolean

// Apply changes asynchronously
editor.apply()
```

Here, apply() is used to save the changes in the background. This method is generally preferred over commit() because it is faster and does not block the main thread.

Retrieving Data from SharedPreferences

To retrieve data from SharedPreferences, you use the getXXX() methods, where XXX represents the data type you want to retrieve (e.g., getString(), getInt(), getBoolean(), etc.).

Code Example:

```
// Access SharedPreferences
val sharedPref = getSharedPreferences("AppPreferences", Context.MODE_PRIVATE)

// Retrieve values using keys
val username = sharedPref.getString("username", "defaultUser")  // Default value if not found
val userAge = sharedPref.getInt("userAge", 18)          // Default value if not found
val isLoggedIn = sharedPref.getBoolean("isLoggedIn", false)   // Default value if not found

// Use the retrieved values
println("Username: $username, Age: $userAge, Logged In: $isLoggedIn")
```

In this example:

- The first argument in getString(), getInt(), or getBoolean() is the key used to store the value.
- The second argument is the default value returned if the key doesn't exist in SharedPreferences.

Removing Data from SharedPreferences

If you need to remove a specific value from SharedPreferences, you can use the remove() method.

Code Example:

```
// Access SharedPreferences
val sharedPref = getSharedPreferences("AppPreferences", Context.MODE_PRIVATE)

// Get SharedPreferences.Editor to edit data
val editor = sharedPref.edit()
```

```
// Remove a specific key-value pair
editor.remove("username")

// Apply changes asynchronously
editor.apply()
```

This will remove the value associated with the key "username", and the next time you retrieve it, it will return the default value instead of the previously stored value.

Clearing All Data from SharedPreferences

If you want to clear all the data stored in SharedPreferences, you can use the clear() method.

Code Example:

```
// Access SharedPreferences
val sharedPref = getSharedPreferences("AppPreferences", Context.MODE_PRIVATE)

// Get SharedPreferences.Editor to edit data
val editor = sharedPref.edit()

// Clear all stored data
editor.clear()

// Apply changes asynchronously
editor.apply()
```

Using clear() will remove all the data in the SharedPreferences file, making it an effective way to reset all user preferences, for example, when a user logs out.

3. Common Use Cases for SharedPreferences

Here are some of the most common use cases for SharedPreferences in Android development:

User Authentication and Session Management:

Storing user login status, tokens, and session information. For example, saving an authentication token or the user's session ID to keep them logged in between app launches.

editor.putString("auth_token", "user123token")
editor.putBoolean("isLoggedIn", true)

App Preferences:

Saving user preferences such as theme settings, language selection, or notification preferences.

editor.putBoolean("dark_mode", true)
editor.putString("language", "en")

Flags for Feature Toggles:

Storing simple flags to check whether the user has completed a task (e.g., tutorial completion) or enabled a feature.

editor.putBoolean("hasCompletedTutorial", true)

Tracking App States:

Saving app states or user progress that can be easily retrieved when the app restarts.

4. Best Practices for Using SharedPreferences

While SharedPreferences is simple and convenient, there are a few best practices you should follow to use it effectively:

- **Use Default Values**: Always provide default values when retrieving data. This ensures that your app doesn't crash or behave unexpectedly if the key doesn't exist.
- **Avoid Storing Large Data**: SharedPreferences is not suitable for storing large datasets. It is designed for small pieces of data such as strings, booleans, or integers. For larger or more complex data, consider using a database like SQLite or Room.

- **Store Sensitive Data Securely**: SharedPreferences is not secure by default. If you need to store sensitive information like passwords or tokens, consider using EncryptedSharedPreferences, a more secure variant that encrypts the data.
- **Asynchronous Access**: Always use apply() instead of commit() for asynchronous saving, as it does not block the UI thread.

SharedPreferences is a powerful and simple tool for saving small amounts of data locally on an Android device. It is ideal for storing user settings, flags, preferences, and other non-complex data that should persist across app launches. While it's not suitable for large or complex data, its simplicity and efficiency make it an essential tool for most Android developers. By following the best practices outlined above, you can make effective use of SharedPreferences in your Android apps, ensuring a smooth and user-friendly experience.

10.3 Storing Complex Data in SQLite Databases

In Android development, SQLite databases provide a powerful and flexible way to store complex, structured data locally on a device. Unlike SharedPreferences, which is suited for small key-value pairs, SQLite allows developers to manage large datasets, perform complex queries, and maintain relational data models. SQLite is an embedded database, meaning it's part of the Android operating system and doesn't require any external server. It's highly efficient, making it ideal for apps that require persistent storage of large amounts of structured data, such as user information, transaction records, or app data.

This section will cover how to use SQLite databases in Android apps, including how to create, manage, and interact with databases, and best practices for storing complex data efficiently.

1. Introduction to SQLite in Android

SQLite is a lightweight, relational database engine that comes embedded in Android. It is used to store structured data in tables with rows and columns. SQLite supports SQL syntax, which allows you to execute queries such as SELECT, INSERT, UPDATE, and DELETE. While SQLite does not require a network connection or server-side management, it can handle relational data and is highly optimized for mobile devices.

Key Features of SQLite in Android:

- **Relational Database**: Data is stored in tables, which can be related to one another.
- **SQL Syntax**: Supports standard SQL for querying and managing data.
- **Lightweight**: No external dependencies or servers required, making it suitable for mobile environments.
- **Built-in**: It is included in the Android SDK and doesn't require any additional libraries to be added.

2. Setting Up SQLite in Android

To begin using SQLite in an Android app, you'll need to interact with the SQLiteDatabase class and create a custom SQLiteOpenHelper. The SQLiteOpenHelper helps manage the database, including creating, upgrading, and downgrading the database schema. It also handles opening and closing the database connection.

Creating a SQLiteOpenHelper Class

To define and manage your database, you need to create a class that extends SQLiteOpenHelper. This class will provide methods for creating the database, upgrading its version, and managing database connections.

Code Example:

```
class MyDatabaseHelper(context: Context) : SQLiteOpenHelper(context,
DATABASE_NAME, null, DATABASE_VERSION) {

    override fun onCreate(db: SQLiteDatabase) {
        // Create the table schema
        val createTableQuery = "CREATE TABLE $TABLE_NAME (" +
            "$COLUMN_ID INTEGER PRIMARY KEY," +
            "$COLUMN_NAME TEXT," +
            "$COLUMN_EMAIL TEXT)"
        db.execSQL(createTableQuery)
    }

    override fun onUpgrade(db: SQLiteDatabase, oldVersion: Int, newVersion: Int) {
        // Drop the old table and recreate it if the schema is changed
        db.execSQL("DROP TABLE IF EXISTS $TABLE_NAME")
        onCreate(db)
    }
```

```kotlin
    companion object {
        const val DATABASE_NAME = "my_database.db"
        const val DATABASE_VERSION = 1
        const val TABLE_NAME = "users"
        const val COLUMN_ID = "_id"
        const val COLUMN_NAME = "name"
        const val COLUMN_EMAIL = "email"
    }
}
```

In this example, we define a database with one table, users, which stores user information with columns id, name, and email. The onCreate() method is called when the database is first created, and onUpgrade() handles upgrading the schema when the database version changes.

3. Storing and Retrieving Data in SQLite

Once the database and table have been set up, you can perform CRUD operations: Create, Read, Update, and Delete data in the database.

Inserting Data into SQLite

To insert data into an SQLite table, you can use the insert() method of the SQLiteDatabase class. The data is inserted as a set of key-value pairs, where the key corresponds to the column name, and the value is the data to be inserted.

Code Example:

```kotlin
fun insertUser(name: String, email: String) {
    val db = writableDatabase
    val values = ContentValues().apply {
        put(COLUMN_NAME, name)
        put(COLUMN_EMAIL, email)
    }
    db.insert(TABLE_NAME, null, values)
    db.close()
}
```

In this code, we create a ContentValues object and insert the name and email into the database. The insert() method handles the actual database insertion.

Retrieving Data from SQLite

To retrieve data, you use the query() or rawQuery() method of SQLiteDatabase. These methods allow you to execute SQL queries and return the results as a Cursor object, which you can iterate over to access individual records.

Code Example:

```
fun getAllUsers(): List<User> {
    val users = mutableListOf<User>()
    val db = readableDatabase
    val cursor = db.query(TABLE_NAME, null, null, null, null, null, null)

    if (cursor.moveToFirst()) {
        do {
            val id = cursor.getLong(cursor.getColumnIndex(COLUMN_ID))
            val name = cursor.getString(cursor.getColumnIndex(COLUMN_NAME))
            val email = cursor.getString(cursor.getColumnIndex(COLUMN_EMAIL))
            users.add(User(id, name, email))
        } while (cursor.moveToNext())
    }
    cursor.close()
    db.close()
    return users
}
```

In this example, we use query() to fetch all users from the users table. We iterate over the Cursor to retrieve each user's details and store them in a User object, which is added to a list.

4. Updating and Deleting Data in SQLite

Updating and deleting data in SQLite is straightforward and uses the update() and delete() methods of SQLiteDatabase.

Updating Data:

To update a specific record, you use the update() method, specifying the table name, the values to be updated, and a WHERE clause to identify the record.

Code Example:

```
fun updateUser(id: Long, name: String, email: String) {
    val db = writableDatabase
    val values = ContentValues().apply {
        put(COLUMN_NAME, name)
        put(COLUMN_EMAIL, email)
    }
    val selection = "$COLUMN_ID = ?"
    val selectionArgs = arrayOf(id.toString())
    db.update(TABLE_NAME, values, selection, selectionArgs)
    db.close()
}
```

Deleting Data:

To delete a record, you use the delete() method, specifying the table and a WHERE clause to identify the record to be deleted.

Code Example:

```
fun deleteUser(id: Long) {
    val db = writableDatabase
    val selection = "$COLUMN_ID = ?"
    val selectionArgs = arrayOf(id.toString())
    db.delete(TABLE_NAME, selection, selectionArgs)
    db.close()
}
```

In both cases, after modifying the database, we close the database connection to avoid memory leaks.

5. Best Practices for Using SQLite

- **Use ContentValues for Inserting and Updating**: Always use ContentValues when inserting or updating data. It ensures that data is properly formatted and makes it easier to handle different data types.

- **Avoid Memory Leaks**: Always close the Cursor and database after use. Use try-catch-finally or use in Kotlin to ensure that resources are closed properly.
- **Use Database Transactions**: When performing multiple operations, wrap them in a transaction to ensure atomicity and improve performance. Use beginTransaction(), setTransactionSuccessful(), and endTransaction() to manage transactions.
- **Perform Operations on a Background Thread**: SQLite operations are blocking and can cause the app's UI to freeze. Always perform database operations on a background thread using AsyncTask, ExecutorService, or Kotlin coroutines.

SQLite databases provide a robust solution for storing complex data locally in Android apps. With its support for SQL queries, relational data modeling, and efficient storage, SQLite is ideal for managing large datasets and performing complex data operations. By using the SQLiteOpenHelper to manage your database schema, and leveraging the SQLiteDatabase methods for CRUD operations, you can create efficient, scalable, and responsive Android apps that handle complex data storage needs.

10.4 Simplifying Database Management with Room

While SQLite provides a powerful and flexible method for managing databases in Android, it can be cumbersome to handle manually, especially when dealing with more complex data models or maintaining migrations. To simplify database management, Android provides Room, an abstraction layer over SQLite that facilitates database operations while offering the full power of SQLite. Room is part of Android's Jetpack libraries and aims to make working with databases easier, safer, and more efficient by reducing boilerplate code and promoting best practices.

In this section, we'll explore how to use Room for database management in Android apps. We will cover how to define entities, create data access objects (DAOs), and interact with the database in a more structured and object-oriented way.

1. Introduction to Room Database

Room provides an easy-to-use API that allows developers to define entities (data classes) and access them with simple methods. It abstracts the raw SQL queries and maps Java/Kotlin objects to database tables, ensuring that developers can focus on interacting with objects rather than worrying about SQL syntax.

Key Benefits of Using Room:

- **Object-Oriented Approach**: Maps data to entities and provides an abstraction over SQL, making it easier to interact with the database using objects.
- **Compile-Time Verification**: Room checks SQL queries at compile-time, which reduces the chances of runtime errors due to SQL syntax mistakes.
- **Lifecycle-Aware**: Room is integrated with the Android lifecycle, making it easy to manage database queries in a way that is safe for asynchronous operations.
- **Easier Migration**: Room simplifies database version management and schema migration.

2. Setting Up Room in Your Android Project

To use Room, you need to add the necessary dependencies to your project. This can be done by including Room's libraries in your build.gradle file:

In the build.gradle file (app level):

```
dependencies {
    def room_version = "2.5.0" // Check for the latest version of Room
    implementation "androidx.room:room-runtime:$room_version"
    annotationProcessor "androidx.room:room-compiler:$room_version" // For Java users
    kapt "androidx.room:room-compiler:$room_version" // For Kotlin users
    implementation "androidx.room:room-ktx:$room_version" // Kotlin extensions for
Room
}
```

Once the dependencies are added, you can sync your project, and you're ready to start using Room.

3. Defining Entities

Entities in Room represent the tables in the database. Each entity corresponds to a class annotated with @Entity, and each field within that class corresponds to a column in the database.

Code Example:

```
@Entity(tableName = "users")
data class User(
    @PrimaryKey(autoGenerate = true) val id: Long = 0,
```

```
@ColumnInfo(name = "name") val name: String,
@ColumnInfo(name = "email") val email: String
)
```

In this example, the User class is an entity representing the users table. It has three fields:

- **id**: The primary key of the table, which auto-generates its value.
- **name and email**: Columns in the table, with custom names defined using @ColumnInfo.

4. Creating Data Access Objects (DAOs)

In Room, DAOs (Data Access Objects) are interfaces that provide methods for interacting with the database. DAOs define the queries used to access data and the operations such as insert, update, delete, and query. Room automatically implements these methods at compile-time.

Code Example:

```
@Dao
interface UserDao {

    @Insert
    suspend fun insert(user: User)

    @Update
    suspend fun update(user: User)

    @Delete
    suspend fun delete(user: User)

    @Query("SELECT * FROM users WHERE id = :userId")
    suspend fun getUserById(userId: Long): User?

    @Query("SELECT * FROM users")
    suspend fun getAllUsers(): List<User>
}
```

In this example:

- The @Insert, @Update, and @Delete annotations automatically map to SQL operations.
- The @Query annotation is used to define custom queries, such as fetching a user by id or getting all users.

By using DAOs, you can keep your database interactions in a separate class, making the code cleaner, more maintainable, and less error-prone.

5. Creating the Room Database

To access the Room database, you need to define a database class that extends RoomDatabase. This class serves as the main access point for the database, and it provides access to DAOs.

Code Example:

```
@Database(entities = [User::class], version = 1)
abstract class AppDatabase : RoomDatabase() {
    abstract fun userDao(): UserDao
}
```

Here, the @Database annotation specifies the entities associated with the database (User) and the version number. The AppDatabase class provides an abstract method userDao() to access the UserDao interface.

6. Accessing the Database

Once the database and DAOs are set up, you can create and access the database instance using Room's Room.databaseBuilder() method. This method should be called within the Application or Activity class, and it returns a singleton instance of the database to ensure that only one instance is used throughout the app.

Code Example:

```
val db = Room.databaseBuilder(applicationContext, AppDatabase::class.java,
"my_database")
    .build()

val userDao = db.userDao()
```

```
// Inserting a user (in a coroutine or background thread)
CoroutineScope(Dispatchers.IO).launch {
    val newUser = User(name = "John Doe", email = "john.doe@example.com")
    userDao.insert(newUser)
}
```

In this example, the database instance db is created using Room.databaseBuilder(), and the userDao() method is used to interact with the UserDao. Note that database operations should be done in a background thread, like using coroutines or AsyncTask.

7. Room Migrations

Room handles schema migrations through the Migration class. When you change the structure of the database (e.g., adding or removing a column), you must provide a migration strategy to ensure data integrity and smooth transitions.

Code Example:

```
val MIGRATION_1_2 = object : Migration(1, 2) {
    override fun migrate(database: SupportSQLiteDatabase) {
        // Add a new column to the users table
        database.execSQL("ALTER TABLE users ADD COLUMN phoneNumber TEXT")
    }
}
```

In this migration example, we add a new phoneNumber column to the users table. You would then pass the migration object to Room.databaseBuilder():

```
val db = Room.databaseBuilder(applicationContext, AppDatabase::class.java,
"my_database")
    .addMigrations(MIGRATION_1_2)
    .build()
```

Room ensures that database migrations are smooth, and developers don't need to worry about managing changes manually.

8. Best Practices for Using Room

- **Use Coroutines**: Since Room supports Kotlin coroutines natively, it's best to use coroutines for database operations to prevent blocking the UI thread.

- **Use LiveData or StateFlow for Observing Data**: Room supports returning LiveData or StateFlow from DAO methods, allowing you to observe changes to the database in real-time.
- **Version Management**: Always maintain proper version management and provide migration strategies to ensure the app handles database changes smoothly.
- **Avoid Long Queries on the Main Thread**: Always perform long-running database queries in the background to prevent UI freezes.

Room simplifies working with databases in Android by providing an object-oriented abstraction over SQLite while maintaining the flexibility and power of SQL. It reduces boilerplate code, helps prevent runtime errors, and integrates well with modern Android components like LiveData and ViewModel. By using Room, developers can focus on writing clean, efficient, and maintainable database code without worrying about the complexities of SQL syntax and database management. Room is a great choice for any Android project that requires local data persistence.

10.5 Syncing Local Data with Cloud Solutions

One of the key challenges in modern app development is ensuring that local data on users' devices remains consistent with cloud-based storage. Whether you're building a simple mobile app or a complex enterprise solution, users expect their data to sync seamlessly across devices and platforms. In Android development, this requires implementing reliable synchronization strategies between local storage and cloud solutions.

This section will explore how to manage the synchronization of local data (such as information stored in SQLite databases or Room) with cloud-based databases and storage solutions. We'll discuss various strategies, best practices, and tools to make this process seamless and efficient, ensuring that your app performs well even in low-connectivity situations.

1. Introduction to Syncing Local Data with the Cloud

Syncing local data with cloud solutions means ensuring that data stored on a user's device (e.g., in an SQLite database or using Room) is correctly mirrored or updated in the cloud and vice versa. This is essential for apps that require data persistence across devices, or in cases where users might operate the app offline and later need to sync their actions once the network is available.

Key cloud solutions for data syncing include:

- **Firebase Realtime Database or Firestore**: Google's backend-as-a-service solutions that offer real-time data syncing.
- **Amazon Web Services (AWS):** Includes services like AWS Amplify, which integrates cloud data storage with mobile applications.
- **REST APIs**: Custom APIs that allow mobile apps to interact with cloud storage solutions.

These solutions offer different levels of control, scalability, and complexity. The best choice depends on the specific requirements of your app, such as the need for real-time updates, offline capabilities, and cost considerations.

2. Firebase for Syncing Local Data

Firebase offers two popular databases for Android apps: Firebase Realtime Database and Cloud Firestore. Both databases offer seamless integration with Android apps and automatic syncing of local data with the cloud.

Firebase Realtime Database syncs data in real-time across all clients, while Firestore offers more advanced querying capabilities and scalability. Both databases offer offline support, allowing apps to operate even when there is no internet connection. Once the device reconnects to the network, Firebase automatically syncs the local data with the cloud.

Steps for Firebase Syncing:

- **Setting up Firebase**: Add Firebase to your Android project using Firebase Assistant in Android Studio.
- **Data Model**: Map your local data models to Firebase database structures.
- **Local Data Sync**: Implement listeners in your app to track changes in the local database and automatically push updates to Firebase.

Code Example:

```
val database = FirebaseDatabase.getInstance()
val myRef = database.getReference("users")

// Write to Firebase
myRef.setValue(user)
```

```
// Read from Firebase
myRef.addValueEventListener(object : ValueEventListener {
    override fun onDataChange(dataSnapshot: DataSnapshot) {
        val user = dataSnapshot.getValue(User::class.java)
    }

    override fun onCancelled(databaseError: DatabaseError) {
        // Handle possible errors
    }
})
```

By setting up Firebase listeners and syncing local changes, the app automatically handles syncing and conflict resolution when needed.

3. Using AWS Amplify for Cloud Sync

AWS Amplify is a development platform for building cloud-powered mobile apps. It integrates well with Android apps and provides powerful cloud storage solutions, including Amazon DynamoDB (a NoSQL database) and Amazon S3 (for file storage). AWS Amplify simplifies the setup and management of cloud resources, making it an ideal choice for syncing local data with the cloud.

Steps for AWS Syncing:

- **Set up Amplify**: Initialize Amplify in your project using the AWS Amplify SDK.
- **Use DataStore**: Amplify's DataStore is a persistent storage engine that automatically synchronizes data between the app and the cloud.
- **Local and Cloud Sync**: DataStore syncs data both locally and remotely by handling offline and online scenarios automatically.

Code Example:

```
Amplify.addPlugin(AWSDataStorePlugin())
Amplify.configure(applicationContext)

val post = Post("Hello world", "My first post")
Amplify.DataStore.save(post,
    { Log.i("Tutorial", "Saved item: $it") },
    { error -> Log.e("Tutorial", "Could not save item to DataStore", error) }
```

)

Amplify handles synchronization in the background, making it easy to integrate cloud-based data syncing with minimal setup. The local database automatically syncs changes to the cloud when the network is available, and the app can operate offline without issues.

4. Syncing with REST APIs

For more custom solutions or when working with cloud providers that don't offer direct mobile app synchronization (like AWS or Firebase), you can implement your own API to sync local data with cloud databases. This involves creating a backend service (using technologies like Node.js, Python, Java, etc.) that receives data from the mobile app, updates the cloud database, and sends any necessary updates back to the app.

Steps for API-Based Syncing:

- **Create a Cloud Backend**: Build a REST API that allows your Android app to send and retrieve data from the cloud.
- **Store Local Changes**: Whenever local data changes, the app should store these changes in a queue or a temporary storage.
- **Send Data to the API**: When the device is online, send the local changes to the cloud through the API.
- **Handle Conflicts**: The backend service needs to handle data conflicts if two devices modify the same record concurrently.

Code Example (sending data to an API with Retrofit):

```
interface ApiService {
    @POST("/sync")
    suspend fun syncData(@Body localData: List<MyDataModel>): Response<Void>
}

// Retrofit call
val apiService = Retrofit.Builder()
    .baseUrl("https://api.example.com")
    .build()
    .create(ApiService::class.java)

val response = apiService.syncData(localData)
if (response.isSuccessful) {
```

```
    Log.i("Sync", "Data synced successfully")
}
```

This approach gives you full control over how syncing is handled but requires more effort to implement. You'll need to manage issues such as network retries, offline storage, and conflict resolution.

5. Handling Conflicts and Data Integrity

When syncing data between local storage and the cloud, especially in an offline-first approach, it's essential to have a strategy to manage conflicts. A conflict occurs when two different devices make changes to the same data, and these changes need to be merged correctly.

Common Conflict Resolution Strategies:

- **Last Write Wins (LWW):** The last update received by the cloud database is the one that is considered final.
- **Merge Conflicts**: More sophisticated systems merge changes based on specific rules, such as combining updates from both devices.
- **User Conflict Resolution**: In some cases, it might be necessary to ask the user to resolve conflicts manually.

Firebase and AWS provide built-in conflict resolution mechanisms, but with custom APIs, you'll need to define your approach, whether it's timestamp-based or merge-based.

6. Best Practices for Syncing Data

- **Efficient Syncing**: Instead of syncing entire databases or large sets of data, only sync changed or newly added records. Use tools like Change Data Capture (CDC) or timestamps to detect modifications.
- **Retry Mechanisms**: Implement retry mechanisms for failed network requests to ensure that sync attempts succeed when connectivity is restored.
- **Data Compression**: For large data, compress data before sending it to reduce network usage and improve performance.
- **Batch Updates**: Batch multiple data sync requests together to improve efficiency rather than syncing each record individually.

Syncing local data with cloud solutions is an essential aspect of modern mobile app development, especially for apps that need to operate offline and later sync with the cloud.

Whether using Firebase, AWS Amplify, or custom REST APIs, there are several methods to ensure your app's data stays consistent across devices. By using these cloud solutions and following best practices for conflict resolution, efficient syncing, and managing offline data, you can create a seamless user experience that works reliably in all scenarios.

11. Integrating Modern Technologies

To stay competitive in the ever-evolving tech landscape, integrating modern technologies into your Android apps is crucial. In this chapter, you'll learn how to leverage cutting-edge tools and frameworks like machine learning, augmented reality (AR), and IoT (Internet of Things) to enhance your apps with advanced features. You'll also explore how to implement these technologies effectively, using libraries and APIs that simplify the integration process. By incorporating these innovations, you'll be able to create apps that push the boundaries of what's possible, offering users new and immersive experiences.

11.1 Using TensorFlow Lite for On-Device ML

Machine learning (ML) has become a significant part of modern mobile applications, enabling functionalities like image recognition, voice commands, predictive typing, and more. With the rise of mobile technology, developers are increasingly looking to incorporate machine learning directly into their Android apps. However, running complex machine learning models on mobile devices can be computationally expensive and may strain device resources like memory and battery life.

This is where TensorFlow Lite, an open-source framework developed by Google, comes into play. TensorFlow Lite is a lightweight solution designed specifically for mobile and embedded devices, providing a way to run machine learning models efficiently and with low latency on Android devices.

This section will guide you through the essentials of using TensorFlow Lite to integrate on-device machine learning into your Android app. By the end of this section, you'll be able to set up TensorFlow Lite, load pre-trained models, and perform inference directly on Android devices, improving the overall performance and user experience of your app.

1. Introduction to TensorFlow Lite

TensorFlow Lite is the mobile-optimized version of the widely-used TensorFlow machine learning framework. It was designed to meet the unique requirements of mobile devices, including limited processing power, memory, and battery life. TensorFlow Lite offers a set of tools and APIs to convert, optimize, and run ML models directly on Android devices with minimal latency and low power consumption.

TensorFlow Lite has multiple key advantages:

- **Efficiency**: It's optimized to run ML models with reduced memory and CPU footprint.
- **Cross-Platform**: While we focus on Android here, TensorFlow Lite also works across iOS and other embedded systems.
- **Flexibility**: Supports a wide range of ML models such as image classification, natural language processing, and regression models.
- **Pre-Trained Models**: TensorFlow Lite supports a large collection of pre-trained models, making it easy to get started without needing to train models from scratch.

2. Setting Up TensorFlow Lite in Your Android Project

Before you can use TensorFlow Lite, you'll need to set up your Android project. This involves adding TensorFlow Lite dependencies to your project and ensuring the necessary tools are available.

Steps:

Add Dependencies: In your build.gradle file, add TensorFlow Lite dependencies under the dependencies block:

```
implementation 'org.tensorflow:tensorflow-lite:2.12.0'
implementation 'org.tensorflow:tensorflow-lite-support:2.12.0'
implementation 'org.tensorflow:tensorflow-lite-task-vision:2.12.0' // For image models
```

Sync Project: Once the dependencies are added, sync the project to download the required libraries.

Prepare TensorFlow Lite Model: You can either convert an existing TensorFlow model into a TensorFlow Lite model or use one of the pre-trained models available from TensorFlow Hub or the TensorFlow Lite Model Zoo. To convert a model, use the TensorFlow Lite converter to optimize and reduce its size.

Example TensorFlow Lite conversion:

```
import tensorflow as tf
model = tf.keras.models.load_model('model.h5')
converter = tf.lite.TFLiteConverter.from_keras_model(model)
tflite_model = converter.convert()
open("model.tflite", "wb").write(tflite_model)
```

Add the Model to Your Project: Place the .tflite model file into the assets folder of your Android project.

3. Loading and Running a TensorFlow Lite Model on Android

Once you've set up the environment and added the TensorFlow Lite model to your project, the next step is loading and running inference with the model.

Steps:

Load the Model: Use the Interpreter class from TensorFlow Lite to load your model into memory.

```
val tfliteOptions = Interpreter.Options()
val interpreter = Interpreter(loadModelFile("model.tflite"), tfliteOptions)
```

Prepare the Input Data: Depending on the type of model (e.g., image classification, speech recognition), you need to format your input data correctly. For an image classification model, you would typically preprocess the image to a fixed size (e.g., 224x224 for a pre-trained model) and normalize pixel values to a range between 0 and 1.

Run Inference: Once the input data is ready, you can pass it to the model for inference:

```
val input = arrayOf<FloatArray>(FloatArray(224 * 224)) // Example input for image
val output = Array(1) { FloatArray(1000) }  // Output array for the results

interpreter.run(input, output)
```

Post-Process the Output: The model will output the results in a specific format. For image classification, it might return a set of probabilities for each class. You can post-process the output to interpret the result (e.g., finding the class with the highest probability).

4. Optimizing TensorFlow Lite Models for Mobile Devices

While TensorFlow Lite is already optimized for mobile devices, there are further optimizations you can make to ensure your app performs well, especially for more complex models or devices with lower resources.

Optimizations to consider:

Quantization: This reduces the precision of the numbers used by the model, typically from 32-bit floating point to 8-bit integers, leading to smaller model sizes and faster inference.

converter.optimizations = [tf.lite.Optimize.DEFAULT]
converter.target_spec.supported_ops = [tf.lite.OpsSet.TFLITE_BUILTINS_INT8]

Model Pruning: This involves removing unnecessary weights from the model, reducing its size and improving inference time without losing accuracy.

Delegate Support: TensorFlow Lite supports hardware acceleration via delegates (e.g., GPU delegate, NNAPI delegate, or DSP delegate). You can enable this to take advantage of hardware-specific optimizations for faster processing:

val tfliteOptions = Interpreter.Options().addDelegate(NnApiDelegate())

Edge Devices and Accelerators: If you are working with specialized hardware like Google's Edge TPU or other ML accelerators, you can use TensorFlow Lite's Edge TPU delegate for hardware-accelerated inference. This allows for high-speed ML processing on resource-constrained devices.

5. Use Cases for On-Device Machine Learning with TensorFlow Lite

There are many practical applications for TensorFlow Lite in Android apps, including:

- **Image Recognition**: TensorFlow Lite can be used for real-time object detection, facial recognition, and image classification in apps.
- **Natural Language Processing (NLP):** Use models for text classification, sentiment analysis, or even chatbots that function offline.
- **Voice Recognition**: Integrate on-device speech-to-text or voice command recognition in your apps.
- **Anomaly Detection**: For apps that monitor systems or track sensor data (e.g., health or fitness apps), TensorFlow Lite can be used for real-time anomaly detection.

Example: Using TensorFlow Lite for Object Detection For an image classification model, you can use TensorFlow Lite to recognize objects in an image and take action based on the results. Here's how it might work in an app:

```
val inputImage = preprocessImage(bitmap)
val result = runObjectDetectionModel(inputImage)
displayResults(result)
```

TensorFlow Lite empowers Android developers to integrate powerful machine learning models directly into their apps, allowing for real-time, on-device inference. By setting up TensorFlow Lite, loading models, and optimizing them for mobile devices, developers can create intelligent apps that are responsive, efficient, and able to function even in offline scenarios. Whether you're building apps with image recognition, voice assistants, or other AI-driven features, TensorFlow Lite makes it possible to perform high-performance machine learning tasks on mobile devices without compromising user experience.

11.2 Integrating Augmented Reality with ARCore

Augmented Reality (AR) has rapidly gained traction in the mobile app development space, offering users immersive and interactive experiences that blend the real world with virtual objects. From gaming to education, retail, and healthcare, AR is transforming how we interact with the world around us. With the advent of ARCore, Google's platform for building AR experiences, Android developers can easily create apps that incorporate AR elements, enhancing the user experience.

ARCore allows you to develop AR apps on Android devices with powerful features such as motion tracking, environmental understanding, and light estimation. By integrating ARCore into your Android apps, you can create dynamic, real-time interactions with virtual content overlaid onto the physical world.

This section will walk you through the steps of integrating ARCore into your Android projects, including setting up the environment, creating a basic AR experience, and enhancing the functionality of your AR app with advanced features.

1. Introduction to ARCore

ARCore is Google's software development kit (SDK) for building augmented reality experiences on Android devices. ARCore enables your device to detect and track its surroundings and place virtual content overlaid on the real world in real-time. It does this through three core features:

- **Motion Tracking**: ARCore tracks the position and orientation of the device by detecting feature points in the environment, allowing virtual objects to stay in place as the device moves.
- **Environmental Understanding**: ARCore detects flat surfaces like tables and floors, providing a foundation for virtual objects to be anchored and interact with the real world.
- **Light Estimation**: ARCore estimates the lighting conditions of the environment, enabling virtual objects to match the lighting and shadows of the physical world for a more realistic experience.

Together, these features provide the foundation for building compelling AR apps that can integrate with the real world.

2. Setting Up ARCore in Your Android Project

To get started with ARCore, you need to integrate it into your Android Studio project. This involves adding dependencies, setting up your app's manifest, and ensuring that your device supports ARCore.

Steps:

Add ARCore Dependencies: Begin by adding the ARCore SDK dependencies in your build.gradle (Module: app) file.

```
dependencies {
    implementation 'com.google.ar:core:1.31.0'  // ARCore SDK
    implementation 'com.google.ar.sceneform:core:1.17.1'  // Sceneform for 3D content rendering
}
```

Sync Your Project: Once you've added the necessary dependencies, sync your project with Gradle.

Update Your Android Manifest: You need to declare the ARCore features in your app's AndroidManifest.xml file. This ensures that the app only runs on devices that support ARCore.

```
<uses-feature android:name="android.hardware.camera" android:required="true" />
<uses-feature android:name="android.hardware.camera.ar" android:required="true" />
<uses-permission android:name="android.permission.CAMERA" />
```

ARCore Supported Devices: ARCore is supported on a range of Android devices. Ensure your target device supports ARCore by checking the ARCore device list provided by Google.

3. Creating a Simple AR Experience

Once your environment is set up, you can create a simple AR experience by displaying a 3D object or image on a flat surface in the user's environment. For this example, we will place a virtual object (such as a 3D model) in the user's physical space.

Steps:

Create a SceneView: Use the ArFragment from Sceneform (a library that simplifies ARCore integration) to display AR content. The ArFragment manages the session, rendering, and touch events for your AR app.

In your activity layout XML, add the ArFragment to the view:

```
<com.google.ar.sceneform.ux.ArFragment
    android:id="@+id/fragment"
    android:name="com.google.ar.sceneform.ux.ArFragment"
    android:layout_width="match_parent"
    android:layout_height="match_parent" />
```

Add 3D Models: ARCore uses Sceneform to display 3D models in the AR scene. You can either create custom 3D models or use pre-built models in .glb or .gltf format. Once you have your 3D model, you can load it into your AR scene.

Example of loading a 3D model:

```
val modelUri = Uri.parse("model.sfb")  // Load model from assets
ModelRenderable.builder()
    .setSource(this, modelUri)
    .build()
    .thenAccept { modelRenderable ->
        placeObject(modelRenderable)
    }
```

Place Objects in the AR World: Use touch gestures to place the object on detected surfaces. ARCore allows you to detect flat surfaces (such as floors or tables) and place your virtual objects accordingly.

Example code to place the object:

```
fun placeObject(modelRenderable: ModelRenderable) {
    val frame = arFragment.arSceneView.arFrame
    val hitResult = frame?.hitTest(x, y)?.firstOrNull()

    if (hitResult != null) {
        val anchor = hitResult.createAnchor()
        val anchorNode = AnchorNode(anchor)
        val modelNode = TransformableNode(arFragment.transformationSystem)
        modelNode.renderable = modelRenderable
        anchorNode.addChild(modelNode)
        arFragment.arSceneView.scene.addChild(anchorNode)
    }
}
```

Handle Touch Events: You can allow users to interact with the AR scene by adding touch event handlers. For example, tapping on the screen will place the virtual object at the tapped location.

4. Enhancing the AR Experience with Additional Features

Once you have a basic AR experience running, you can enhance it with more interactive features, such as object scaling, rotation, or multiple object placement.

Examples of advanced features:

Object Scaling and Rotation: Use gestures such as pinch-to-zoom or drag to scale and rotate 3D objects in the AR world.

```
modelNode.setOnTapListener { hitTestResult, motionEvent ->
    // Handle rotation or scaling of the model
}
```

Multiple Object Placement: Allow the user to place multiple objects within the scene by detecting additional touch events or gestures.

AR-based Games and Experiences: Add interactivity and logic to your AR experience, such as using AR for gaming applications (e.g., placing virtual characters in the real world).

Adding Light Estimation: Use ARCore's light estimation feature to adjust the lighting and shadows of the 3D model to make it look more realistic. The LightEstimate can provide values for ambient light and the environmental light direction, which you can apply to your objects.

```
val lightEstimate = frame?.getUpdatedLightEstimate()
val intensity = lightEstimate?.pixelIntensity ?: 1.0f
```

5. Debugging and Testing ARCore Apps

Testing AR apps can be tricky, as they rely on real-world environments and hardware sensors. To ensure that your AR app works correctly, consider the following tips:

- **ARCore Device Simulation**: Use ARCore's simulation features in Android Studio to simulate different lighting conditions and surfaces.
- **Real-World Testing**: Test your app on physical devices that support ARCore to verify performance and functionality in actual environments.
- **Device Calibration**: Ensure that the device's sensors (e.g., accelerometer, gyroscope, camera) are calibrated properly for accurate motion tracking and surface detection.

Integrating ARCore into your Android apps allows you to create immersive and interactive augmented reality experiences that enhance user engagement. By leveraging ARCore's motion tracking, environmental understanding, and light estimation, developers can place virtual objects in the real world, allowing users to interact with and explore their surroundings in innovative ways. Whether you are building a gaming app, an educational tool, or a shopping app with AR product previews, ARCore provides the tools and capabilities to bring your ideas to life with augmented reality on Android devices.

11.3 Connecting IoT Devices to Android Apps

The Internet of Things (IoT) has revolutionized how devices communicate with one another, and Android apps play a key role in enabling users to control, monitor, and interact with a wide range of IoT devices. Whether you're developing smart home systems, wearables, industrial sensors, or health devices, Android offers numerous ways to connect to and manage IoT devices, making it an ideal platform for building connected applications.

In this section, we'll explore the key concepts of integrating IoT devices with Android apps, the various communication protocols used in IoT, and how you can seamlessly establish and manage these connections. We'll cover everything from setting up Bluetooth and Wi-Fi communications to using cloud-based services and real-time communication platforms, ensuring that your app can interact with IoT devices in a variety of contexts.

1. Overview of IoT in Android Development

IoT refers to the network of physical objects—devices, vehicles, home appliances, sensors—that are embedded with sensors, software, and other technologies that allow them to collect and exchange data. As Android devices are increasingly becoming central hubs for managing and controlling IoT devices, Android development must support a variety of protocols and services to interact with these smart devices.

IoT-enabled Android apps allow users to connect to and manage devices remotely, providing a seamless interaction between the physical and digital world. With Android's built-in support for technologies like Bluetooth, Wi-Fi, NFC, and cloud platforms, developers can build rich IoT experiences directly within their apps.

2. Common Communication Protocols for IoT Devices

Before diving into integrating IoT devices with Android apps, it's important to understand the communication protocols commonly used in IoT ecosystems. These protocols are responsible for enabling data exchange between devices and your app.

Key Communication Protocols:

- **Bluetooth Low Energy (BLE):** BLE is widely used for low-power communication over short distances. IoT devices like smart wearables, health trackers, and home automation systems often use BLE to communicate with Android devices.
- **Wi-Fi**: Wi-Fi is commonly used for IoT devices that require a stable and high-speed connection. Devices like smart thermostats, security cameras, and smart speakers often use Wi-Fi to connect to a home or office network.
- **Zigbee and Z-Wave**: These are wireless communication protocols commonly used in smart home devices. While Android doesn't natively support these

protocols, developers can use additional hardware bridges or gateways to communicate with Zigbee and Z-Wave devices.

- **NFC (Near Field Communication):** NFC is a short-range wireless technology used for simple communication, such as tapping a phone to an IoT device for quick configuration or data exchange.
- **MQTT (Message Queuing Telemetry Transport):** MQTT is a lightweight messaging protocol used in cloud-based IoT applications. It is widely used for real-time communication between IoT devices and cloud servers.

By understanding these protocols, you can determine the best method to connect your Android app to the target IoT devices.

3. Using Bluetooth to Connect IoT Devices

One of the most common methods for connecting Android apps to IoT devices is Bluetooth Low Energy (BLE). BLE is energy-efficient and suitable for applications where devices need to communicate over short distances, such as connecting an Android phone to a smart lightbulb or a wearable device.

Steps for Bluetooth Integration:

Enable Bluetooth Permissions: Before you can use Bluetooth in your app, you must request the necessary permissions in your AndroidManifest.xml file.

```
<uses-permission android:name="android.permission.BLUETOOTH"/>
<uses-permission android:name="android.permission.BLUETOOTH_ADMIN"/>
<uses-permission android:name="android.permission.ACCESS_FINE_LOCATION"/>
```

Initialize Bluetooth Adapter: Use Android's BluetoothAdapter to detect available Bluetooth devices.

```
val bluetoothAdapter: BluetoothAdapter? = BluetoothAdapter.getDefaultAdapter()
if (bluetoothAdapter == null || !bluetoothAdapter.isEnabled) {
    // Prompt the user to enable Bluetooth
}
```

Scan for Devices: Use BluetoothLeScanner to scan for nearby BLE devices. Devices can be filtered based on their advertising data.

```
val scanner = bluetoothAdapter.bluetoothLeScanner
```

scanner.startScan(scanCallback)

Connect to a Device: Once a target device is found, establish a connection by creating a BluetoothGatt object to handle communication with the device.

val gatt = device.connectGatt(context, false, gattCallback)

Read/Write Data: Once connected, you can read and write data to the device's characteristics.

val characteristic =
bluetoothGattService.getCharacteristic(UUID.fromString(SAMPLE_CHARACTERISTIC)
)
bluetoothGatt.readCharacteristic(characteristic)

Disconnect: After the interaction is complete, remember to disconnect from the device to save power.

bluetoothGatt.disconnect()
bluetoothGatt.close()

4. Using Wi-Fi for IoT Connectivity

Wi-Fi-based IoT devices are increasingly common due to their reliable and high-speed connection. These devices typically connect to a local network or the internet, allowing users to control and monitor them remotely.

Steps for Wi-Fi Integration:

Connect to the Device's Network: Many IoT devices, such as smart cameras or smart speakers, have their own Wi-Fi networks that you need to connect to first for configuration.

You can either use Android's native Wi-Fi APIs or direct device configuration methods to establish this initial connection.

Establish a Cloud Connection: After the device is connected to the network, you can interact with it by connecting to a cloud service (such as Firebase or AWS IoT). These services can facilitate communication between your Android app and IoT devices over the internet.

HTTP or MQTT Communication: Once connected, you can send commands to the device via HTTP requests or through protocols like MQTT.

Use Retrofit or Volley libraries to send HTTP requests to an IoT device's RESTful API. Alternatively, you can use MQTT for real-time communication with the device or cloud.

5. Using Cloud Services for IoT Integration

Cloud platforms play a critical role in the IoT ecosystem, providing scalable storage, real-time communication, and device management. Platforms like Firebase, Google Cloud IoT, and AWS IoT allow developers to connect Android apps to a wide variety of IoT devices.

Steps for Cloud-based IoT Integration:

Firebase Cloud Messaging (FCM): Firebase offers Cloud Messaging (FCM) to send real-time notifications to Android devices. You can use FCM to notify users of status updates or alerts from IoT devices.

IoT Cloud Platforms: AWS IoT, Google Cloud IoT, and Microsoft Azure IoT provide SDKs and APIs that facilitate the integration of Android apps with cloud-connected devices. These platforms allow devices to send data to the cloud, and Android apps can retrieve or control them remotely.

MQTT Protocol: Many IoT systems rely on MQTT as a lightweight messaging protocol for real-time communication. Using the MQTT protocol, you can publish and subscribe to topics on a cloud service to exchange data between the Android app and the IoT device.

6. Real-Time Communication with WebSockets

For IoT devices that require real-time bidirectional communication, WebSockets can provide a persistent connection between the Android app and the device. WebSockets are ideal for applications like home automation, where immediate feedback and control are needed.

Steps for Real-Time Communication with WebSockets:

Integrating WebSocket Library: To implement WebSocket communication in your Android app, you can use libraries like OkHttp or Java-WebSocket.

```
implementation 'com.squareup.okhttp3:okhttp:4.9.1'
```

Open a WebSocket Connection: Establish a WebSocket connection to the server or IoT device.

```
val client = OkHttpClient()
val request = Request.Builder().url("ws://example.com/socket").build()
val webSocket = client.newWebSocket(request, webSocketListener)
```

Send and Receive Data: Once connected, you can send and receive data in real-time.

```
webSocket.send("Command to Device")
webSocket.onMessage { message -> processMessage(message) }
```

Integrating IoT devices with Android apps offers endless possibilities for building innovative, connected experiences. By leveraging Bluetooth, Wi-Fi, cloud services, and real-time communication protocols like MQTT and WebSockets, Android developers can enable users to interact with and control IoT devices seamlessly. Whether building a smart home app, wearable device, or a health-tracking system, understanding the communication protocols and integration strategies will ensure that your app can connect to the broad spectrum of IoT devices that make the world smarter and more connected.

11.4 Leveraging Google APIs for Maps and Location

The integration of location-based services into Android apps is a crucial feature for many applications today, from navigation apps to delivery services and real-time tracking systems. Google provides a powerful set of APIs—known as Google Maps and Location Services—designed to help Android developers easily incorporate location-based features. These APIs offer robust solutions for mapping, location tracking, geofencing, and more, enabling developers to create seamless and interactive experiences for users.

In this section, we'll explore how to leverage Google's Maps and Location APIs to enhance your Android apps. You will learn how to integrate maps, access real-time location data, and use geospatial features such as reverse geocoding, places search, and geofencing to enrich your app's functionality.

1. Introduction to Google Maps and Location APIs

Google's location-based services are split into several key components, which can be used individually or in combination, depending on the needs of the app. Two of the most important Google services for location-based functionality are:

- **Google Maps API**: Provides access to Google's rich map data, including map rendering, markers, camera controls, polygons, routes, and more.
- **Google Location Services API**: Offers location data, such as the current location of the device, and allows tracking and managing user locations, as well as geofencing and location updates.

Both these APIs simplify the process of working with geographical data, helping you avoid reinventing the wheel for tasks like showing a map or retrieving the user's current location.

2. Setting Up Google Maps API in Your Android App

To get started with Google Maps, you'll need to set up your Android app to use the Google Maps API by following these steps:

Create a Google Cloud Project:

- Go to the Google Cloud Console.
- Create a new project, and enable the Maps SDK for Android and Places API.

Get an API Key:

- Once you've enabled the necessary APIs, generate an API key from the Cloud Console. This key will be used to authenticate your app's requests to the Google Maps service.

Add Google Play Services to Your App:

In your build.gradle (app-level) file, add the necessary dependencies to integrate Google Play Services:

implementation 'com.google.android.gms:play-services-maps:17.0.1'
implementation 'com.google.android.gms:play-services-location:17.0.0'

Add API Key to the Manifest:

Include the generated API key in your app's AndroidManifest.xml file:

```
<application>
  <meta-data
    android:name="com.google.android.geo.API_KEY"
    android:value="@string/google_maps_api_key"/>
</application>
```

Display a Map:

In your activity, use MapFragment or SupportMapFragment to display the map:

```
class MapActivity : AppCompatActivity(), OnMapReadyCallback {
  private lateinit var mMap: GoogleMap

  override fun onCreate(savedInstanceState: Bundle?) {
    super.onCreate(savedInstanceState)
    setContentView(R.layout.activity_map)

    val mapFragment = supportFragmentManager
      .findFragmentById(R.id.map) as SupportMapFragment
    mapFragment.getMapAsync(this)
  }

  override fun onMapReady(googleMap: GoogleMap) {
    mMap = googleMap
    // Custom map configurations or add markers here
  }
}
```

3. Adding Markers and Customizing the Map

Once the basic map is set up, you can add markers to the map, customize the view, and allow users to interact with the map.

Adding a Marker: You can add markers to represent places of interest on the map.

```
val markerOptions = MarkerOptions().position(LatLng(37.7749, -122.4194)).title("San Francisco")
mMap.addMarker(markerOptions)
```

Camera Controls: You can also change the view of the map by adjusting the camera position.

```
val cameraPosition = CameraPosition.Builder()
    .target(LatLng(37.7749, -122.4194)) // San Francisco
    .zoom(12f)
    .build()
mMap.moveCamera(CameraUpdateFactory.newCameraPosition(cameraPosition))
```

Polylines and Shapes: You can draw routes or boundaries on the map using polylines and polygons.

```
val polylineOptions = PolylineOptions().add(LatLng(37.7749, -122.4194),
LatLng(34.0522, -118.2437))
mMap.addPolyline(polylineOptions)
```

4. Using Google Location Services API

Google Location Services provides a simple and efficient way to access location data from the device. You can retrieve the current location, track location changes, and manage geofences.

Getting the Current Location: To get the current location of the device, you can use the FusedLocationProviderClient, which provides a simple API for accessing location data.

```
val fusedLocationClient = LocationServices.getFusedLocationProviderClient(this)
fusedLocationClient.lastLocation.addOnSuccessListener { location: Location? ->
    if (location != null) {
        val lat = location.latitude
        val lng = location.longitude
        // Do something with the location
    }
}
```

Requesting Location Updates: If you want to track the user's location over time, you can request periodic updates.

```
val locationRequest = LocationRequest.create().apply {
    interval = 10000 // 10 seconds
    fastestInterval = 5000 // 5 seconds
```

```
        priority = LocationRequest.PRIORITY_HIGH_ACCURACY
}

val locationCallback = object : LocationCallback() {
    override fun onLocationResult(locationResult: LocationResult?) {
        locationResult?.locations?.let { locations ->
            // Handle location updates
        }
    }
}

fusedLocationClient.requestLocationUpdates(locationRequest, locationCallback,
Looper.getMainLooper())
```

5. Geofencing with Google APIs

Geofencing allows you to define geographical boundaries around specific locations.
When a user enters or exits a geofenced area, the app can trigger events like notifications.

Creating a Geofence: To create a geofence, you need to define a geographical area
using a Geofence object and a GeofencingRequest to specify how the system should
react when the user crosses the boundary.

```
val geofence = Geofence.Builder()
    .setRequestId("geo_fence_id")
    .setCircularRegion(
        37.7749, // Latitude
        -122.4194, // Longitude
        100f // Radius in meters
    )
    .setExpirationDuration(Geofence.NEVER_EXPIRE)
    .setTransitionTypes(Geofence.GEOFENCE_TRANSITION_ENTER or
Geofence.GEOFENCE_TRANSITION_EXIT)
    .build()
```

Monitoring Geofence Events: After setting up the geofence, register it with the
GeofencingClient to start monitoring the region.

```
val geofencingClient = LocationServices.getGeofencingClient(this)
val geofenceRequest = GeofencingRequest.Builder()
```

```
    .addGeofence(geofence)
    .setInitialTrigger(GeofencingRequest.INITIAL_TRIGGER_ENTER)
    .build()

val geofencePendingIntent: PendingIntent = // Create a pending intent to receive
geofence events
geofencingClient.addGeofences(geofenceRequest, geofencePendingIntent)
```

6. Reverse Geocoding and Places Search

Google also offers APIs for reverse geocoding (converting coordinates to a physical address) and searching for places (like restaurants, parks, etc.).

Reverse Geocoding: Reverse geocoding allows you to obtain a human-readable address from latitude and longitude.

```
val geocoder = Geocoder(this, Locale.getDefault())
val addresses = geocoder.getFromLocation(latitude, longitude, 1)
if (addresses.isNotEmpty()) {
    val address = addresses[0].getAddressLine(0)
}
```

Places Search: You can search for places nearby using the Google Places API, which helps users find businesses, landmarks, and other locations of interest.

```
val placesClient = Places.createClient(this)
val request = FindCurrentPlaceRequest.newInstance(fields)
placesClient.findCurrentPlace(request).addOnSuccessListener { response ->
    for (placeLikelihood in response.placeLikelihoods) {
        val place = placeLikelihood.place
        // Handle places search results
    }
}
```

Leveraging Google Maps and Location APIs in Android apps allows you to integrate powerful location-based features, such as mapping, geofencing, reverse geocoding, and places search. By using Google's tools, you can create interactive and intuitive apps that help users navigate the world around them. Whether you're developing a navigation app, real-time tracking system, or a location-based service, integrating Google's Maps and

Location Services will enhance the user experience and provide dynamic, location-aware functionality.

11.5 Exploring WearOS and Smartwatch Integration

WearOS, Google's operating system for smartwatches and wearable devices, opens up exciting possibilities for extending your Android app's reach and functionality. With the increasing popularity of wearable technology, integrating WearOS into your app allows you to deliver seamless, on-the-go user experiences that complement smartphones. WearOS provides a robust framework to create apps that interact with Android devices, share data, and take advantage of unique wearable features like sensors, notifications, and fitness tracking.

This section provides an overview of WearOS and explores how to integrate it into your Android app. You will learn about the WearOS ecosystem, tools for development, and strategies to create engaging smartwatch experiences that keep users connected and informed.

1. Introduction to WearOS

WearOS is designed to provide a lightweight, hands-free user experience optimized for smaller screens. It integrates tightly with Android and Google services, offering:

- **Customizable Watch Faces**: Users can personalize their smartwatch with interactive, stylish watch faces.
- **Health and Fitness Features**: WearOS supports activity tracking, heart rate monitoring, and integration with fitness APIs.
- **Notifications and Quick Actions**: Users can receive notifications and interact with apps directly from their wrists.
- **Voice Commands**: Google Assistant is built into WearOS, enabling hands-free interactions.

WearOS apps can either run standalone on smartwatches or work as companion apps that synchronize with an Android smartphone.

2. Setting Up WearOS Development Environment

Developing for WearOS requires specific tools and configurations. Here's how to get started:

Install Android Studio:

Ensure that you have the latest version of Android Studio installed.

Enable WearOS Modules:

Create a WearOS module in your existing project by selecting File > New > New Module > Wear OS Module in Android Studio.

Configure the Emulator:

Use the Android Virtual Device (AVD) Manager to create a WearOS emulator for testing.

Choose a WearOS device profile, such as a round or square watch face, and configure its specifications.

Dependencies:

Add the necessary dependencies in your app's build.gradle file for WearOS support:

implementation 'com.google.android.wearable:wearable:2.9.0'
implementation 'androidx.wear:wear:1.2.0'

Testing on Physical Devices:

For a realistic testing experience, connect a WearOS smartwatch to your development machine via Bluetooth or Wi-Fi.

3. Designing for WearOS

Wearable devices have unique design constraints, including smaller screens and different interaction patterns. Follow these design principles to create intuitive and efficient WearOS apps:

Compact and Focused Interfaces:

- Use concise layouts and large touch targets to ensure usability on small screens.
- Avoid overcrowding the interface with too much information.

Voice and Gesture Inputs:

- Leverage voice commands and simple gestures for hands-free interactions.
- Use Google's Actions on Google to implement voice actions.

Watch Faces:

Create custom watch faces using the Watch Face API, allowing users to personalize their device while providing relevant app data.

Consistency with Material Design:

Follow WearOS design guidelines, which are an extension of Android's Material Design principles, tailored for wearables.

Battery Optimization:

Minimize background activity and optimize code to reduce power consumption on limited-capacity smartwatch batteries.

4. Developing WearOS Features

WearOS supports a range of features that can enhance your app's functionality. Here are a few key use cases:

4.1 Notifications for Wearables

WearOS supports notifications synchronized with the paired smartphone. Customize notifications to make them actionable and informative:

Add wearable-specific actions using NotificationCompat.Action.

Use WearableExtender to extend notifications for the smartwatch display:

```
val notification = NotificationCompat.Builder(context, CHANNEL_ID)
    .setContentTitle("Reminder")
    .setContentText("It's time to exercise!")
    .extend(NotificationCompat.WearableExtender())
    .build()
```

4.2 Fitness and Health Integration

WearOS is heavily used in fitness tracking. Use the Google Fit API to access health and activity data like step counts, heart rates, and workout details.

Collect fitness data:

```
val fitnessOptions = FitnessOptions.builder()
   .addDataType(DataType.TYPE_STEP_COUNT_DELTA,
FitnessOptions.ACCESS_READ)
   .build()

val steps = Fitness.getHistoryClient(this, GoogleSignIn.getAccountForExtension(this,
fitnessOptions))
   .readDailyTotal(DataType.TYPE_STEP_COUNT_DELTA)
```

4.3 Data Synchronization with Smartphones

The Data Layer API enables data sharing between a WearOS device and a connected smartphone. Use it to synchronize app states, settings, or user inputs.

Send data:

```
val dataClient = Wearable.getDataClient(context)
val putDataMapReq = PutDataMapRequest.create("/path").apply {
   dataMap.putString("key", "value")
}
val putDataReq = putDataMapReq.asPutDataRequest()
dataClient.putDataItem(putDataReq)
```

Listen for data changes:

```
Wearable.getDataClient(context).addListener { dataEventBuffer ->
   for (event in dataEventBuffer) {
     if (event.type == DataEvent.TYPE_CHANGED) {
        val dataMap = DataMapItem.fromDataItem(event.dataItem).dataMap
     }
   }
}
```

4.4 Standalone Apps

Develop standalone WearOS apps that work independently of a smartphone. This approach is useful for fitness apps or utilities that require minimal interaction with other devices.

Add the standalone capability in the manifest:

```
<meta-data
  android:name="com.google.android.wearable.standalone"
  android:value="true" />
```

5. Testing and Deployment

WearOS apps require rigorous testing to ensure smooth operation on various devices and configurations.

Test on Emulators and Devices:

- Use the WearOS emulator to simulate different screen sizes and interactions.
- Test on physical devices to evaluate performance, gestures, and user comfort.

Debugging:

Use Android Studio's debugging tools to troubleshoot issues, especially with data synchronization and battery consumption.

App Deployment:

Publish your app to the Google Play Store with the WearOS category selected to ensure proper discovery by smartwatch users.

6. Real-World Applications

WearOS integration can add value to various types of apps:

- **Health and Fitness**: Apps like step counters, workout trackers, and heart rate monitors benefit from smartwatch capabilities.
- **Productivity Tools**: Calendar reminders, task managers, and voice-to-text note apps keep users organized.

- **Navigation**: Display turn-by-turn directions on a watch face for on-the-go convenience.
- **IoT and Home Automation**: Smartwatch controls for smart home devices enhance user accessibility.

WearOS provides a versatile platform for expanding your Android app's functionality and engaging with users in innovative ways. By creating tailored experiences for smartwatches, you can meet the needs of the modern user who values convenience, connectivity, and style. As the wearable market continues to grow, mastering WearOS integration will ensure your apps remain relevant and appealing in this rapidly evolving ecosystem.

Part 4: Performance, Deployment, and Beyond

Building a great Android app doesn't end with development—it's equally important to ensure your app performs well, reaches users effectively, and continues to evolve. Part 4 of this book covers critical topics like optimizing app performance, managing memory, and reducing battery consumption. You'll also learn how to prepare your app for deployment, from testing and debugging to publishing it on the Google Play Store. Finally, this section explores strategies for app maintenance, updates, and scaling, ensuring your app stays relevant and continues to provide an exceptional user experience long after launch.

12. Optimizing App Performance

Performance is a critical factor in user satisfaction, and a slow or resource-hungry app can drive users away. In this chapter, you'll learn how to optimize the performance of your Android app by improving speed, responsiveness, and efficiency. You'll explore techniques for memory management, reducing app load times, optimizing UI rendering, and minimizing battery usage. With a focus on best practices and profiling tools, this chapter will help you fine-tune your app, ensuring it runs smoothly and delivers a seamless experience to users, even on low-end devices.

12.1 Identifying Memory Leaks with Profiler Tools

Memory management is critical for ensuring the performance and stability of Android applications. Memory leaks, which occur when objects are not properly released after they are no longer needed, can lead to increased memory usage, app slowdowns, and even crashes. Identifying and addressing these leaks early in development is essential for creating robust applications.

In this section, we'll explore how to identify memory leaks using Android Profiler tools. These tools provide insights into memory usage patterns, help locate problematic objects, and assist in diagnosing issues related to garbage collection and memory retention. By mastering these techniques, you can optimize your app's performance and improve the user experience.

Understanding Memory Leaks

A memory leak occurs when an object in memory is unintentionally held by another reference, preventing it from being garbage collected. Common causes include:

- **Static References**: Static variables that continue to hold references to objects.
- **Activity/Fragment Leaks:** Keeping references to an activity or fragment after it has been destroyed.
- **Listener or Callback Mismanagement**: Forgetting to unregister listeners or callbacks.
- **Inner Classes**: Non-static inner classes that hold implicit references to their enclosing classes.

These leaks lead to increased memory usage, which, over time, can cause the app to run out of memory.

Using Android Profiler Tools

The Android Profiler in Android Studio is a powerful suite of tools that helps monitor your app's performance, including memory usage. Here's how to use it effectively:

1. Open Android Profiler

- Launch your app in Android Studio.
- Open the Profiler by navigating to View > Tool Windows > Profiler.
- Select your device or emulator to start profiling.

2. Switch to the Memory Tab

- In the Profiler window, click on the Memory tab.
- Observe real-time memory usage, including allocated memory, garbage collection events, and native memory usage.

3. Capturing a Heap Dump

Heap dumps are snapshots of memory usage at a specific point in time. They show all objects in memory and their references.

- Click Dump Java Heap to capture a heap dump.
- Analyze the captured dump to identify objects consuming excessive memory or persisting unnecessarily.

4. Analyzing Memory Allocation

The Allocation Tracker lets you see which parts of your code allocate specific objects.

- Enable memory allocation tracking by clicking Record Allocations.
- Perform actions in your app that might lead to memory leaks.
- Stop the recording and review allocations to pinpoint excessive or unnecessary object creation.

Detecting Memory Leaks

Once you've gathered profiling data, focus on identifying patterns that suggest memory leaks:

1. Look for Retained Objects

In the heap dump, review retained objects—those still held in memory but no longer needed. Large lists or collections without proper clearing are common culprits.

2. Analyze Reference Chains

The References view in the heap dump reveals how objects are interconnected.

- Identify strong references preventing objects from being garbage collected.
- Pay attention to objects with long reference chains, as they often lead to leaks.

3. Monitor Garbage Collection

Frequent garbage collection events with increasing memory usage indicate potential leaks. Review the memory graph for suspicious spikes or sustained increases.

Best Practices to Avoid Memory Leaks

To reduce the likelihood of memory leaks, follow these best practices:

Use Weak References:

Replace strong references with weak references when objects do not need to stay in memory.

Example:

val weakContext = WeakReference(context)

Unregister Listeners and Callbacks:

Always unregister listeners and callbacks in onDestroy() or onPause() to prevent lingering references.

Avoid Static References to Context:

Never store Activity or Context in static fields, as this prevents the garbage collector from releasing them.

Watch Out for Anonymous Inner Classes:

Use static inner classes or explicit lifecycle management to prevent holding references to outer classes.

Use Tools Like LeakCanary:

LeakCanary is a third-party library that detects memory leaks during development and provides detailed insights.

Practical Example: Identifying and Fixing a Leak

Scenario: An Activity uses a static Handler to post delayed messages but doesn't clean up references on destruction. This leads to a memory leak because the Handler holds a reference to the Activity.

Code Before Fix:

```
class MainActivity : AppCompatActivity() {
    companion object {
        val handler = Handler(Looper.getMainLooper())
    }

    override fun onCreate(savedInstanceState: Bundle?) {
        super.onCreate(savedInstanceState)
        handler.postDelayed({ /* do something */ }, 10000)
    }
}
```

Code After Fix:

Use a weak reference to the Activity and properly remove callbacks in onDestroy().

```
class MainActivity : AppCompatActivity() {
    private val handler = Handler(Looper.getMainLooper())

    override fun onCreate(savedInstanceState: Bundle?) {
```

```
    super.onCreate(savedInstanceState)
    handler.postDelayed({ /* do something */ }, 10000)
  }

  override fun onDestroy() {
    super.onDestroy()
    handler.removeCallbacksAndMessages(null)
  }
}
```

Memory leaks can severely impact app performance and user experience. By leveraging Android Profiler tools, you can detect and resolve these issues effectively. Regular profiling, combined with proactive memory management practices, ensures that your apps remain efficient, stable, and ready to meet the demands of modern users.

12.2 Improving App Start-Up Time

App start-up time is one of the first metrics users notice when launching an application. A fast and smooth start-up not only enhances user experience but also reflects the app's overall quality and performance. Long delays during this crucial moment can lead to user dissatisfaction and even app abandonment. As such, optimizing start-up time is an essential task for developers.

This section explores strategies to improve your app's start-up time, from analyzing performance bottlenecks to implementing best practices for resource management and initialization. By reducing delays and prioritizing essential tasks during app launch, you can create an app that feels responsive and engaging from the very first interaction.

Understanding App Start-Up Phases

App start-up is typically divided into two main phases:

- **Cold Start**: Occurs when the app is launched from scratch (not in memory). All resources, data, and components need to be loaded.
- **Warm Start**: Happens when the app is reopened while still partially in memory. Less initialization is required compared to a cold start.

Optimizing both phases ensures a faster and more seamless user experience.

Analyzing App Start-Up Performance

Before making optimizations, it's important to measure and analyze your app's current performance. Tools like Android Profiler and Traceview in Android Studio can help pinpoint bottlenecks.

1. Enable Start-Up Profiling

- Open Android Studio and navigate to View > Tool Windows > Profiler.
- Select the CPU Profiler and record app start-up traces.
- Identify time-consuming methods, excessive resource loads, or redundant operations.

2. Log Start-Up Events

Use custom logs or timestamps to track key moments during app launch, such as the time taken to inflate the first screen or initialize components.

Key Techniques to Improve Start-Up Time

1. Minimize Application Class Initialization

- The Application class is executed at launch and should be kept lightweight.
- Avoid initializing heavy resources or running complex logic here.

Example:

```
override fun onCreate() {
    super.onCreate()
    // Move heavy initializations to background threads
}
```

2. Delay Non-Essential Tasks

Use lazy initialization or deferred loading for components that are not immediately required.

Example:

```
val analytics by lazy { Analytics.initialize(context) }
```

3. Optimize Resource Loading

- Reduce the size of images and assets used during start-up by compressing or resizing them.
- Use VectorDrawable or WebP formats for better efficiency.
- Preload necessary resources intelligently using background threads.

4. Use Splash Screens Effectively

- A properly designed splash screen gives the illusion of faster loading while essential tasks complete in the background.
- Use the Jetpack SplashScreen API for a seamless experience.

5. Optimize Main Thread Usage

Ensure heavy operations like database queries, file I/O, or network requests run on background threads using Coroutine or AsyncTask.

6. Trim Dependencies

Unused libraries or dependencies in your app can slow down initialization. Regularly review and remove redundant dependencies.

Example:

implementation("com.some.library") // Remove if unused

Code Example: Optimizing Start-Up

Here's how to optimize the initialization process for a sample app:

Before Optimization

```
class MyApplication : Application() {
    override fun onCreate() {
        super.onCreate()
        DatabaseHelper.init(this) // Heavy database initialization
        Analytics.setup(this) // Time-consuming setup
    }
```

```kotlin
}
After Optimization
kotlin
Copy code
class MyApplication : Application() {
    override fun onCreate() {
        super.onCreate()
        // Move heavy tasks to background threads
        CoroutineScope(Dispatchers.IO).launch {
            DatabaseHelper.init(this@MyApplication)
        }
        Analytics.initializeLater(this)
    }
}
```

In this example, non-essential initializations are deferred or moved to background threads.

Additional Tips

Use ProGuard and R8 for Code Shrinking:

Minimize the APK size by removing unused code and resources.

Enable shrinking and obfuscation in your build.gradle file:

```
minifyEnabled true
shrinkResources true
```

Reduce Dependency on External APIs During Launch:

Avoid network calls or API requests during start-up. If necessary, load this data in the background.

Preload Critical Data:

Cache frequently used data to avoid delays during launch.

Keep the Launch Activity Lightweight:

Minimize operations in the onCreate() method of your main activity. Focus on inflating the UI quickly.

Optimize Background Services:

Review and limit background services that start during app launch.

Testing and Validation

After implementing optimizations, test your app across a range of devices, from low-end to high-end models, to ensure consistent performance. Measure start-up times before and after changes to validate improvements.

Tools for Testing Start-Up Time

ADB Shell: Measure app start-up time using:

adb shell am start -W <package_name>/<activity_name>

Firebase Performance Monitoring: Track app performance metrics, including cold and warm starts.

Improving app start-up time is a vital step in delivering a polished user experience. By profiling performance, prioritizing essential tasks, and deferring unnecessary initializations, you can significantly reduce launch delays. A fast-loading app not only enhances user satisfaction but also reinforces your commitment to quality and performance.

12.3 Minimizing Power Consumption and Battery Usage

Efficient power management is critical for modern mobile apps, as battery life is one of the most valued aspects of smartphone performance. Apps that drain the battery excessively are more likely to be uninstalled or receive negative feedback. By understanding the factors contributing to power consumption and implementing optimization techniques, developers can create apps that are both feature-rich and energy-efficient.

This section explores strategies to minimize battery usage, focusing on optimizing resource-heavy processes such as network operations, background tasks, and hardware access. These techniques not only improve the user experience but also align your app with Android's battery-saving features and policies.

Understanding Power Consumption in Android Apps

Power consumption in mobile devices is influenced by several components:

- **CPU Usage**: High computational load or inefficient algorithms can lead to excessive CPU usage.
- **Network Operations**: Frequent or redundant data transfers consume significant battery power.
- **Background Services**: Unnecessary tasks running in the background can drain battery life.
- **Sensors and Hardware**: Constant use of GPS, camera, or other sensors can quickly deplete power.

To reduce battery usage, developers must optimize these aspects without compromising app functionality.

Analyzing Power Consumption

1. Android Battery Historian

- Use the Battery Historian tool to analyze your app's power usage patterns.
- It provides a visual representation of battery-draining components, helping identify areas for improvement.

2. Android Profiler

The Profiler in Android Studio includes an energy profiler to monitor CPU, network, and other resource usage in real time.

Techniques for Minimizing Power Consumption

1. Optimize Network Usage

Batch Network Requests: Combine multiple network calls into a single request to reduce the frequency of data transfers.

fun batchRequests() {

```
    // Combine multiple API calls into one
}
```

- **Use Efficient Protocols**: Prefer HTTP/2 for reduced overhead and better connection management.
- **Cache Data**: Implement caching strategies to minimize redundant network calls.

2. Manage Background Work

Use WorkManager for background tasks to ensure they are run efficiently and only when necessary.

```
val workRequest = OneTimeWorkRequestBuilder<MyWorker>().build()
WorkManager.getInstance(context).enqueue(workRequest)
```

Limit background services to essential tasks and avoid long-running processes.

3. Reduce GPS and Sensor Usage

Access location services sparingly and use the Fused Location Provider API for more power-efficient location tracking.

```
locationRequest.priority =
LocationRequest.PRIORITY_BALANCED_POWER_ACCURACY
```

Disable unused sensors or reduce the frequency of updates.

4. Minimize Wake Locks

Wake locks prevent the device from entering low-power states. Use them judiciously and release them as soon as possible.

```
val wakeLock =
powerManager.newWakeLock(PowerManager.PARTIAL_WAKE_LOCK,
"MyApp::WakeLockTag")
wakeLock.acquire(10 * 60 * 1000L /*10 minutes*/)
wakeLock.release()
```

5. Optimize UI Rendering

- Reduce overdraw and avoid unnecessary UI updates to lower GPU usage.
- Use ConstraintLayout and flatten view hierarchies for better efficiency.

6. Respect Doze Mode and App Standby

- Android's Doze Mode and App Standby manage background activities to save battery. Ensure your app complies with these power-saving mechanisms.
- Avoid triggering unnecessary alarms or wakeups when the device is idle.

7. Efficient Data Storage and Processing

- Use optimized data structures and algorithms to reduce CPU and memory usage.
- Compress large files and use streams for processing data incrementally.

8. Optimize Multimedia Usage

- Load images and videos efficiently using libraries like Glide or Picasso, which include built-in optimizations for memory and power usage.
- Adjust video playback quality based on network conditions and device capabilities.

Code Example: Reducing Battery Usage

Below is an example of efficient location tracking using the Fused Location Provider API:

Inefficient Code

```
val locationRequest = LocationRequest.create().apply {
    interval = 1000 // High frequency updates
    priority = LocationRequest.PRIORITY_HIGH_ACCURACY
}
```

Optimized Code

```
val locationRequest = LocationRequest.create().apply {
    interval = 60000 // Lower frequency updates
    fastestInterval = 30000
    priority = LocationRequest.PRIORITY_BALANCED_POWER_ACCURACY
}
```

Best Practices for Battery Optimization

- **Use Battery-Friendly Libraries**: Leverage libraries like WorkManager, Retrofit, and Glide that are designed with efficiency in mind.
- **Perform Background Tasks Sparingly**: Limit background processes to essentials and schedule them intelligently.
- **Test Across Devices**: Battery usage varies across devices and Android versions. Test on multiple devices to ensure consistent performance.
- **Monitor Energy Impact**: Use tools like adb shell dumpsys batterystats to monitor energy impact over time.

Validation and Testing

After implementing optimizations, validate your app's energy efficiency using the following methods:

ADB Battery Stats:

adb shell dumpsys batterystats > stats.txt

- **Device Testing**: Test on physical devices with varying battery capacities and operating conditions.
- **User Feedback**: Monitor reviews and feedback for complaints related to battery usage.

Minimizing power consumption is essential for creating apps that respect user preferences and stand out in a competitive market. By optimizing network operations, background tasks, and hardware usage, and adhering to Android's energy-saving guidelines, you can significantly improve battery efficiency. These efforts lead to happier users, better app ratings, and a more sustainable mobile experience.

12.4 Optimizing Graphics and Animations

Graphics and animations play a crucial role in creating visually appealing and engaging Android apps. However, poorly optimized visual elements can degrade performance, increase power consumption, and lead to a subpar user experience. To ensure smooth rendering and responsiveness, developers must focus on optimizing graphics and animations while balancing aesthetics and efficiency.

In this section, we delve into strategies to reduce rendering overhead, optimize resource usage, and maintain high frame rates. You'll learn practical techniques to create polished graphics and animations that are efficient, scalable, and aligned with Android's performance guidelines.

The Impact of Graphics and Animations on Performance

Animations and graphics significantly affect an app's performance by consuming CPU, GPU, and memory resources. Common issues include:

- **Jank and Frame Drops**: When rendering takes longer than the 16ms frame time (to achieve 60fps), the UI appears sluggish.
- **Overdraw**: Rendering the same pixel multiple times wastes GPU resources.
- **Large Bitmap Memory Usage**: Loading unoptimized or oversized images can lead to memory leaks and crashes.
- **Battery Drain**: Complex animations and high frame rates increase power consumption.

Optimizing Graphics

1. Use Vector Drawables Over Bitmaps

Vector Drawables scale efficiently across devices and consume less memory compared to bitmaps.

```
<vector xmlns:android="http://schemas.android.com/apk/res/android"
    android:width="24dp"
    android:height="24dp"
    android:viewportWidth="24"
    android:viewportHeight="24">
    <!-- Vector content -->
</vector>
```

2. Compress Bitmap Images

Use tools like ImageAsset Studio or third-party tools to compress PNG and JPG images.

Implement in-app compression with libraries like Glide or Picasso:

```
Glide.with(context)
```

```
.load(imageUrl)
.override(200, 200) // Optimize dimensions
.into(imageView)
```

3. Reduce Overdraw

- Use the Debug GPU Overdraw feature in Developer Options to identify areas where the UI is rendered unnecessarily.
- Flatten view hierarchies with layouts like ConstraintLayout to minimize redundant layers.

4. Leverage Hardware Acceleration

Hardware acceleration uses the GPU for rendering. It's enabled by default for apps targeting API 14 and above, but ensure specific heavy tasks like animations are offloaded effectively.

5. Optimize OpenGL and Vulkan Graphics

If your app uses OpenGL or Vulkan, streamline shaders and reduce the complexity of 3D models to improve performance.

Optimizing Animations

1. Use Motion Layout for Complex Animations

MotionLayout provides an efficient way to handle animations with minimal overhead, offering better control over transitions and interactions.

```
<MotionScene>
  <Transition
    motion:constraintSetStart="@id/start"
    motion:constraintSetEnd="@id/end">
    <OnSwipe
      motion:touchAnchorId="@id/view"
      motion:dragDirection="dragUp" />
  </Transition>
</MotionScene>
```

2. Avoid Overly Complex Animations

Simplify animations to avoid performance degradation, especially on older devices. Stick to lightweight animations like fades and slides.

3. Utilize Android's Animation APIs

Use built-in APIs like ObjectAnimator, ValueAnimator, and AnimatorSet for smoother animations.

```
val animator = ObjectAnimator.ofFloat(view, "translationY", 0f, 100f)
animator.duration = 300
animator.start()
```

4. Reduce Animation Frame Rates

If high frame rates aren't necessary, reduce the animation frame rate to conserve power and GPU usage.

5. Cache Animation States

Reuse pre-rendered animation frames or states to minimize computational overhead.

Best Practices for Graphics and Animation Optimization

Testing and Profiling

Use the Android Profiler to monitor GPU rendering and frame time:

- Enable the Profile GPU Rendering tool to visualize the rendering performance.
- Test animations across devices with different hardware capabilities.

Responsive Design

- Ensure graphics and animations adapt seamlessly to different screen sizes and densities.
- Avoid hardcoded values and use scalable resources like dp and sp units.

Preloading and Caching

Preload images and animations during idle times to prevent stuttering during runtime.

Implement caching for reusable assets with libraries like Glide.

Using Lottie for Lightweight Animations

Use Lottie for rendering JSON-based animations exported from design tools like Adobe After Effects. These animations are lightweight and efficient.

```
val animationView: LottieAnimationView = findViewById(R.id.animation_view)
animationView.setAnimation("animation.json")
animationView.playAnimation()
```

Avoid Blocking the Main Thread

Perform complex computations or asset loading off the main thread using Coroutines or AsyncTask.

Code Example: Optimizing Animation with ObjectAnimator

Inefficient Code

```
val animation = AnimationUtils.loadAnimation(context, R.anim.slide_in)
view.startAnimation(animation)
```

Optimized Code

```
val animator = ObjectAnimator.ofFloat(view, "translationX", -100f, 0f)
animator.duration = 300
animator.start()
```

Reducing Power Consumption with Graphics

Graphics-intensive apps are notorious for draining batteries. To address this:

- **Limit Frame Rates**: Set a maximum frame rate for animations to prevent unnecessary GPU usage.
- **Optimize Transitions**: Use efficient transitions between activities and fragments to reduce rendering overhead.
- **Minimize GPU Overload**: Test with tools like GPU Inspector to identify bottlenecks in rendering pipelines.

Optimizing graphics and animations is essential for delivering smooth and efficient apps that delight users. By employing techniques like vector graphics, efficient layouts, and streamlined animations, you can reduce resource usage while maintaining visual quality. Balancing aesthetics with performance ensures your app runs seamlessly across devices, enhancing user satisfaction and extending battery life.

12.5 Reducing APK Size with ProGuard and R8

The size of your app can significantly impact user adoption and retention. Large APKs can deter users with limited storage or slow internet connections, particularly in markets where such constraints are common. By reducing APK size, you improve app performance, download speeds, and overall user experience. Tools like ProGuard and R8 are instrumental in optimizing Android apps by shrinking, obfuscating, and optimizing code and resources.

In this section, you'll explore techniques to leverage ProGuard and R8 to reduce APK size while maintaining functionality and performance. From understanding their core features to configuring them effectively, this guide will help you craft a leaner, more efficient APK.

The Role of ProGuard and R8 in APK Optimization

What is ProGuard?

ProGuard is a tool that optimizes and obfuscates Java bytecode. It shrinks your app by removing unused code, renames classes and methods to reduce their size, and performs optimizations like inlining methods.

What is R8?

R8 is the successor to ProGuard and is now the default code shrinker and obfuscator for Android apps built with Android Gradle Plugin 3.4.0 and higher. It offers all the capabilities of ProGuard but with improved performance and additional optimizations.

Steps to Enable and Configure ProGuard/R8

1. Enable ProGuard/R8 in Your Project

R8 is enabled by default for apps built with the release build type. To confirm or enable ProGuard for earlier configurations, add the following to your build.gradle file:

```
buildTypes {
  release {
    minifyEnabled true
    shrinkResources true
    proguardFiles getDefaultProguardFile('proguard-android-optimize.txt'), 'proguard-rules.pro'
  }
}
```

- **minifyEnabled**: Activates code shrinking.
- **shrinkResources**: Removes unused resources like images or strings.
- **proguardFiles**: Specifies the ProGuard configuration files.

2. Configure ProGuard Rules

Create or edit the proguard-rules.pro file to define specific rules for retaining necessary code and resources. For example:

```
# Keep essential classes and methods
-keep class com.example.app.** { *; }

# Avoid obfuscating Gson model classes
-keep class com.google.gson.** { *; }
```

Techniques for Reducing APK Size

1. Shrink Unused Code and Resources

R8 and ProGuard automatically identify and remove unused classes, methods, and libraries. Use shrinkResources in your Gradle configuration to remove unused resources.

2. Obfuscate Code

Code obfuscation renames classes and methods to reduce size and enhance security. For example:

Before obfuscation:

```
public class UserManager {
    public void getUserDetails() { ... }
}
```

After obfuscation:

```
class a {
    void a() { ... }
}
```

3. Optimize Libraries

Modern libraries like Retrofit, Glide, and Jetpack are modular. Import only the required modules instead of the entire library. For example:

```
implementation 'com.squareup.retrofit2:retrofit:2.9.0'
implementation 'com.squareup.retrofit2:converter-gson:2.9.0' // Only needed converter
```

4. Split APKs by Configuration

Use Android App Bundles to generate APKs tailored to specific device configurations, reducing the size of each APK. Add the following in your build.gradle:

```
android {
    bundle {
        language { enableSplit = true } // Split by language
        density { enableSplit = true } // Split by screen density
        abi { enableSplit = true }    // Split by CPU architecture
    }
}
```

Tips for Effective ProGuard/R8 Use

1. Retain Essential Code

Some libraries dynamically load code or use reflection, which might get stripped during shrinking. Use -keep rules to ensure critical code is retained.

Example for keeping Glide modules:

-keep class com.bumptech.glide.** { *; }

2. Optimize Image Resources

Use tools like pngcrush or Android Studio's built-in image optimizer to reduce image sizes. For scalable graphics, prefer vector drawables over raster images.

3. Compress and Optimize Resources

Use resource shrinking to remove unused resources:

shrinkResources true

Debugging and Testing Optimized APKs

1. Test APK Thoroughly

After shrinking and obfuscating, test your app extensively to ensure all features work as expected.

2. Analyze APK Size

Use Android Studio's APK Analyzer to inspect your APK's contents and identify size contributors. To open the APK Analyzer:

- Build your APK.
- Go to Build > Analyze APK.

3. Inspect ProGuard Mappings

To debug obfuscated code, use the mapping.txt file generated by ProGuard/R8. Keep this file secure, as it's essential for decoding crash reports.

Common Issues and Solutions

1. Missing or Broken Functionality

If ProGuard removes necessary code:

- Identify the affected classes or methods using the stack trace.
- Add appropriate -keep rules in proguard-rules.pro.

2. Increased APK Size

Sometimes, overuse of libraries or unnecessary dependencies inflates APK size. Audit dependencies with Gradle:

./gradlew app:dependencies

3. Obfuscation Causing Crashes

Libraries that rely on reflection (e.g., Gson) might break if obfuscated. Add rules to keep such classes.

By leveraging ProGuard and R8 effectively, you can significantly reduce the size of your APK without compromising its performance or functionality. A leaner APK not only improves user experience but also enhances your app's adoption rates, particularly in resource-constrained markets. Combining code and resource shrinking with thoughtful library usage and APK splitting ensures that your app remains optimized for diverse devices and users.

13. Publishing and Monetizing Your App

Building a great app is just the beginning—getting it into the hands of users and generating revenue is the next crucial step. In this chapter, you'll learn how to prepare your app for release, from final testing and debugging to creating an effective app store listing on Google Play. You'll also explore various monetization strategies, including in-app purchases, subscriptions, and ads, to turn your app into a sustainable business. With insights into marketing and app store optimization (ASO), this chapter will guide you through the process of launching and profiting from your Android app.

13.1 Preparing Your App for Google Play Submission

Launching your app on Google Play is an exciting milestone that requires careful preparation. A polished submission process ensures your app meets Google's standards, stands out in the crowded marketplace, and attracts potential users. From ensuring your app adheres to guidelines to preparing assets like screenshots and descriptions, this step is pivotal for a successful release.

This section provides a comprehensive guide to getting your app ready for Google Play submission. You'll learn about the necessary checks, documentation, and assets required to make your app attractive to users and compliant with Google's policies.

Key Steps to Prepare for Submission

1. Adhering to Google Play Guidelines

Before submission, your app must comply with the Google Play Developer Policy. Key aspects include:

- **Content compliance**: Ensure your app doesn't contain prohibited content like malware, hate speech, or adult material.
- **Data privacy**: Implement a privacy policy if your app collects user data and ensure proper data handling practices.
- **Adherence to technical standards**: Test your app for crashes, ANRs (Application Not Responding), and proper performance on supported devices.

2. Testing and Debugging

Thoroughly test your app to ensure it performs reliably across devices and screen sizes. Key tests include:

- **Device compatibility**: Test on physical devices and emulators with various Android versions.
- **Network conditions**: Simulate poor connectivity to ensure robust offline and online performance.
- **Edge cases**: Handle rare or extreme user inputs gracefully.

3. Configuring Your App

Set up your app's technical metadata for submission:

Versioning: Update your app's version name and version code in build.gradle:

versionCode 2
versionName "1.1"

Signing: Use a release keystore to sign your app. Without this, Google Play won't accept your submission.

Target API level: Ensure your app targets the latest API level required by Google Play.

4. Creating an App Bundle or APK

Generate an optimized Android App Bundle (AAB) or APK file for upload. Google Play requires an AAB for new submissions. To generate it:

- Open Build > Build Bundle(s)/APK(s) > Build Bundle(s) in Android Studio.
- Locate the generated AAB in the outputs directory.

5. Preparing Graphic Assets

Visuals play a crucial role in attracting users. Prepare the following assets:

- **App icon**: A 512x512px high-resolution PNG.
- **Screenshots**: Clear, well-lit screenshots that showcase key features. Ensure they comply with required resolutions.
- **Feature graphic**: A compelling 1024x500px image that highlights your app.

- **Promo video (optional):** A short video showcasing the app's functionality and benefits.

Setting Up a Google Play Developer Account

To submit your app, you'll need a Google Play Developer account. Follow these steps:

- Visit the Google Play Console.
- Create an account and pay the one-time $25 registration fee.
- Complete your account details, including a business email, phone number, and website (if applicable).
- Submitting App Details on the Google Play Console

1. Create a New Application

Log in to the Google Play Console and select Create App.
Provide your app's name, default language, and application type (e.g., game or app).

2. Complete App Information

Fill out details in the following sections:

Store listing:

- App name, short description, and full description.
- Add graphic assets (icon, screenshots, feature graphic).

Pricing and distribution:

- Choose whether the app is free or paid.
- Specify countries for distribution.

Content rating:

Complete the content rating questionnaire to help users understand the app's age suitability.

3. Upload the AAB or APK

Navigate to Release > Production and upload your app bundle or APK. Ensure your build is signed with your release keystore.

Final Checks Before Submission

1. Perform a Pre-Launch Report

Google Play offers a pre-launch testing tool that analyzes your app for crashes, ANRs, and compatibility issues. Run the report to catch potential problems.

2. Verify Privacy and Security Settings

Privacy policy: Host your privacy policy on a public URL and link it in the Play Console. Data safety: Provide details about data collection and sharing in the Data Safety section.

3. Double-Check Metadata

Ensure your app's descriptions, screenshots, and graphics align with its functionality and target audience.

Submitting Your App

Once you've completed all steps, hit the Submit for Review button in the Play Console. Google typically reviews apps within a few days, although complex apps may take longer.

By following these steps, you're setting the stage for a smooth Google Play submission process and a successful app launch.

13.2 Creating Compelling App Store Listings

A great app store listing is your app's first chance to make a lasting impression. The listing serves as your digital storefront, enticing potential users to download your app. By showcasing your app's unique features, benefits, and value proposition in a visually appealing and concise manner, you increase your app's chances of standing out in a crowded marketplace.

This section dives into the key elements of an effective app store listing. From crafting engaging descriptions to optimizing your listing for search and discoverability, you'll learn how to maximize downloads and build a strong first impression.

Key Components of a Compelling App Store Listing

1. App Name and Subtitle

- **App Name**: Choose a name that's memorable, easy to spell, and reflects your app's purpose. For example, "FitTrack: Your Personal Fitness Companion" clearly conveys the app's utility.
- **Subtitle (optional):** Use a subtitle to highlight a unique feature or benefit, such as "Track Workouts & Stay Motivated."

2. Icon Design

Your app icon is often the first visual element users notice. Make it count:

- **Simplicity**: Use a clean, uncluttered design with bold colors.
- **Brand Identity**: Ensure the icon aligns with your app's theme and branding.
- **Scalability**: Test how your icon looks at smaller sizes.

3. Screenshots

Screenshots are a visual representation of your app's functionality and design:

- **Highlight Key Features**: Showcase your app's most impressive features, such as a sleek dashboard or unique tools.
- **Use Captions**: Add short, descriptive captions to explain each screenshot.
- **Prioritize Visual Flow**: Arrange screenshots in a logical sequence to tell a story about your app.

4. Promotional Video

If applicable, include a short promo video that highlights your app's features and user experience:

- **Keep it Brief**: Limit the video to 30–60 seconds.
- **Focus on Benefits**: Show users how the app solves a problem or improves their life.
- **High Quality**: Use professional editing and clear audio narration.

5. App Description

Your app description is your chance to persuade users:

- **First Sentence Matters**: Begin with a compelling statement or question that hooks readers.
- **Example**: "Looking for a better way to manage your daily tasks? Try TaskMaster!"
- **Highlight Benefits**: Focus on what users gain from the app, such as increased productivity or entertainment.

Use Bullet Points: Break down features for easy readability:

- Stay organized with customizable task lists.
- Sync across all devices for seamless access.
- Enjoy a clean, intuitive interface.

6. Ratings and Reviews

Positive user feedback can significantly influence potential downloads:

- **Encourage Reviews**: Prompt satisfied users to leave reviews.
- **Respond to Feedback**: Show users you care by addressing both praise and concerns in the review section.

7. Category and Keywords

Choosing the right category and keywords is essential for discoverability:

- **Accurate Categorization**: Select a category that best describes your app (e.g., "Health & Fitness" for a workout tracker).
- **Keyword Optimization**: Use relevant keywords in your app name, subtitle, and description to improve search rankings.

8. Privacy and Data Safety

Transparency builds trust. Ensure users can easily access:

- **Privacy Policy**: Link a detailed, easy-to-understand privacy policy.
- **Data Usage**: Clearly state how user data is collected and protected.

Optimizing Your Listing for Discoverability

1. Conduct Keyword Research

Identify keywords users are likely to search for when looking for apps like yours. Use tools like Google Keyword Planner or App Store Optimization (ASO) platforms.

2. Leverage User Personas

Understand your target audience's needs and tailor your listing to resonate with their interests and pain points.

3. Update Regularly

Keep your listing fresh by:

- Highlighting new features in the description.
- Updating screenshots to reflect recent design changes.
- Adding seasonal promotions or limited-time offers.

Tips for Success

- **A/B Testing**: Experiment with different versions of your app icon, screenshots, and descriptions to see what performs best.
- **Competitor Analysis**: Study successful apps in your category to identify effective strategies and areas for improvement.
- **Localization**: Translate your listing into multiple languages to reach a broader audience. Adapt visuals and descriptions for cultural relevance.

Creating a compelling app store listing is both an art and a science. By focusing on clear communication, strong visuals, and user-centric language, you can create a listing that attracts downloads and showcases your app's unique value.

13.3 Strategies for In-App Advertising and Purchases

Monetization is a critical component of app development, and mastering in-app advertising and purchase strategies can transform your app into a revenue-generating platform. A well-balanced approach ensures a positive user experience while maximizing your earnings. This chapter covers best practices for implementing advertising and in-app purchases, so your app remains engaging and profitable.

Key Strategies for In-App Advertising

1. Types of In-App Ads

- **Banner Ads**: Displayed at the top or bottom of the screen, banner ads are unobtrusive but often less effective than other formats.
- **Interstitial Ads**: Full-screen ads that appear during transitions, such as between levels in a game. Use them sparingly to avoid frustrating users.
- **Native Ads**: Blended seamlessly into the app's content, native ads provide a non-disruptive user experience.
- **Rewarded Ads**: Encourage users to watch an ad in exchange for rewards, such as virtual currency or extra lives in a game. These ads often result in higher engagement.

2. Choosing the Right Ad Network

Select an ad network that aligns with your app's goals and audience:

- **Popular Networks**: Google AdMob, Facebook Audience Network, and Unity Ads.
- **Key Considerations**: CPM (cost per thousand impressions), fill rate, and ad quality.

3. Ad Placement and Frequency

- **Strategic Placement**: Ensure ads don't interfere with core functionality. For example, avoid covering critical navigation buttons.
- **Frequency Management**: Too many ads can lead to user churn. Balance ad display frequency to maintain a positive user experience.

4. Personalization

Use user data (with consent) to deliver personalized ads:

- **Targeted Ads**: Leverage demographic and behavioral data to show relevant ads.
- **Improved Engagement**: Personalized ads tend to have higher click-through rates and conversions.

5. Monitoring and Optimization

Track ad performance and make adjustments:

- **Metrics**: Monitor click-through rates (CTR), impressions, and revenue per user.
- **A/B Testing**: Test different ad formats and placements to identify the most effective setup.

Key Strategies for In-App Purchases (IAPs)

1. Types of In-App Purchases

- **Consumable Purchases**: Items that can be used once, such as game coins, extra lives, or power-ups.
- **Non-Consumable Purchases**: One-time purchases that provide permanent benefits, like unlocking premium features or removing ads.
- **Subscription Models**: Recurring payments for access to exclusive content or features. This model is ideal for apps offering ongoing value, such as fitness programs or streaming services.

2. Creating a Seamless Purchase Experience

- **Intuitive Design**: Ensure in-app purchase options are easy to find and use. Avoid cluttered interfaces that confuse users.
- **Transparent Pricing**: Clearly display prices and avoid hidden fees. Include details on what the user will receive.
- **Simplified Payment**: Support multiple payment methods, including credit cards, PayPal, and mobile wallets.

3. Encouraging Purchases

- **Freemium Model**: Offer a free version of your app with optional paid upgrades.
- **Limited-Time Offers**: Create urgency by offering discounts or bonuses for a limited time.
- **Exclusive Content**: Provide valuable features or content accessible only through purchases.

4. Retaining Paying Users

- **Loyalty Rewards**: Incentivize repeat purchases with loyalty points or exclusive rewards.

- **Dynamic Pricing**: Tailor pricing strategies to different user segments based on their engagement levels or geographic location.

5. Compliance and Security

- **Regulatory Compliance**: Follow guidelines set by app stores and local laws regarding payments and data privacy.
- **Secure Transactions**: Use encrypted payment gateways to protect user information.

Combining Ads and Purchases for Maximum Revenue

1. Complementary Strategies

- Use rewarded ads to encourage in-app purchases by giving users a taste of premium features.
- Combine a freemium model with interstitial ads in the free version, nudging users to upgrade to an ad-free premium experience.

2. Analyzing User Behavior

- Identify user segments likely to make purchases and adjust ad frequency for these users to avoid deterring them.
- For non-purchasing users, focus on optimizing ad revenue through higher engagement with rewarded or native ads.

3. Testing and Iteration

- Experiment with different combinations of ads and purchases to find the optimal mix for your audience.
- Regularly update offerings based on analytics and user feedback.

Best Practices for Ethical Monetization

- **User-Centric Design**: Prioritize user experience over aggressive monetization tactics. Happy users are more likely to engage with ads and make purchases.
- **Transparency**: Clearly communicate how ads and in-app purchases work within your app.
- **Value for Money**: Ensure users feel that their purchases provide tangible benefits or enjoyment.

Tracking and Improving Performance

- **Key Metrics**: Measure ARPU (Average Revenue Per User), LTV (Lifetime Value), and conversion rates for both ads and purchases.
- **Continuous Improvement**: Analyze data to identify trends and refine monetization strategies.

By implementing well-thought-out strategies for in-app advertising and purchases, you can create a sustainable revenue model while delivering value to your users. Whether your goal is to monetize a free app or enhance the profitability of a paid one, the principles outlined here will guide you toward success.

13.4 Managing App Updates and User Feedback

Keeping an app relevant and user-friendly requires ongoing updates and an active feedback loop. A successful update strategy ensures your app evolves with user needs, technology advancements, and market trends. In this chapter, we'll explore how to manage app updates effectively while leveraging user feedback to enhance your app's quality and engagement.

The Importance of Regular Updates

1. Staying Competitive

- Regular updates help maintain compatibility with new operating system versions, ensuring your app remains functional and bug-free.
- Updates also allow you to introduce new features and stay ahead of competitors in functionality and design.

2. User Trust and Retention

- An updated app signals that developers are actively improving the experience, which builds user confidence.
- Users are more likely to stay engaged with an app that evolves to meet their needs.

3. Security Enhancements

Frequent updates patch vulnerabilities, protecting user data and maintaining compliance with privacy standards.

Best Practices for Managing App Updates

1. Planning the Update Cycle

- **Major Updates**: Introduce significant new features, often coinciding with major OS releases.
- **Minor Updates**: Focus on bug fixes, performance improvements, and small feature additions.
- **Emergency Updates**: Address critical issues or security vulnerabilities as soon as they arise.

2. Version Control and Documentation

- Clearly define version numbers (e.g., major.minor.patch) to communicate the scale of changes.
- Maintain detailed documentation of changes for internal use and user communication.

3. Testing Before Release

- **Beta Testing**: Involve a subset of users in testing new updates to identify bugs and gather feedback.
- **Automated Testing**: Use testing frameworks to ensure functionality across devices and screen sizes.
- **Manual Testing**: Validate user experience by manually testing key features.

4. Rollout Strategies

- **Phased Rollout**: Release updates to a small percentage of users before a full launch to monitor performance and address potential issues.
- **Rollback Plan**: Prepare a strategy to revert updates if critical problems are detected.

Gathering and Utilizing User Feedback

1. Channels for Collecting Feedback

- **In-App Feedback Tools**: Use feedback forms, surveys, or chatbots directly within the app.
- **App Store Reviews**: Monitor reviews and ratings for user opinions and trends.
- **Social Media and Support Emails**: Track mentions and messages for additional insights.

2. Categorizing Feedback

- **Feature Requests**: Identify new features users want to see.
- **Bug Reports**: Address recurring issues reported by users.
- **Usability Concerns**: Improve UI/UX based on user pain points.

3. Responding to Feedback

- **Timely Responses**: Reply to user reviews and messages promptly to build rapport.
- **Acknowledgment**: Let users know their feedback has been noted and considered.
- **Actionable Changes**: Implement feasible suggestions and communicate these changes in update notes.

Crafting Effective Update Notes

1. Transparency

Clearly describe what has been updated, including new features, bug fixes, and performance enhancements.

2. User-Centric Language

Avoid technical jargon and focus on how the changes improve the user experience.

3. Highlight Key Features

Emphasize major improvements or exciting new features to encourage users to update. Engaging Users Post-Update

1. In-App Tutorials for New Features

Use tooltips or guided tours to introduce significant changes or new functionality.

2. Encouraging Feedback

After an update, ask users for their thoughts to refine future iterations.

3. Monitoring Metrics

Track KPIs such as crash rates, user retention, and engagement to evaluate the impact of updates.

Leveraging Analytics for Continuous Improvement

1. Usage Data

Analyze user behavior to identify underused features or frequent pain points.

2. A/B Testing

Experiment with different designs or workflows to find the most effective solutions.

3. Sentiment Analysis

Use AI tools to gauge user sentiment from feedback and reviews, helping prioritize changes.

Avoiding Common Pitfalls

1. Overloading Users with Updates

Avoid frequent updates that disrupt the user experience. Aim for meaningful and impactful changes.

2. Ignoring Backward Compatibility

Ensure updates don't break functionality for users on older devices or operating systems.

3. Lack of Communication

Failing to inform users about changes can lead to confusion or frustration. Use update notes and notifications effectively.

Managing app updates and user feedback is a dynamic, ongoing process that ensures your app remains relevant, functional, and engaging. By adopting a structured approach to updates and actively listening to user input, you can foster loyalty, attract new users, and maintain a competitive edge in the ever-evolving Android ecosystem.

13.5 Analytics and A/B Testing for Monetization

To maximize revenue and user satisfaction, leveraging analytics and A/B testing is a must in modern app monetization strategies. These tools help developers make informed decisions, optimize user experiences, and refine monetization methods. In this chapter, we'll dive into the role of data-driven techniques in monetization and how to implement them effectively.

The Role of Analytics in Monetization

1. Understanding User Behavior

- Analytics tools provide insights into how users interact with your app, from session length to frequently accessed features.
- Behavioral trends help identify user preferences and bottlenecks in the monetization process.

2. Identifying Monetization Opportunities

- Analyze which features or content segments users engage with the most.
- Use this data to decide where to place ads, offer premium upgrades, or introduce in-app purchases (IAPs).

3. Tracking Key Performance Indicators (KPIs)

- **Retention Rate**: Measures how often users return to the app after installation.
- **Lifetime Value (LTV):** Calculates the total revenue generated by a user over their lifetime in the app.
- **Conversion Rate**: Tracks the percentage of users who complete desired actions, such as making a purchase.

Choosing the Right Analytics Tools

1. Built-In Solutions

- **Google Analytics for Firebase**: Provides real-time tracking of user behavior and engagement metrics.
- **Android Vitals**: Focuses on app performance data, including crashes and ANRs (Application Not Responding errors).

2. Third-Party Tools

- **Mixpanel**: Offers advanced user segmentation and funnel analysis.
- **Amplitude**: Ideal for cohort analysis and retention tracking.
- **App Annie**: Provides competitive benchmarking and app store performance metrics.

A/B Testing in Monetization

1. What is A/B Testing?

- A/B testing involves creating two or more versions of an app feature, interface, or monetization method and testing them with different user groups.
- The goal is to identify which variation performs better based on predefined metrics.

2. Benefits of A/B Testing

- Minimize guesswork by relying on data to make informed decisions.
- Increase revenue by optimizing user experiences around ads, IAPs, or subscriptions.
- Reduce churn by testing user preferences for design, content, or pricing.

3. Common Areas for A/B Testing

- **Ad Placement**: Test different locations for banner ads to see where they generate the most clicks without disrupting user experience.
- **Subscription Models**: Compare pricing tiers or trial periods to determine which model yields the highest conversion.
- **UI/UX Elements**: Experiment with button designs, text labels, or color schemes for calls to action.

Steps to Implement A/B Testing

1. Define Objectives and Hypotheses

- Set clear goals, such as increasing ad click-through rates or boosting IAP conversions.
- Formulate hypotheses like, "Users are more likely to click ads when placed at the bottom of the screen."

2. Segment Your Audience

- Divide users into evenly distributed test groups to ensure results are statistically valid.
- Consider demographics, usage patterns, or location for segmentation.

3. Run Controlled Experiments

- Introduce one change at a time to isolate its impact on performance.
- Use analytics tools to track user interactions and measure success.

4. Analyze Results

- Compare metrics like engagement, conversion rates, and revenue between test groups.
- Look for statistically significant differences to draw conclusions.

5. Implement Winning Variations

- Roll out the successful version to your entire user base and continue monitoring its performance.

Maximizing Revenue with Data-Driven Insights

1. Fine-Tuning In-App Purchases

- Analyze purchase trends to identify popular price points and adjust offerings accordingly.
- Test bundled packages or discounts to increase purchase frequency.

2. Optimizing Ad Strategies

- Use analytics to determine the best-performing ad formats (e.g., banners, interstitials, or rewarded videos).

- Test different ad networks to maximize fill rates and eCPM (effective cost per mille).

3. Improving Subscription Models

- Experiment with free trial durations or feature unlocks to encourage upgrades.
- Monitor churn rates to identify and address pain points for subscribers.

Common Pitfalls in Analytics and A/B Testing

1. Testing Too Many Variables at Once

- Changing multiple elements simultaneously can obscure the true impact of individual changes.

2. Ignoring Sample Size and Duration

- Insufficient sample sizes or short testing periods can lead to unreliable results.

3. Overlooking User Segments

- Aggregating all data without segmenting by user type can mask valuable insights.

4. Misinterpreting Data

- Correlation does not imply causation; validate conclusions with additional tests or analysis.

Ethical Considerations in Monetization Testing

1. User Transparency

- Avoid intrusive experiments that disrupt user experiences without prior notice.

2. Fairness in Pricing

- Ensure that pricing tests don't disadvantage specific user groups unfairly.

3. Data Privacy Compliance

- Adhere to GDPR, CCPA, and other data protection regulations when collecting and analyzing user data.

Analytics and A/B testing are indispensable tools for optimizing monetization strategies in Android apps. By understanding user behavior, running experiments, and making data-driven decisions, developers can enhance user satisfaction while boosting revenue. This chapter equips you with the knowledge to implement these techniques effectively, ensuring your app's financial success and sustainability in the competitive Android market.

14. Future Trends in Android Development

The world of Android development is constantly evolving, and staying ahead of the curve is essential for long-term success. In this chapter, you'll explore the emerging trends and technologies that are shaping the future of Android app development, including advancements in artificial intelligence, 5G, foldable devices, and augmented reality. You'll also learn about the growing role of Kotlin, Jetpack Compose, and other tools that will define the next generation of Android apps. By understanding these trends, you'll be better equipped to adapt and innovate, ensuring your skills and apps remain relevant in an ever-changing ecosystem.

14.1 Exploring New Features in Android 14+

As Android continues to evolve, each new release introduces features and updates that enhance the user experience, increase developer capabilities, and refine app performance. Android 14, along with subsequent versions, brings significant improvements that shape the way apps are developed, tested, and experienced. In this chapter, we will explore the key new features of Android 14+ and how these changes impact both app developers and users.

1. Enhanced Privacy and Security Features

1.1 Privacy Improvements

- **Notification Access and Data**: Android 14 has introduced tighter controls over how apps access sensitive data, such as location and camera. Users are now provided with more granular control over which apps can access their data and for how long.
- **Data Deletion for Unused Apps**: Android 14 introduces a feature that allows apps to automatically delete unused data after a certain period, increasing user control and enhancing privacy.

1.2 Security Enhancements

- **Biometric Authentication**: Android 14+ strengthens biometric authentication security by adding additional layers of protection for fingerprint and face recognition, ensuring that apps using these technologies are more secure against unauthorized access.

- **Improved Encryption**: New methods for data encryption have been introduced, allowing developers to implement even more robust encryption mechanisms for sensitive user data.

2. Improved Performance and Efficiency

2.1 Performance Optimization

- **App Launch Improvements**: Android 14 focuses on reducing app launch times with optimizations to both the system and app initialization processes. Apps that adopt the new launch optimizations will experience faster startup times, providing users with a smoother experience.
- **Memory Efficiency**: Enhanced memory management improves the way Android 14+ handles background processes, reducing the strain on system resources and ensuring better battery life for users.

2.2 Battery Life Enhancements

- **Battery Saving Features**: Android 14 includes features that optimize how apps manage background tasks and activities. Developers are encouraged to design their apps with more efficient energy consumption in mind, reducing the app's battery drain during idle periods.

3. User Interface and Design Changes

3.1 Adaptive UI for Diverse Devices

- **Larger Screens**: Android 14 introduces features designed to better support foldable devices and large-screen devices like tablets. This includes better support for multi-window applications and split-screen functionality, offering users a more versatile experience.
- **Dynamic Color Palette**: New design tools have been introduced to help developers implement a consistent and dynamic color scheme that adjusts based on the user's wallpaper and themes. This allows for a more personalized and visually appealing user interface (UI).

3.2 Gesture Enhancements

- **Advanced Gesture Controls**: Android 14 brings support for new gesture types, particularly for foldable and dual-screen devices. These gestures make navigation smoother and more intuitive, particularly on devices with non-traditional form factors.

4. New APIs and Development Tools

4.1 Enhanced APIs for App Development

- **Permission System Updates**: Android 14 introduces an updated permission system, which enables more precise control over what apps can do with system resources. For example, apps can now request permissions more explicitly, leading to a more secure and user-friendly experience.
- **New Jetpack Libraries**: With Android 14+, Google continues to improve Jetpack libraries, offering new functionalities that make it easier for developers to create high-performance apps, such as more efficient handling of background tasks and improved UI components.

4.2 App Compatibility with Android 14+

- **Compatibility Checks**: Android 14 includes improved backward compatibility tools, helping developers ensure that their apps work seamlessly across multiple versions of the Android operating system. The updated compatibility frameworks reduce fragmentation, allowing apps to target multiple Android versions with ease.
- **App Compatibility Testing Tools**: Android Studio now offers improved testing tools to help developers validate that their apps will work properly on Android 14+ devices. These tools include simulators for new form factors like foldable devices and improved test cases for privacy and security features.

5. Support for New Form Factors and Hardware

5.1 Foldable and Dual-Screen Devices

- **Foldable Device Optimization**: Android 14 introduces enhanced support for foldable devices, allowing apps to adapt to the unique form factors of these devices. Developers can now use dedicated APIs to handle dynamic screen sizes and multi-window operations more effectively.
- **Dual-Screen Integration**: Android 14 brings new tools for developers to design apps that seamlessly support dual-screen devices, offering better multitasking and continuous experiences when users switch between screens.

5.2 Support for Wearables and Automotive

- **Wear OS Improvements**: Android 14+ brings deeper integration with Wear OS, allowing developers to create more feature-rich and responsive apps for smartwatches. This includes improvements in health tracking APIs, better battery management, and more efficient connectivity.
- **Automotive Integration**: Android 14+ also continues the expansion of Android Auto, with enhanced features for in-car experiences. Apps can now more effectively interact with vehicle systems, improving user safety and convenience in automotive environments.

6. AI and Machine Learning Enhancements

6.1 TensorFlow Lite and ML Kit Integration

- **On-Device Machine Learning**: Android 14 introduces better support for on-device machine learning models, allowing developers to implement real-time AI features without relying on server-side processing. TensorFlow Lite has been enhanced to offer faster and more efficient machine learning capabilities for a wide range of applications, from image recognition to predictive analytics.

6.2 Improved AI-Powered Features

- **Natural Language Processing (NLP):** Android 14+ introduces updates to ML Kit that improve natural language processing tasks, such as text translation, sentiment analysis, and text summarization. This opens up new possibilities for apps that require advanced text understanding, including chatbots, language learning tools, and accessibility features.

7. Multi-Device Support

7.1 Seamless Cross-Device Experiences

- **Continuity Features**: Android 14 introduces enhanced support for continuity features, making it easier for users to switch between their phone, tablet, and other Android devices without losing their app context. This ensures that developers can create more fluid and connected experiences for users across their devices.
- **Cross-Platform Integration**: With Android 14, apps can better integrate with other platforms, such as web or desktop versions, ensuring a more cohesive experience for users who use multiple devices.

Android 14+ marks a major step forward in the evolution of the Android operating system, with new features designed to enhance both user experience and app development. Developers are encouraged to embrace these innovations, as they provide opportunities to create more secure, efficient, and engaging apps across a range of devices. With improvements in performance, UI design, machine learning, and multi-device support, Android 14+ continues to set the stage for a new era of app development that is faster, smarter, and more user-centric than ever before.

14.2 Designing for Foldable and Large-Screen Devices

With the rapid growth of foldable and large-screen devices in the market, Android developers must embrace new design principles and practices to ensure their apps provide seamless and engaging experiences on these devices. The unique form factors of foldable phones, tablets, and large-screen devices create opportunities and challenges for app design, requiring flexibility in how apps are structured, navigated, and optimized for these screens. In this chapter, we will explore best practices and techniques for designing Android apps for foldable and large-screen devices.

1. Understanding the Impact of Foldable and Large Screens

1.1 The Rise of Foldables and Large Screens

Foldable devices, such as the Samsung Galaxy Z Fold series, offer multiple screen configurations, allowing users to switch between compact and expanded screen states. Large-screen devices, including tablets and high-resolution displays, also provide extra space for multitasking and more immersive experiences. These devices allow users to engage with content in new ways, so it is essential to design apps that take advantage of these large, flexible screen spaces.

1.2 Challenges and Opportunities

The diverse screen sizes, folding mechanisms, and aspect ratios present a unique challenge for app developers. However, these devices also offer opportunities for creating more dynamic and feature-rich user interfaces, such as:

- **Multi-window interactions**: Users can run multiple apps simultaneously or switch between apps with ease.

- **App continuity**: Apps can maintain a continuous user experience across different screen configurations (e.g., transitioning from the phone screen to the expanded tablet view).
- **Enhanced multitasking**: Larger screens offer the potential to display more content, such as side-by-side views or detailed, split-screen modes.

2. Designing Adaptive Layouts for Flexibility

2.1 Flexibility with Layouts and Views

To ensure your app works well on foldable and large-screen devices, it's important to design layouts that adjust dynamically to the screen size and form factor. Android provides several tools and layouts for responsive design:

- **ConstraintLayout**: This layout allows you to design flexible, responsive user interfaces that adapt to different screen sizes. By setting constraints and guidelines, you can create UIs that adjust fluidly without requiring additional layouts for each screen size.
- **LinearLayout and GridLayout**: Both layouts offer a way to create structured layouts that align children dynamically. These layouts are useful for organizing content in rows and columns that adjust as the screen size changes.

2.2 Supporting Multiple Screen Sizes

Android apps need to scale smoothly across various screen sizes and densities, especially when supporting foldable and large-screen devices. The res/ directory includes different folders for various screen sizes, such as values-large/ or values-sw600dp/. These help ensure that your app appears properly on different-sized devices.

2.3 Multi-Window and Resizable Activities

Foldable and large-screen devices often support multi-window mode, where users can interact with two or more apps simultaneously. To take full advantage of this feature, developers should:

- Ensure your app supports Resizable Activities, which allows it to resize dynamically when the screen is split.
- Handle changes in screen dimensions gracefully, adjusting layout elements, such as resizing buttons or reflowing text to fit.

3. Using Foldable-Specific Features and APIs

3.1 Detecting Foldable Devices and Their State

Android 10 and above offer APIs to detect when your app is running on a foldable or large-screen device and whether the device is in its folded or unfolded state. The FoldableFeature API provides information about the hinge position, screen size, and whether the screen is folded or unfolded. This allows developers to adjust the app's UI and behavior based on the device's state.

3.2 Seamless Transitions Between Screen States

Foldable devices can transition between different screen modes, such as compact mode (folded) and expanded mode (unfolded). Developers should ensure their apps can:

- **Transition smoothly**: Apps should continue displaying content in an uninterrupted way as the user unfolds or folds the device.
- **Handle screen state changes**: For instance, when switching from a smaller, folded view to a larger unfolded view, apps should reflow their content to fit the new screen dimensions, whether it's a list, image, or video.

3.3 Managing UI Across Multiple Panels

Foldable devices may have multiple panels, which means an app might need to display different content across each panel. This is particularly useful for apps like messaging, video streaming, or email, where you might want to display a list on one screen and the details on another.

Example Use Case: An email app can show the inbox in one panel while displaying the email content in the second panel when unfolded, improving user workflow and multitasking.

4. Optimizing for Multi-Tasking and Multi-Window Support

4.1 Supporting Multi-Tasking

Multi-tasking is a key feature of large-screen devices. For apps to effectively utilize this feature:

- Ensure that your app supports multi-window mode, allowing users to drag and resize app windows on the screen.
- Avoid UI elements that could interfere with the multi-window experience, such as fixed header bars that do not adjust when the window size changes.

4.2 Using Multi-Window APIs

Android supports multi-window functionality, which allows multiple apps or instances of the same app to be open at the same time. Developers should use the following best practices:

- **Allow resizable activity windows**: Your app should respond well when resized, making UI elements fluid and flexible.
- **Focus on app states**: Ensure that your app saves its state when switched between windows so that users do not lose their place.

4.3 Multi-Display Support

For devices with multiple displays, like foldables or devices with external monitors, developers should:

- Take advantage of the Multiple Display API, which helps apps determine how they should interact across multiple screens.
- Allow for seamless transitions when moving between screens or when apps are stretched across two displays.

5. Enhancing User Experience with Adaptive Navigation

5.1 Flexible Navigation Patterns

On large-screen devices, it's crucial to use navigation patterns that optimize the extra space available. The standard single-column design may not be sufficient to fill up larger screens effectively.

- **Two-Pane Layout**: A common navigation pattern for tablets and foldables is the two-pane layout. The main content is shown on one side, while the secondary content is shown on the other side. For example, an email app might show a list of emails on the left side and the email content on the right.

- **Navigation Drawer**: Consider using a navigation drawer that adapts to larger screens, enabling users to easily switch between different sections of the app without wasting screen space.

5.2 Large-Screen Gesture Support

Gesture-based navigation is particularly useful on larger screens, where traditional buttons may take up too much screen real estate. Android 14+ provides built-in support for gestures, such as:

- **Swipe gestures**: These can be used to navigate between sections of the app or to minimize/maximize windows.
- **Edge gestures**: Support gestures that allow users to quickly interact with menus or pull up additional options from the sides of the screen.

6. Testing and Optimizing for Foldable and Large-Screen Devices

6.1 Testing Across Devices and Form Factors

Testing is essential to ensure your app functions properly on all foldable and large-screen devices. Android Studio provides emulators to test your app on different screen sizes and orientations, including foldable devices and large tablets. Test the following scenarios:

- App layout adjustment when switching between screen sizes.
- User interactions such as multi-window or split-screen mode.
- Hinge position detection and content reflow.

6.2 Performance Considerations

Larger screens and foldable devices may place additional strain on performance, particularly when it comes to graphics and memory usage. To optimize your app:

- Avoid heavy graphics rendering and animations that could impact performance, especially when the app is used in multi-window mode.
- Profile your app to identify memory leaks or bottlenecks that could degrade the user experience on these devices.

Designing for foldable and large-screen devices requires thoughtful consideration of flexible layouts, navigation, and performance optimizations. By embracing new design paradigms and taking advantage of Android's powerful tools and APIs, developers can create intuitive, dynamic, and engaging experiences for users on these devices. As the market for foldable and large-screen devices grows, mastering these design principles will be essential for staying competitive and delivering high-quality apps.

14.3 Multi-Platform Development with Flutter and Jetpack Compose Multiplatform

As the demand for apps that work seamlessly across a wide variety of devices and operating systems grows, the need for multi-platform development tools has become more critical. Android developers are increasingly looking for ways to create applications that can run on iOS, web, and desktop platforms, while still maintaining a native feel and experience. Two of the most popular frameworks for building multi-platform apps today are Flutter and Jetpack Compose Multiplatform. These technologies allow developers to write code once and deploy it across various platforms, significantly reducing development time and resources. In this chapter, we will explore how both Flutter and Jetpack Compose Multiplatform are changing the landscape of multi-platform development, offering a deep dive into their features, capabilities, and how to choose the right framework for your project.

1. Introduction to Multi-Platform Development

1.1 The Need for Multi-Platform Development

In today's fast-paced app development world, building apps for multiple platforms—such as Android, iOS, web, and desktop—can be time-consuming and expensive if done separately for each. Multi-platform development frameworks allow developers to share a large portion of code across different platforms, making the process faster and more efficient. By using the right tools, you can significantly reduce the need for platform-specific development while ensuring a consistent user experience.

1.2 The Role of Flutter and Jetpack Compose Multiplatform

Flutter and Jetpack Compose Multiplatform are two emerging frameworks that address this challenge by enabling developers to write code that works across multiple platforms, but with a native feel. While Flutter allows you to target both Android and iOS, Jetpack Compose Multiplatform is Google's latest initiative for Kotlin-based UI development, designed to work not just for Android but across web and desktop platforms as well.

2. Introduction to Flutter for Multi-Platform Development

2.1 What is Flutter?

Flutter, developed by Google, is an open-source UI framework designed to build natively compiled applications for mobile, web, and desktop from a single codebase. Using a rich set of pre-built widgets, Flutter makes it easy to create beautiful and performant apps for multiple platforms. The key benefit of using Flutter is that you can write your app in Dart, a language that compiles to native code, ensuring a smooth and responsive experience on both Android and iOS.

2.2 Core Features of Flutter

- **Cross-Platform Support**: Flutter supports Android, iOS, web, and desktop applications, which allows developers to write once and deploy across different platforms.
- **Widgets and UI Customization**: Flutter offers a wide range of customizable widgets, including Material Design components, making it easy to create attractive and responsive user interfaces.
- **Performance**: Since Flutter uses a compiled language (Dart) to generate native code, it provides near-native performance on both Android and iOS devices.

2.3 Flutter's Ecosystem and Development Tools

Flutter comes with a powerful suite of development tools that support the development, testing, and debugging of cross-platform apps:

- **Flutter SDK**: Provides all the necessary tools, libraries, and resources for building Flutter apps.
- **Dart Language**: A modern programming language optimized for UI development.
- **Flutter DevTools**: A suite of debugging tools for performance monitoring, inspection, and debugging.

3. Introduction to Jetpack Compose Multiplatform

3.1 What is Jetpack Compose Multiplatform?

Jetpack Compose is Android's modern UI toolkit built using Kotlin, allowing developers to build UI components declaratively. Jetpack Compose Multiplatform extends this idea by allowing developers to write a single codebase that runs on Android, iOS, web, and desktop, using Kotlin as the shared language. Jetpack Compose Multiplatform aims to make the development of apps for multiple platforms easier and more consistent, leveraging Kotlin's ability to be used across different platforms seamlessly.

3.2 Key Features of Jetpack Compose Multiplatform

- **Declarative UI**: Just like Jetpack Compose for Android, Jetpack Compose Multiplatform allows developers to define UI components declaratively. This simplifies UI development and reduces boilerplate code.
- **Kotlin as the Common Language**: Developers can use Kotlin, a modern and expressive language, for both the app's UI and business logic, making it easier to maintain and share code between different platforms.
- **Platform-Specific UI Customization**: While Jetpack Compose Multiplatform aims to share as much code as possible, it also provides the flexibility to implement platform-specific code when needed, allowing developers to fine-tune the app experience for each platform.

3.3 Jetpack Compose Multiplatform Tools and Libraries

- **Compose UI Libraries**: A set of UI components and libraries that can be used across platforms, offering native UI elements for Android, iOS, web, and desktop.
- **Kotlin Multiplatform**: The foundational technology that allows code sharing between platforms. It allows developers to write business logic once and run it on multiple platforms.
- **Compose for Desktop and Web**: As Jetpack Compose expands, it now supports desktop applications (Windows, macOS, and Linux) and the web, making it an excellent choice for developers who want to target a wide range of platforms.

4. Flutter vs. Jetpack Compose Multiplatform

4.1 Comparing the Two Frameworks

While both Flutter and Jetpack Compose Multiplatform aim to solve similar problems, they each have their strengths and ideal use cases:

- **Flutter**: Best suited for developers who want a fully cross-platform solution with minimal effort required for design and UI consistency across platforms. It is ideal for developers familiar with Dart and those looking for a robust set of tools to build apps quickly.

- **Jetpack Compose Multiplatform**: Best suited for developers who want to leverage Kotlin across all platforms and prefer a declarative UI model. It is ideal for Android developers who are already using Jetpack Compose and want to extend their apps to iOS, web, and desktop.

4.2 Which Framework Should You Choose?

For existing Android developers: If you're already familiar with Kotlin and Jetpack Compose, and you want to extend your app across multiple platforms, Jetpack Compose Multiplatform might be the better choice.

For new developers or those seeking a unified framework: Flutter may be more suitable, especially for developers who want to target multiple platforms with a single framework and language.

5. Building a Multi-Platform App with Flutter and Jetpack Compose Multiplatform

5.1 Flutter Example: Building a Simple Multi-Platform App

To build a simple Flutter app, you would start by setting up Flutter SDK and creating a project. The code for the app can be written in Dart, with most components using Flutter's widget system. Here's an example of a Flutter project setup:

- Install Flutter SDK.
- Create a new Flutter project.
- Define a responsive layout with widgets for Android, iOS, and web.
- Use Flutter's Hot Reload feature for instant UI changes.

5.2 Jetpack Compose Multiplatform Example: Creating a Cross-Platform UI

For Jetpack Compose Multiplatform, you would use Kotlin for both the UI and logic. Start by setting up the Kotlin Multiplatform plugin and the necessary dependencies to target Android, iOS, and desktop.

- Create a shared ViewModel in Kotlin.
- Use Compose UI components to define the layout.
- Implement platform-specific tweaks when needed, such as handling iOS navigation patterns.

The introduction of multi-platform development tools like Flutter and Jetpack Compose Multiplatform has revolutionized app development by reducing the need for separate codebases across platforms. Both frameworks offer unique strengths, and the choice between the two depends on your familiarity with Dart or Kotlin, as well as the specific needs of your app. By mastering these technologies, Android developers can significantly streamline their development process and ensure their apps work seamlessly across a wide variety of platforms, creating richer experiences for users and greater efficiency for developers.

14.4 Trends in AI and Machine Learning for Mobile Apps

Artificial Intelligence (AI) and Machine Learning (ML) have evolved rapidly in recent years, and their integration into mobile apps has become a key trend. The ability of mobile devices to leverage powerful AI and ML tools opens up new possibilities for app developers, enhancing functionality, improving user experiences, and driving innovative solutions across industries. As mobile technology continues to evolve, AI and ML are being increasingly used to create smarter, more efficient apps. This chapter explores the latest trends in AI and ML for mobile apps, discussing their impact on mobile development, and offering insights on how you can leverage these technologies to enhance your own Android apps.

1. The Growing Role of AI in Mobile Apps

1.1 AI-Powered Personalization

One of the most significant ways AI is impacting mobile apps is through personalization. AI algorithms can analyze user data, such as app usage patterns, preferences, and behaviors, to tailor content and experiences in real time. This can range from personalized recommendations in e-commerce apps (like product suggestions) to tailored newsfeeds in social media apps. By using machine learning algorithms, mobile apps can learn from users' actions and continuously improve the quality of personalized experiences.

1.2 Smart Assistants and Natural Language Processing (NLP)

Mobile apps are increasingly integrating smart assistants powered by AI, such as Google Assistant, Siri, and Alexa. These AI-driven assistants use natural language processing (NLP) to understand and respond to voice commands, making the interaction with apps more intuitive and natural. NLP is also being used in chatbots, which are becoming a common feature in customer service applications, enabling businesses to provide 24/7 assistance to users.

2. Integration of Machine Learning on Mobile Devices

2.1 On-Device Machine Learning

One of the most significant trends in mobile app development is the shift towards on-device machine learning. Rather than relying on cloud-based processing, mobile devices are increasingly capable of running machine learning models locally. This reduces latency and reliance on internet connectivity, while also improving privacy by keeping user data on the device. Frameworks like TensorFlow Lite, Core ML, and ML Kit have made it easier for developers to integrate on-device ML capabilities into their Android apps. These technologies can be used for a variety of tasks such as image recognition, language translation, and real-time data processing.

2.2 Edge AI for Real-Time Processing

Edge AI is another trend gaining traction, allowing mobile devices to process AI algorithms at the "edge" of the network rather than relying solely on cloud-based servers. This is especially valuable for apps that require real-time processing, such as augmented reality (AR) or gaming apps. By performing computations locally, mobile devices can process data more quickly and efficiently, creating more responsive experiences for users.

3. AI for Image and Video Recognition

3.1 Computer Vision in Mobile Apps

Computer vision, a subset of AI, allows mobile apps to analyze and interpret visual data, making it useful for a wide range of applications such as facial recognition, object detection, and image classification. AI-driven computer vision is being increasingly integrated into apps for tasks such as unlocking phones through face recognition, scanning barcodes in shopping apps, or enabling real-time augmented reality (AR) experiences.

Applications in fields like healthcare, security, and entertainment are particularly benefitting from computer vision. For instance, healthcare apps can use image recognition to analyze medical images like X-rays, while AR-based gaming apps use computer vision to detect objects in the real world and integrate them into virtual gameplay.

3.2 Deep Learning and Neural Networks for Improved Accuracy

Deep learning techniques and neural networks, which are subsets of machine learning, have proven particularly effective for improving the accuracy of image and video recognition on mobile devices. These algorithms can be trained on vast datasets to recognize objects, people, and scenes with high precision. In mobile apps, deep learning is increasingly used to enhance features such as real-time video editing, facial filters, and object recognition in AR apps.

4. AI and ML in App Security

4.1 Enhancing App Security with AI

Security is a top priority for app developers, and AI is playing an important role in making mobile apps more secure. Machine learning algorithms are being used to detect anomalies in user behavior, identify fraudulent transactions, and strengthen authentication mechanisms. For instance, AI can analyze the user's device behavior to detect potential security threats such as unauthorized access or malware. Additionally, AI-powered biometric authentication methods, such as fingerprint scanning or facial recognition, are improving the security of mobile apps and reducing the reliance on traditional passwords.

4.2 Fraud Prevention and Detection

AI's ability to analyze large amounts of data and identify patterns is also being used to detect fraudulent activities in mobile apps. For example, financial apps and e-commerce platforms are integrating machine learning algorithms to identify and flag suspicious behavior such as credit card fraud or identity theft. By analyzing user behavior, device location, transaction patterns, and other data points, AI-powered systems can quickly identify fraudulent activities and alert users or administrators in real-time.

5. Voice and Speech Recognition for App Interaction

5.1 Enhancing User Experience with Speech Recognition

Speech recognition technology is one of the most significant applications of AI in mobile apps. It allows users to interact with apps through voice commands, enabling hands-free control. Many apps, from virtual assistants like Google Assistant to fitness apps, are incorporating voice recognition for a more seamless and engaging experience. With the growing accuracy of speech-to-text technology, voice interfaces are becoming more reliable, making them an increasingly popular feature in mobile apps.

5.2 Conversational AI and Chatbots

Conversational AI is revolutionizing user interaction with mobile apps. Chatbots powered by AI can provide instant responses to customer queries, make recommendations, or even complete transactions. These bots use machine learning to improve over time, learning from user interactions and enhancing the quality of their responses. AI-powered chatbots are already widely used in customer service, healthcare, and retail apps, improving user engagement and reducing the need for human intervention.

6. Machine Learning for App Optimization and Performance

6.1 Personalizing User Experience

Machine learning algorithms can be used to optimize mobile apps based on user behavior. For example, by analyzing usage patterns, AI can help adjust the app's interface, push notifications, or content recommendations to suit the user's preferences. This level of personalization helps improve user retention and satisfaction, as the app becomes more tailored to individual needs.

6.2 Predictive Analytics for Enhanced Performance

AI can also be used to optimize the performance of mobile apps. Predictive analytics powered by machine learning algorithms can forecast user demand, app traffic, and behavior, allowing developers to fine-tune app performance. This helps ensure that apps run smoothly under varying load conditions and can scale dynamically to handle more users.

7. Conclusion: The Future of AI and Machine Learning in Mobile Apps

As AI and machine learning continue to evolve, their applications in mobile app development will only grow. From smarter, more personalized experiences to enhanced security and performance optimization, AI and ML have the potential to transform the mobile app landscape. Developers who embrace these technologies will be well-positioned to create innovative, engaging, and efficient apps that meet the demands of the modern user. As more advanced AI tools become available, mobile app development will increasingly rely on machine learning to improve functionality and provide deeper insights into user behavior, setting the stage for even more groundbreaking advancements in the years to come.

14.5 Preparing for 5G-Enabled Applications

The advent of 5G technology promises to reshape the mobile app development landscape, offering faster speeds, lower latency, and more reliable connections. With 5G, mobile devices will be able to handle much larger volumes of data in real time, opening the door to a wide range of new opportunities for app developers. As 5G continues to roll out worldwide, it's important for developers to understand the potential impact of this technology and how to prepare their apps for 5G-enabled environments. In this section, we will explore how 5G will influence mobile app development and the key considerations developers should keep in mind as they build for the next generation of mobile networks.

1. The Advantages of 5G for Mobile Applications

1.1 Faster Data Speeds

One of the most significant benefits of 5G is its ability to provide much faster data speeds compared to previous generations of mobile networks. With download speeds of up to 10 gigabits per second (Gbps), 5G will enable mobile apps to transfer large amounts of data in real time. This is particularly valuable for applications that require quick access to large files or data sets, such as high-quality video streaming, cloud gaming, and augmented reality (AR) apps. Developers can leverage 5G speeds to create richer, more data-intensive experiences for users.

1.2 Ultra-Low Latency

5G networks are designed to have incredibly low latency, often as low as 1 millisecond (ms). This reduction in latency will drastically improve the responsiveness of mobile apps, particularly in applications where real-time interaction is critical. For instance, in gaming, telemedicine, and live-streaming applications, users will experience nearly instantaneous feedback and interaction. Developers will be able to create more interactive, immersive, and real-time experiences without the delays that have been common with 4G networks.

1.3 Increased Network Capacity

5G can support a significantly higher number of connected devices than 4G, meaning that app developers will be able to cater to a larger audience, especially in dense urban environments or crowded events. For apps that rely on real-time interactions (such as social media or event-based applications), 5G will ensure that the experience remains smooth even in areas with high device density. This increased network capacity also means that more IoT (Internet of Things) devices can be connected and managed by apps, enabling new use cases in industries like smart homes, healthcare, and transportation.

2. Key App Development Considerations for 5G

2.1 Optimizing for Higher Bandwidth

With 5G enabling higher bandwidth, developers should focus on optimizing their apps to take full advantage of faster data transfers. Apps that rely on large data uploads and downloads (such as video conferencing, gaming, or media streaming apps) will benefit from 5G's faster speeds. Developers should ensure that their apps can handle this increased bandwidth efficiently, ensuring smooth data transmission, seamless media streaming, and faster load times. For instance, video apps could use higher-resolution content (like 4K) without buffering or stuttering, enhancing the user experience.

2.2 Adapting to Low Latency for Real-Time Apps

Low latency opens the door for real-time applications to function better than ever. Apps that require immediate interaction—such as remote gaming, live streaming, or augmented reality—will see dramatic improvements with 5G. Developers should focus on reducing any latency issues in their apps by optimizing backend systems, ensuring faster communication between the device and servers. For instance, cloud gaming platforms can use 5G's ultra-low latency to offer smooth, high-quality gaming experiences directly on mobile devices, without the need for powerful hardware.

2.3 Utilizing Edge Computing with 5G

Edge computing refers to processing data closer to the user's device or the edge of the network, rather than sending it to a central server. When combined with 5G, edge computing can provide low-latency and real-time processing for applications that require fast decision-making, such as autonomous vehicles, industrial automation, and smart city solutions. Developers should consider integrating edge computing into their apps to reduce dependency on the cloud and further optimize app performance.

3. New App Use Cases Enabled by 5G

3.1 Augmented Reality (AR) and Virtual Reality (VR)

5G will be a game-changer for AR and VR apps, as it will provide the necessary bandwidth and low latency for real-time processing and high-quality experiences. For instance, AR-based mobile games like Pokémon Go, which require the device to constantly track the user's location and surroundings, will be able to provide much more interactive and immersive experiences. VR apps, such as those used for remote training or virtual tourism, will also benefit from smoother interactions and faster data transmission, enhancing realism and user immersion.

3.2 Cloud Gaming and Streaming

5G's increased speeds and low latency will unlock the potential for cloud gaming, where games are streamed in real time rather than requiring heavy processing power on the device. Game developers will be able to create richer, more complex games that can be streamed seamlessly to mobile devices without lag or performance issues. Streaming services, such as video or music, will also be able to deliver higher-quality content without buffering, enabling features like 4K video streaming, live broadcasts, and interactive media experiences directly to mobile users.

3.3 Enhanced IoT Applications

The Internet of Things (IoT) will benefit significantly from 5G's enhanced network capacity. IoT apps that connect a large number of devices, such as smart homes or connected health monitoring systems, will be able to operate more efficiently with 5G. 5G's ability to support millions of connected devices means that apps will be able to manage larger networks of sensors, wearables, and connected devices. Developers will need to design apps that can handle data from these devices in real time, while ensuring efficient data processing and privacy protection.

4. Preparing Your App for 5G Integration

4.1 Testing Your App in 5G Environments

To fully take advantage of 5G, it is important to test your app in real 5G environments. Although 5G is still being rolled out in many parts of the world, developers can test their apps on available 5G networks to understand the impact of high bandwidth and low latency. By testing your app on 5G devices, you can ensure that it performs optimally, with faster load times, better responsiveness, and smoother interactions. It's essential to understand how 5G will impact both your app's frontend and backend performance.

4.2 Updating Infrastructure for Scalability

With 5G enabling larger volumes of connected devices and higher levels of data usage, developers will need to ensure their backend infrastructure can handle the increased demand. Optimizing server architectures, using scalable cloud services, and improving database efficiency will be crucial to delivering a seamless experience to users. Apps that leverage cloud-based features should ensure that their servers are ready to handle the large data requests generated by 5G networks.

4.3 Focusing on Efficient Data Usage

Although 5G will provide faster speeds and more bandwidth, developers should still focus on optimizing their apps to minimize data usage wherever possible. For instance, apps that stream video should incorporate adaptive streaming to automatically adjust quality based on the user's connection. Efficient data usage will not only improve performance but also enhance user satisfaction, especially in regions where users may still have data limits or slower network speeds.

5. Conclusion: Embracing the Future with 5G

5G represents the future of mobile connectivity, with the potential to drastically improve mobile app experiences. By embracing the opportunities that 5G brings—such as faster data speeds, lower latency, and increased network capacity—developers can create more powerful, interactive, and efficient apps. While 5G is still in its early stages, it is essential for developers to start preparing their apps now to ensure they are ready to take full advantage of these new capabilities as the technology becomes more widely available. By understanding the trends, testing for 5G environments, and optimizing your apps for faster speeds and lower latency, you can position your apps to lead the next generation of mobile experiences.

<u>Android App Mastery: Developing for the Modern User</u> is your ultimate guide to building world-class Android applications that captivate, engage, and delight. Whether you're an aspiring developer or a seasoned professional, this book takes you step-by-step through the essentials of Android development, from setting up your first project to mastering advanced technologies.

Inside, you'll explore:

- The foundations of Android architecture and Kotlin programming.
- Designing stunning user interfaces with Material Design and Jetpack Compose.
- Optimizing app performance for speed, efficiency, and battery life.
- Seamless integration of APIs, data storage, and cloud services.
- Best practices for accessibility, inclusivity, and user engagement.
- Insights into publishing, monetizing, and future-proofing your app.

Packed with hands-on examples, expert tips, and actionable strategies, this book doesn't just teach you how to code—it empowers you to create impactful apps for today's demanding users.

Whether you aim to build your first app, grow your skills, or launch a successful career in mobile development, Android App Mastery is your trusted companion for mastering the Android platform and turning your ideas into reality.

Take the next step in your journey. The Android world awaits your innovation.

To all the readers of **<u>Android App Mastery: Developing for the Modern User</u>**,

Thank you for embarking on this journey with me. Writing this book has been an incredible experience, and knowing that it might inspire or guide you in your Android development journey is deeply fulfilling.

Your time is one of your most valuable resources, and I am honored that you chose to spend it with this book. I hope the knowledge, insights, and strategies shared here not only empower you to build amazing apps but also ignite a deeper passion for creativity and innovation.

To the aspiring developers, seasoned coders, and dreamers alike—this book is a result of my experiences, challenges, and triumphs, but it's written with you in mind. Your success is my greatest reward.

Please know that every step you take toward mastering your craft matters, and every app you build has the potential to make an impact. Keep learning, experimenting, and creating. The Android ecosystem—and the world—needs your ideas.

Thank you for trusting me to be a part of your learning process. I wish you all the best in your endeavors, and I look forward to seeing the incredible things you'll create.

With deep gratitude,

Biagio Palazzo

www.ingramcontent.com/pod-product-compliance
Lightning Source LLC
LaVergne TN
LVHW081751050326
832903LV00027B/1898